SAN FRANCISCO
FROM THE GOLD RUSH TO CYBERSPACE

Charles A. Fracchia & Thomas Stauffer

Edited by Carol Piasente, VC Irwin and Lauren Hauptman

SAN FRANCISCO CHAMBER OF COMMERCE
and
MARCOA PUBLISHING INC.
2000

The editors wish to thank Selby Collins of the San Francisco History Center for his assistance.

SAN FRANCISCO
FROM THE GOLD RUSH TO CYBERSPACE

Profiles of Success . 168

San Francisco Chamber of Commerce

G. Rhea Serpan, *President & CEO*

Carol Piasente, *Editor in Chief*

Lauren Hauptman, *Managing Editor*

Richard Lu, *Art Director*

San Francisco Chamber of Commerce
235 Montgomery Street, 12th Floor
San Francisco, CA 94104
415-392-4520

MARCOA Publishing Inc.

Victoria Bailey, *Publisher*

V.C. Irwin, *Editor*

Jocelyn Boehm, *Production Director*

Rudy Rey, *Production Manager*

Patricia Cross, *Art Director*

Ginger Owens, *Supervisor of Advertising*

Melody Robinson, *Quality Control*

Andrew Guillen, *Project Consultant*

Bart Lally, *Project Consultant*

John McClure, *Project Consultant*

Stuart Robertson, *President*

Michael J. Martella, *Chair*

Cover Photo, Richard Lu

Prologue

San Francisco. The name is recognized worldwide. Most think kindly, even passionately, about it: its physical beauty, its cosmopolitan qualities, its reputation for diversity.

One magazine selects San Francisco as the best place in the United States to live; others name it as the favorite urban destination for tourists. And yet, the local newspapers are often filled with derogatory articles about the city's problems.

Such adulation and vituperation have been part of the descriptive process of San Francisco since the beginning of its European colonization.

Europeans colonized San Francisco at the beginning of the last quarter of the eighteenth century as a military outpost to guard San Francisco Bay and as a missionary outpost to convert the natives to Christianity. It was an unsuccessful and neglected outpost of the enervated and crumbling Spanish Empire, and it would be, for a quarter of a century, a virtually forgotten outpost of Mexico.

But it was during nominal Mexican rule (1821–1846) that the urban area now known as San Francisco began: in the granting of land to Mexican-Californians, creating the ranchos; in the creation of a pueblo, or town, of San Francisco in 1834; in the appointment of a British-born merchant by the name of William Richardson as customs collector in 1835, and his building of a trading shack and a house on the Yerba Buena Cove.

During the next decade the settlement on the cove grew to a polyglot population of about 200. Even under the aegis of Mexico, what was to become San Francisco was ethnically diverse. It was a small trading town, with those who peopled it primarily engaged in supplying the trading vessels that entered the bay with the hides and tallow they sought.

The United States conquered California in 1846 as part of the Mexican-American War, and in the following year Yerba Buena's small mercantile community changed the settlement's name to San Francisco.

In early 1848, gold was discovered about 150 miles northeast of San Francisco, and as the area where gold was to be found grew larger and larger, the news of its discovery traveled throughout the world. Within the next few years, somewhere between 350,000 and 500,000 individuals descended upon California to seek their fortune.

Those who came by sea landed in the port closest to where gold had been found — San Francisco — and the small trading village became an instantaneous city. Overnight the city became the financial and mercantile center of the West.

Business was not without its challenges, however: In 1849, there took place in San Francisco the city's first strike, when the printers' union successfully sought an eight-hour work day. Relations between capital and labor would remain in dynamic tension for the next century and a half, sometimes in coalition, sometimes with the unions in the ascendancy, other times with business dominant.

The city's affluence enabled it to create an instant cultural complex: Music, theater, opera, books, newspapers and magazines were all part of the city's landscape from the earliest days of the Gold Rush.

Gold had transformed a trading town of a few hundred individuals into one of the largest cities of the country, and in 1859 another discovery — that of silver in the

Comstock Lode — would enhance it even more. San Francisco's capital had been a major factor in financing the Comstock mines, and for two decades they would pour millions of dollars into the pockets of San Franciscans. The population of the city once again skyrocketed, its physical expansion was noticeable, and economic activity quickened.

The city's capital continued to be utilized in the development of the West: in the oil discoveries of Southern California, in real-estate development, in the expansion of utilities (gas, electricity and water), in the movie industry growing in the southern part of the state. The list could go on for pages. At the end of the 20th century, this capital would finance components of the Technological Revolution.

But it was not only the dynamism of its business and financial community for which San Francisco became known. The city developed a spirit as early as the Gold Rush for the unconventional, the innovative, the original. This spirit and these energies were poured into the two principal universities of the Bay Area — Stanford and the University of California, Berkeley — which in turn sparked the Technological Revolution that began in the aftermath of World War II and intensified in the 1980s and '90s. This spirit and these energies gave birth to many aspects of the sexual revolution that marked the pleasure-loving years that followed the tumult of the 1960s. And they sparked the new age that gave such wonder and amusement to millions throughout the United States: Esalen, est and various other components of the human-potential movement.

The optimism that has so marked San Francisco's history has at times been sorely tested. Even during the prosperous, golden years of the Gold Rush, there were sharp financial panics and depression. Lawlessness and corruption were glaring problems at that time as well, and corruption has marked other periods in the city's history. Earthquakes damaged the city in the 1860s and in 1989 and, along with the subsequent fire, virtually destroyed it in 1906.

Paralyzing strikes, with attendant violence, roiled San Francisco in 1901 and 1934. The depression of the last quarter of the 19th century and of the 1930s devastated the city's economy and created vast unemployment.

During the second half of the 20th century, what had once been the third-busiest port in the United States virtually evaporated — the victim of absentee ownership and mismanagement and the fact that the port had been misplaced for the realities of modern transportation.

Twin tragedies of 1978 shocked the world and eroded the confidence of San Franciscans about the city's future. And at various times in San Francisco's history, politics have become so divisive that it was feared that the city would be torn apart.

Nevertheless, the divisions have mended, the tragedies have lessened in their impact, the results of the natural cataclysms have been healed, ever greater prosperity has followed earlier economic dislocations, and San Francisco has survived — survived to become one of the most livable cities in the world and one that often points the way in how urban areas can reconcile their diverse populations and celebrate the synergy that comes from this diversity.

Tensions will continue to exist: between the affluent and the economically marginal, between homosexual and heterosexual, between different ethnic groups, between business owners and labor unions, between political conservatives and liberals. But ever since William Richardson put up a trading shack on the Yerba Buena Cove in 1834, compromise and goodwill have resolved these tensions, sparked the city's rebirth and renewal, and continued the city's prosperity.

As the distinctive wind-blown, salt-filled air fills the nostrils of San Franciscans, as the melancholy counterpoint of its foghorns punctuates a foggy evening, and as the pungent smells of restaurants, grocery stores and bakeries on Columbus Avenue in North Beach, Clement Street in the Richmond and 16th Street in the Mission perfume the air, San Franciscans reach back into the collective consciousness of their cumulative past and seek solutions that will continue to keep this city sitting on its golden hills, the urban oasis that it has been.

CHAPTER 1

When the Water Came up to Montgomery Street

Before 1848

When the Water Came up to Montgomery Street

For millions of years, the upheavals that marked the cooling of the earth's crust and the shifting atmosphere that attended this constant reshaping of the surface of the planet continuously changed the lay of the land. Much of the activity that created the landscape of what we call today the state of California — the deserts, the coastal mountain chains, the Sierra Nevada, the extraordinarily fertile Central Valley, the narrow strait that connects the Pacific Ocean with that extensive body of water known as San Francisco Bay (and its connection with the two principal rivers of California) — occurred relatively late in geological time.

The result was an area favored by nature, with abundant rainfall and rivers, a benign climate, fertile soil and metallic riches — all factors that would shape the historical development of California, making it a populous and affluent part of the United States and one of the most productive regions on earth.

The First Asian Immigrants

In the neighborhood of 10,000 to 12,000 years ago, a migration of Asians into the two American continents over the then-land bridge connecting Asia with Alaska took place. These first inhabitants of the Americas filtered into every part of the two continents, developing societies, many of which were existing when the Europeans arrived in the late 15th century.

Some of these societies achieved a high level of technological advancement; others remained groups of semi-nomads, establishing villages of between 50 and 200 people, hunting and gathering their food, living in huts of tule grass — a life of utmost simplicity.

California Indians did not form into tribes: The names given to them described the territory they occupied or a linguistic grouping. For example, the villages that bracketed San Francisco Bay from the northern end of San Francisco and the opposite side of the bay and then hugged the coast almost to Monterey were named by the Spaniards the Costanoans, because they spoke related languages (as related as one Romance language to another). Today, it is fashionable to refer to them as Ohlones, after one of the villages in what is now northern San Mateo County. The Costanoans — or Ohlones — were the first human inhabitants of San Francisco.

The Coming of the Europeans

Columbus' rediscovery of the Americas for the Europeans in 1492 began a sustained period of European conquest and colonization of the two continents. Just more than a quarter of a century after Spain had conquered and began to colonize Mexico, the

PREVIOUS SPREAD: When the Native Californians came to the missions and accepted Christianity, they were forced to give up their old beliefs.

(LUDOVIK CHORIS ENGRAVING/CALIFORNIA HISTORICAL SOCIETY, TEMPLETON CROCKER COLLECTION)

Coiffures de danse des habitans de la Californie.

The Costanoans — so named by the Spaniards because they lived along the coast — dwelled throughout the region, hunting, fishing and gathering, as well as trading with neighboring groups.

country sent out a mariner by the name of Juan Sebastian Cabrillo to explore the lands to the north. Cabrillo's three ships brought the first Europeans to California's shores when they landed at San Diego in 1542.

Cabrillo (who died on this voyage) was followed 37 years later by an English pirate by the name of Francisco Drake. Drake had decided to round the tip of South America in his search for Spanish plunder, and had realized that his ship needed repairs and fresh supplies. He landed on what is today the shore of Marin County, where he was able to fix his ship and take on fresh supplies before continuing his circumnavigation of the earth.

Drake was followed by the unfortunate Sebastian Rodrigues Cermanho, the captain of a Manila galleon in 1595, who, on his return from Manila, was searching for a harbor, when his ship was beached and destroyed by the surf. Cermanho then made his way back to Mexico on a raft of ships' timbers in a harrowing voyage.

In 1602–1603, Spain sent out yet another official voyage of exploration, headed by Sebastian Vizcaino. Vizcaino discovered Monterey Bay, about which he reported in the most extravagant and exaggerated terms.

And then, for 166 years, no European set foot on California's shores.

The Spanish Colonization of California

Spain was badly defeated in the Seven Years War, which ended in 1763. Its new king, Charles III, decided to reform the administration of the country's dominions, and the visitor-general sent to New Spain (Mexico) resolved that the area northwest of Mexico should be colonized. He convinced the Spanish crown to do so.

Thus, in 1769, the governor of Baja California, Don Gaspar de Portola, led a four-part expedition (two by different land routes coupled with two supply ships) to Alta — or Upper — California, where all were to rendezvous at the Bay of San Diego.

The supply ships did not arrive, and many of the soldiers fell ill. Portola's orders were to establish the first settlements — a fort (or presidio) and a mission to evangelize the Native Americans to Christianity — at Monterey. He soon set out with a handful of his men to reconnoiter the area.

Loma Alta was the name of Telegraph Hill when San Francisco was still called Yerba Buena.

Portola marched northward, hugging the coast where he could, but failed to recognize Monterey Bay when he came to it (Vizcaino had greatly exaggerated its excellence in his report). While in present-day San Mateo County, Portola realized that he was too far north and decided to reverse his march.

Before camp was broken, Portola sent a Sergeant Ortega to explore a bit farther. Simultaneously, two soldiers went up the hills behind the camp to shoot a couple of deer for dinner. These three men were to discover what the four great explorers of the 16th and 17th centuries had failed to find: one of the greatest harbors in the world, San Francisco Bay.

The connection between the strait known as the Golden Gate and the body of the bay was not discovered at that time. Three years would go by before the Spanish determined that Portola's men were the first Europeans to discover the bay.

Portola marched back to San Diego without finding Monterey Bay, but when one of the two supply ships finally arrived, the expedition was able to reach the elusive bay by sea. In 1770, the Presidio of Monterey and Mission San Carlos de Borromeo were started, and the European colonization of California had begun.

Spain soon decided to place a presidio and a mission on the shores of spectacular San Francisco Bay. A soldier-administrator by the name of Juan Bautista de Anza was chosen to blaze a trail from northern Mexico across what is today the southwestern part of the United States into Southern California. Anza successfully did this, returned to Mexico, gathered up colonists for the new settlement and led them along the route he had pioneered all the way to Monterey, from whence he came. Anza and a few men traveled north to the end of the peninsula now known as San Francisco, where they located sites for a mission and a presidio.

Having accomplished this, Anza returned to Mexico. The colonists were led into San Francisco to inaugurate the two founding settlements in late June 1776 by one of his subordinates, Captain José Moraga. Spain's California colonists were largely soldiers and officers and their families. It was they who, in the summer of 1776, began the Presidio of San Francisco, both a military outpost and a fledgling civilian center.

Trivia

The Officers' Club at the Presidio, built by the Spaniards in 1776, is the oldest surviving building in San Francisco.
The Presidio is now part of the Golden Gate National Recreation Area.

The Presidio of San Francisco was founded by the Spanish in the summer of 1776. It served as both a military outpost and a civilian center for the families of the military officers.

Jasper O'Farrell laid out San Francisco, building on the original survey by Jean Jacques Vioget. He gave San Francisco the wide boulevard he called Market Street.

SAN FRANCISCO HISTORY CENTER, SAN FRANCISCO PUBLIC LIBRARY

Two Spanish Franciscan missionaries, Father Francisco Palou and Father Benito Cambon, founded the sixth of California's missions, Mission San Francisco de Asis, which would be known by the popular name of Mission Dolores because it was located on a lagoon named for Our Lady of Sorrows.

In the beginning, the mission flourished. Thousands of the Native Americans in the San Francisco Bay Area converted to Roman Catholicism. They moved onto the mission compound, where they led the simple, rhythmical life of peasants, learning various skills and being instructed in ranching and farming.

But this paternalistic life would end in sadness and tragedy. Those Native Americans who could not adapt to their new life and tried to escape would be brought back by soldiers and punished for their desertion. Then the natives began to succumb to diseases of the colonizers, for which they had developed no immunities. Year after year, Native Americans died by the thousands.

During the four and a half decades of Spanish colonization, San Francisco was little more than a remote outpost of a crumbling Spanish empire. The adobe quadrangle in the northwestern part of the peninsula was usually in disrepair, its walls crumbling, its cannon rusted and inoperable. Two gun emplacements — one at today's Fort Mason, the other where Fort Point is — were added in the 1790s, but these did little to augment either the Presidio's defenses or its status as a civilian colony.

For most of this time, Spain was involved in the wars of the French Revolution and those of Napoleon. Just a few years after Napoleon's defeat at Waterloo, Mexico successfully completed its own revolution against Spain, becoming an independent republic. Thus, in 1821, California learned it was now part of Mexico.

Before 1848

Mexico Rules

The world began to change rapidly after the defeat of Napoleon: There would be no world war for a century; the Industrial Revolution, begun during the late 18th century, would gather momentum; international trade would expand, and social mobility would increase. The European powers and the rising United States began to cast about for territorial expansion.

California, loosely controlled by Mexico, mirrored these changes. An increasing number of foreigners began to migrate to California, many of them becoming naturalized citizens of Mexico and marrying into local Hispanic families. Trade, not allowed under Spanish rule, soon began to be a factor as European, Latin American and American ships began to exchange manufactured goods for the hides and tallow from the innumerable herds of cattle that wandered on California's rolling hills.

Political strife was endemic. Groups of families struggled against each other for control of the region, a north-south antipathy arose, and locals found fault with the governors sent by the central government in Mexico City. But such contention did not hamper the daily pastoral rhythms of life in California, nor did it result in bloodshed. It was, largely, an opera buffa type of civil strife.

Yet another of the developments during the quarter century of Mexican rule of California was the removal of the Franciscan missionaries from the control of the mission lands. These lands had never belonged to the church or any of its agencies: They were held in trust for the Native American mission communities, who would hold them communally until such a time as they could demonstrate the capacity for self-rule.

With the removal of Franciscan rule, Native Americans were stripped of their patrimony, and the lands were granted to more than 800 individuals — both Hispanic and naturalized citizens — during the decade after the implementation of the secularization legislation. Thus began what is called the rancho period of California history.

By the end of 1834, a few such ranchos had been granted in the San Francisco Bay Area, and in November of that year, the California territorial assembly created the pueblo, or town, of San Francisco. Its dimensions were considerably greater than today, stretching from the northern waterfront of the San Francisco peninsula to present-day Stanford University, and incorporating substantial portions of today's Alameda and Contra Costa counties.

The creation of the Pueblo of San Francisco enabled its inhabitants to establish a municipal corporation and give it municipal lands, and allowed it to elect municipal officers — the equivalents of a mayor, a town council and justices of the peace.

During the following year, a naturalized citizen of Mexico (an Englishman by birth) who had been living in Southern California, came to the pueblo and settled on the best anchorage on the peninsula's northeastern waterfront: Yerba Buena Cove.

William Richardson had jumped ship in San Francisco Bay in 1822, married a local woman and gone to live in Southern California. He returned to San Francisco in 1835 to establish himself as a merchant and to hold the position of customs collector for the port.

When he arrived, the Presidio had recently been abandoned and its troops removed to Sonoma. The mission was virtually inoperative and starting to crumble. Richardson was the first to establish himself on Yerba Buena Cove. (The cove resembled a half-moon, stretching from the area of today's Spear and Folsom streets to lower Broadway, with the beach largely along what is today's Montgomery Street.) On the beach, where present-day Montgomery and Clay streets intersect across from the Transamerica Pyramid, Richardson put up a trading shack; up the hill — on today's Grant Avenue — he built a crude dwelling, which was replaced in 1837 with a two-story adobe house.

Richardson's establishment was viewed during the winter following his arrival by a young Bostonian on a New England trading vessel anchored in the cove. "Over a region far beyond our sight there were no human habitations, except that an enterprising Yankee (sic), years in advance of his time, had put up on the rising ground above the landing, a shanty of rough boards, where he carried on a very small retail trade between the hide ships and the Indians," wrote Richard Henry Dana in *Two Years Before the Mast*.

Born of a Danish father and a black mother in the West Indies, William Leidesdorff arrived in San Francisco in 1841 and became a merchant. He acquired real estate, including a warehouse at what is now the corner of California and Leidesdorff streets, and launched a steamship on San Francisco Bay to ply the rivers up to Sacramento. Leidesdorff also served on the city's first municipal council and its first school board.

In 1836, Jacob Leese, a merchant from the United States, joined Richardson on the banks of Yerba Buena Cove. Others, mostly foreigners, drifted into the fledgling settlement during the next years. Adobe structures, wooden shanties and the superstructure of a ship cropped up along the cove and around the plot of land that had been designated a plaza for the trading settlement of Yerba Buena. The *alcalde* — the Hispanic term for the pueblo's chief magistrate or mayor — began to grant lots along the cove to those requesting them.

By the end of the decade, there were about 50 people living in Yerba Buena, and the alcalde decided to have a former Swiss sea captain turned San Francisco grocer, Jean Jacques Vioget, make a survey of the settlement. Vioget's survey was modest: an area bounded by the beach (Montgomery Street), Grant Avenue, Sacramento Street and Pacific Avenue. Vioget imposed the grid system (streets at right angles to each other) and fixed the future pattern for San Francisco's development.

Yerba Buena's modest beginnings were based upon a mercantile trade. Richardson and Leese were eventually joined by an agent of the Hudson Bay Co., by Nathan Spear and William Hinckley, and by the merchant William A. Leidesdorff (born of a Danish father and a black mother in the Danish West Indies). By the mid-1840s, there were also several grocery stores, a couple of bars, a restaurant, a blacksmith and three carpenter shops. It has been estimated that by mid-1846 Yerba Buena contained about 200 inhabitants.

The United States Takes Over

The United States had cast a covetous eye on California since the early days of the republic. By the mid-1840s, the rising tide of Manifest Destiny created a conflict with Mexico, whose former province of Texas the United States had recently annexed.

A harbinger of the conflict was seen in the arrogant and hostile expedition of a captain in the US topographical engineers, that of John C. Fremont. Fremont crossed the Sierra Nevada into California and approached Monterey with his soldiers, Kit Carson and Indian guides. The Mexican California authorities told him to leave. Instead, Fremont barricaded himself on a mountain near Monterey, eventually progressing toward Oregon. At the Oregon border, he turned back into California, where he began to agitate among the settlers in the Sacramento Valley, Sonoma and Marin — settlers who had largely come from the United States — against the Mexican California authorities. His activities led to the so-called Bear Flag Revolt.

In late June 1846, Fremont crossed the strait between Marin County and San Francisco and "captured" the Presidio (abandoned 13 years before).

Several days later, his foolhardiness was sanctioned when news reached California that war had broken out between Mexico and the United States in May.

When word of the war reached the commandant of the US Naval Pacific Squadron on July 8, Commodore John Sloat immediately seized Monterey and ordered his subordinate, Captain John B. Montgomery, to seize Yerba Buena and the northern settlements.

Montgomery marched to the plaza on the morning of July 9, raised the American flag, and read a proclamation in Spanish and English that the United States was occupying the village. All parties then retreated to Ridley's bar for libations, and a peaceful occupation followed. By the following January, all hostilities had ceased in California, and the United States was in peaceful possession of the land it had long coveted.

During the next year and a half, Yerba Buena became a bustling trading town. In late January 1847, at the behest of the town's merchants who were concerned about the founding of a town across the bay, which was to be named Francisca, the alcalde, Lieutenant Washington Bartlett, issued a proclamation changing the name of Yerba Buena to San Francisco. Thus, by the stroke of the pen of a naval officer acting as a chief magistrate of the trading settlement, the small town appropriated for itself the name of the bay, the former presidio, the mission and the pueblo.

That same year, the alcalde and the town council petitioned the military governor of California to issue to the municipality certain lands in the public domain, which could then be subdivided and sold for the town's treasury.

Franciscan fathers established Mission Delores in 1776.

CLIFF CROSS

Before 1848

GARY STRENG

The Mission Dolores compound was once home to thousands of Native Americans who converted to Catholicism.

Trivia

John Frémont gave the Golden Gate its prophetic name in 1846 as he watched the sun set over the ocean, framed by lustrous hills.

General Stephen Watts Kearny gave the desired permission, and the town proceeded to hire an Irish-born surveyor by the name of Jasper O'Farrell to survey the designated area. Vioget's earlier survey had set the grid pattern, which had been extended in 1844; O'Farrell's mandate was much larger. First, he had to correct Vioget's five-degree miscalculation (the so-called "O'Farrell swing"). Then he produced three separate surveys: one of the Yerba Buena Cove itself (the shallow cove had been designated as landfill); the second, an extension of the Vioget/1844 survey; and the third an entirely new area to be surveyed to the south of the established settlement.

O'Farrell decided to bisect his survey with a wide boulevard sighted from the middle of the cove to Twin Peaks. The 110-foot–wide street (possibly the widest street in the United States at that time), existing only on the paper of his survey and in actuality a series of high sand dunes, he called Market Street. For the survey of the area south of Market Street, O'Farrell plotted lots twice the size of those north of Market and blocks twice the size. Thus, only every other street south of Market Street would correspond with one north of the proposed boulevard.

The city's government proceeded to sell off the lots in a series of sales and auctions. The more valuable lots on the beach sold for between $50 and $200 each. The less desirable — around today's Union Square and in the South of Market area, for example — sold for $12.62.

The bustling town in mid-1847 had a population of about 500. Its *raison d'être* was entirely as a trading town, the head of a superb bay and harbor and of a complex of waterways that reached extensively throughout Northern California. While many predicted a continuation of a prosperous business community, no one foresaw the change in San Francisco's destiny that an event that took place in early 1848, about 150 miles to the northeast, would effect on the town's future.

CHAPTER 2

Dreams of Gold

1848–1859

Dreams of Gold

One of the non-Hispanics who came to California during its Mexican period was the German immigrant John A. Sutter. Sutter was given a large rancho in the Sacramento Valley, where he built a combination house and business center for his many enterprises.

After the US occupation of California, Sutter thought there would be a substantial increase in migration from the United States to the newly acquired territory, and such migration would require a huge amount of lumber to build homes and businesses. Thus, he added to his string of business operations a sawmill on the south fork of the American River at a place known by the name of Coloma.

For this venture, Sutter hired a recent immigrant to California, James Marshall, who would be a partner and the foreperson for the building of the sawmill.

The construction was nearly completed when, on Jan. 24, 1848, Marshall was wading in the river and spotted a shiny object in the bed of the stream. He stooped to pick it up and saw it was a yellowish rock. For the next four days, Marshall continued to pick up such rocks and, thinking they might be gold nuggets, decided to ride to Sutter's hacienda.

Sutter and Marshall checked an encyclopedia and applied detailed tests to determine whether the rocks were true gold. The specimens were, indeed, the genuine metal.

Both men rode their horses to the sawmill, announcing to the workers that real gold had been found and that they were free to prospect for it during the time they were not engaged in the construction of the sawmill. Neither Sutter nor Marshall suspected the extent of the riches yet to be uncovered, and presumably thought only some surface placers, soon to be exhausted, had been found.

The workers on the sawmill started to search for the gold nuggets in their spare time, going up and down the river. Soon, they laid down their tools and began spending all their time in the pursuit of gold.

The California Gold Rush was on.

The Gold Rush Is On

Such a modest beginning to one of the most important events of the 19th century, in a remote corner of California, took a comparatively long time to come to public attention. Slowly, rumors began to circulate around Northern California, then spread to Southern California, the Hawaiian Islands and Oregon; word reached northern Mexico and the countries of western Latin America.

It was not until mid-March that a small notice of the gold discovery appeared in the back page of one of San Francisco's two newspapers. Two months later, on May 12, the owner of the other newspaper — Sam Brannan, a savvy entrepreneur — ran down Montgomery Street, holding two bottles of gold nuggets, yelling "Gold! Gold! On the American River!"

PREVIOUS SPREAD: The many abandoned ships in San Francisco Bay were pressed into service. Some were used for buildings, as shown in this illustration — a warehouse, a hotel, even a jail. Many were dismantled for their wood, and still others slipped into the bay mud, where their remains are still found when excavating.

With this dramatic pronouncement, the town's several hundred residents emptied out, rushing to the ever-expanding area where gold was being found. Using spoons and knives, pans, picks and shovels, and an assortment of other utensils and equipment, they set up camps of lean-tos, tents and log cabins, and eagerly worked from sunup to sundown in search of the precious metal.

In June 1848, a letter from a Californian describing the discovery was published in a St. Louis newspaper, and soon, rumors ran rampant throughout the United States. In early December, President James K. Polk officially announced that gold had been found in sizable quantities in California. With that, thousands upon thousands of people, not just in the United States but throughout the world, left for the gold fields. Historians estimate that within the next few years somewhere between 350,000 and half a million individuals journeyed to California.

The Rush to California

What motivations could have impelled such a large number of people to leave hearth and home, their occupations, wives and children, sweethearts, friends and aged parents to undertake a long, often dangerous and expensive journey to a land about which little was known, to engage in an enterprise for which they had no previous experience and no certainty about their prospects?

One such motivation hinged on the social restlessness that follows a war. The United States had just concluded its first foreign war, and the returning soldiers were eager candidates for further adventures.

The desire for wealth — a common lure for human beings — was yet another powerful motivation. The yeoman farmer in Illinois who once a year slaughtered his hogs and sent the dressed carcasses to New Orleans to be sold, making $300 for his efforts, read about individuals taking out $300 a day in California gold fields, and would then decide to go himself. A few — such as David Broderick, defeated for the Congress in New York, and William Gwin, a congressmember from Mississippi — saw substantial opportunities for political advancement in California. Others wished to escape debts, family responsibilities and the long hours and crushing labors of most mid-19th century occupations.

In Europe, 1848 was a year of revolution. The resulting tumult motivated many to escape Europe's repressive political climate to begin life anew. Mexico and other countries in Latin America had had ongoing mining ventures for centuries. Many Hispanics from these countries sought to improve their fortunes in the gold fields of what had only recently been part of Mexico.

In the regions of Canton, the traditional center of Chinese entrepreneurship, there had been a civil war that had resulted in lawlessness, extraordinary poverty and social dislocation. The discovery of gold in California prompted a number of merchants to migrate, taking with them many poor Cantonese who would repay them for their transportation costs after they had worked in the their new home.

The governor of the British penal colony of Australia decided to release the least violent of the criminals under his control and allow them to go to California, where they became known as the "Sydney Ducks" and where they would be a troublesome group.

And so, from every part of the country and from every part of the world, eager gold-seekers left their homes for California, where they expected to become rich and then return to their homes.

They came by two methods of transportation: the land route and the journeys by sea. The former required the gold-seeker to join a covered wagon train in St. Joseph, Mo., for departure in April, which would arrive in California in October or November. The sea routes gave travelers a choice of a relatively safe but long and tedious voyage around the tip of South America to San Francisco, a voyage of up to several months.

Two faster, but much more dangerous, routes were by sea to the Isthmus of Panama or to Nicaragua, crossing these areas by a combination of some type of vessel, muleback and walking, and then waiting on the Pacific side of these Central American areas for a

SAN FRANCISCO HISTORY CENTER, SAN FRANCISCO PUBLIC LIBRARY

Levi Strauss, who arrived in San Francisco as a dry-goods dealer in 1849, made clothing for miners, using rivets to make the garments more durable. Today, the company is still family-owned and headquartered in San Francisco.

OVERLEAF: The Bella Union and the Verandah, two of San Francisco's popular music halls, stand proudly on Portsmouth Square in the mid-1850s.

(SAN FRANCISCO HISTORY CENTER, SAN FRANCISCO PUBLIC LIBRARY)

ship bound for San Francisco. Panama and Nicaragua were filled with possibilities of disease — yellow fever, malaria, cholera — which took many lives and impaired the health of many more.

The experience of the eager prospectors once they got to California was usually disappointing. Although many millions of dollars of gold were extracted from the streams and gullies of the Sierra Nevada, there were too many gold-seekers for the available gold. Inflation bid up the cost of goods and services; the miners were often able only to find enough gold to maintain themselves in the basic necessities. Homesickness and physical illness afflicted many. The back-breaking labor of digging or panning for gold from dawn to sunset was in many cases more difficult than the prior occupation of the gold-seekers. And then, many would lose their hard-earned gold through gambling and resorting to the brothels that proliferated through the mining camps and in San Francisco and Sacramento.

Many returned to their homes; others decided to stay in California. Of these, most abandoned the pursuit of gold and turned instead to farming, to business, to the professions, to the trades they thought they had left behind. Some went on to reap fortunes, not from finding gold, but from the numerous economic opportunities unleashed by the discovery of gold.

FROM THE GOLD RUSH TO CYBERSPACE

Trivia

The secret ingredient in the original sourdough bread was yogurt, which provided the bacteria that causes the bread to ferment and rise, just like yeast. In fact, bacteria originating in the mother dough used by Isidore Boudin to bake his first loaf in 1849 still thrive at Boudin bakeries.

Italian Domingo Ghirardelli arrived in San Francisco in 1849 and headed for the gold country. He soon returned to the city to open a shop off Portsmouth Square, where he sold candy, fruits, coffee and pastries. By 1885, he was importing 450,000 pounds of cocoa beans for his California Chocolate Manufactory. In 1893, the company moved to what is now the shopping and entertainment complex known as Ghirardelli Square.

Instant City

San Francisco had been a burgeoning trading village since William Richardson had placed his shack on Yerba Buena Cove in 1835. By mid-1848, the town could boast a population of perhaps 800. After Brannan's announcement that spring the town emptied out and business came to an end. But before long, San Francisco re-emerged as the commercial emporium and the mercantile center for California's exploding population. It was the nexus for people and goods both entering and leaving California.

Each month brought increasing numbers of argonauts, most of whom left almost immediately for the mines. Many came back to work in San Francisco, and those who saw the business opportunities in the city stayed to take advantage of them.

Between Dec. 14, 1848, and Jan. 18, 1849, 61 ships sailed to California from Atlantic ports. By February, the numbers had increased to 130, and the sailings continued at that rate for the remainder of the year. Every vessel that could float was pressed into service, and when the ships arrived in San Francisco, not only did the passengers depart, so did the crews.

The authors of *The Annals of San Francisco*, the first history of the city (1856), present a vivid picture of San Francisco in mid-1848:

About the end of May we left San Francisco almost a deserted place, and such it continued during the whole summer and autumn months. Many ships with valuable cargoes had meanwhile arrived in the bay, but the seamen deserted. The goods at great expense had somehow been landed, but there was nobody to care of them, or remove them from the wharves where they lay exposed to the weather... The merchants who remained were in a feverish bustle. They were selling goods at high prices, but could get no hands to assist them in removing and delivering the articles... Here, therefore, as at the mines, the prices of labor and all necessities rose exceedingly. The common laborer, who had formerly been content with his dollar a day, now proudly refused ten; the mechanic (a 19th century word for a skilled laborer) who had recently been glad to received two dollars, now rejected twenty for his day's services.

This inflation was a common feature in every aspect of San Francisco's urban life, with prices from 10 to 20 times what they would have been back home. Walter Colton's book about his three years in California talks about simple breakfasts for $6, boots for $50, haircuts for $4.

Real-estate prices skyrocketed. A lot facing Portsmouth Plaza was purchased in 1847 for $16.50; in the late spring of 1848, it sold for $6,000; and before the end of the year resold for $43,000. Another lot that had been purchased for $15 sold a year later for $40,000.

Similarly, rents spiraled upward. A one-story building across from Portsmouth Plaza rented for $6,000 per month; one-room offices went for $1,000 per month. Spaces for gambling houses often rented by the day or by the shift. Newspapers from the East, a few months old, were often sold for hundreds of dollars each.

The bustling instantaneous city was a marvel to all visitors, often for the heterogeneity of its inhabitants. New York newspaperperson Bayard Taylor wrote his impression of leaving the ship that brought him to San Francisco:

A furious wind was blowing down through a gap in the hills, filling the streets with clouds of dust. On every side stood buildings of all kinds, begun or half-finished, and the greater part of them were canvas shacks, open in front, and covered with all kinds of signs, in all languages. Great quantities of goods were piled up in the open air, for there was no place to store them. The streets were full of people, hurrying to and fro, and of as diverse and bizarre a character as the houses. Yankees of every possible variety, native Californians in serapes and sombreros, Chileans, Sonorians (sic), Kanakas from Hawaii, Chinese with long (pig) tails, Malays armed with their everlasting creeses, and others on whose embrowed and bearded visages it was impossible to recognize any special nationality.

Tumult and Turbulence

John Geary had been sent out in 1849 as San Francisco's first postmaster. During the same year he was elected alcalde (and in 1850, when the legislature began the reorganization of the state into counties and chartered towns and cities, became San Francisco's first mayor), delivered a statement to his constituents in August 1849:

At this time we are without a dollar in the public treasury, and it is to be feared that the city is greatly in debt. You have neither an office for your magistrate, nor any other public edifice. You are without a single police officer or watchman, and have not the means of confining a prisoner for an hour; neither have you a place to shelter, while living, sick and unfortunate strangers who may be cast upon our shores, or to bury them when dead. Public improvements are unknown in San Francisco. In short, you are without a single requisite necessary for the promotion of prosperity, for the protection of property, or the maintenance of order.

This indictment began to be addressed by the city's political authorities, not always with happy results. A piece of property — on the site of today's Asian Art Museum (the previous location of the Main Library) — was purchased for a cemetery. The attempt to take care of the indigent sick resulted in a massive scam, the so-called Dr. Peter Smith Sales, in which many of the city fathers were involved. A building was secured for a city hall (also fraught with financial chicanery). And the beginnings of a police department were put together.

The city's insolvency, and the combination of business and political corruption that kept the city in debt and its credit nonexistent, would continue until 1856. But such instability paled next to the series of fires that successively destroyed much of the city — six times — between Christmas Eve 1849 and June 1851, a period of only a year and a half.

Fires in urban areas were the bane of the 19th century, and San Francisco's poorly built, crowded structures were prime flammable materials. The stiff prevailing winds helped to fuel fires once they started. The use of kerosene lamps and stoves aided in starting fires. And the ever-present suspicion that arson was the cause of some of the fires was probably justified.

The most disastrous of these fires took place on May 4, 1851. The burned district was three-quarters of a mile long and a quarter-mile wide. Sixteen blocks were destroyed, including 10 bounded by Pine, Jackson, Kearney and Sansome; five bounded by Sansome, Battery, Sacramento and Broadway; one bounded by Kearny, Montgomery, Washington and Jackson; and fractions of five other blocks.

This photograph from 1851, taken from Second and Howard streets looking toward Market, shows early city dwellings.

Lotta Crabtree

A common scene at Wells Fargo:
A miner exchanges his gold for cash.

In early 1850, almost immediately after the first fire, a group of men gathered to form a volunteer fire company. Others would be subsequently begun, and by the time the city inaugurated a municipal fire department in 1867, there were about 20 volunteer fire companies in San Francisco.

The companies became a major factor in the social, political and even business history of San Francisco for more than a decade and a half. Many successful business and professional leaders gave unstintingly of their time and money to the volunteer company to which they belonged. Place of origin was usually the basis for which volunteer company one joined: New Englanders to the Howard Engine Company No. 1, for example; those from New York City to the Knickerbocker Engine Company No. 5.

Crime, Punishment and Vigilantes

The instantaneous transformation of the small trading village of Yerba Buena in 1847 to the bustling metropolis of San Francisco in 1849 was not accomplished without ongoing problems: notably, rampant crime.

Any event such as the Gold Rush is going to attract the off-scourings of humanity from throughout the world. In addition, there were the actual criminals from the British penal colony in Australia.

Augmenting serious criminal activity — murder, mugging, arson and robbery — were the rambunctious activities of a largely male population principally composed of those from their late teens to age 30. And to cap off such depredations was the corrupt collusion between the political authorities and many businesspeople, which resulted in an ongoing looting of public assets for private gain.

The first instance of a major public confrontation to temper lawlessness occurred in 1849, when a group known as the Hounds, inhabiting a tent community on the slope of Telegraph Hill overlooking Broadway, spent an evening committing mayhem on an adjoin-

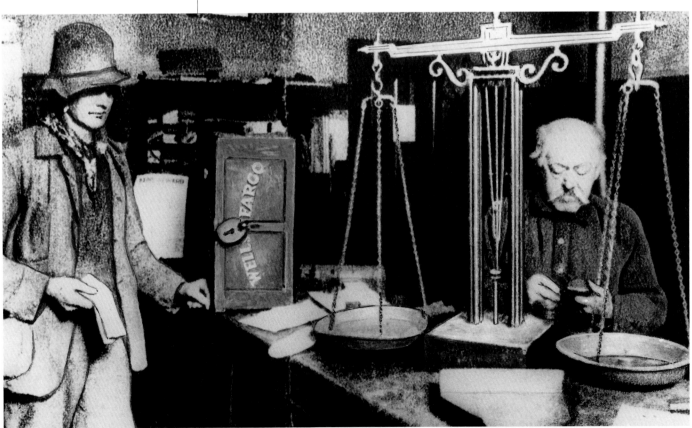

ing tent community of Hispanics. Merchants and other respectable citizens in the city armed and offered their services to the authorities to end such lawlessness.

Although their services were not needed, it was an early experience among the class with most to lose from continuing crime — the business class — in cooperative action to end criminal activities.

Even so, crime did not decline; rather, it worsened. The authorities, often reliant on criminals for their election to office, did little to end or punish criminal activities. Witnesses to crime frequently left the city before the accused came to trial. Business leaders themselves were at fault for the ineffective system of justice because of their reluctance to take time from their occupation to sit on juries. Further, the plethora of fires and the resultant substantial losses had made indignant many a business owner who believed the fires had been set by criminals as a way of looting various stores and places of business.

The merchants became incensed when one of their number, a popular man by the name of Jansen, was set upon and brutally beaten. Two suspects were arrested, but the judge let them go. The arrogance of criminals was boundless, and in early June, a group of about 200 merchants and professional men signed a document that pledged them to take extraordinary means to protect life and property.

The next day, a burglar by the name of John Jenkins was apprehended by two men who had signed the document, taken to the group's headquarters on Sansome Street near Bush, tried, found guilty and sentenced to death. Shortly before 2 am, he was taken by a number of the signatories to the adobe custom house on Portsmouth Plaza and hanged. Thus came into being what is called the First Committee of Vigilance.

This action led to opposition, both on the part of criminals and their allies in government, as well as from those who sincerely deplored individuals taking justice into their own hands.

A month later, a Sidney Duck by the name of James Stuart was tried by the vigilantes, found guilty of murder and hanged. In mid-August, two more criminals were tried and executed.

During its 10 weeks of operation, the Committee of Vigilance had executed four men, deported many others (and caused yet others to flee) and had prevented the landing of ships they believed were bringing criminals into San Francisco.

Within a few months after the Committee of Vigilance had disbanded, however, criminal activity in San Francisco was back in full swing. The authorities remained lax, but no vigilante activity resumed.

Gold production peaked in 1853, and in the following year, the beginning of a decline triggered a depression. By the end of 1854, more than one-third of the city's 1,000 stores stood vacant. During the next 12 months, more than 200 people went bankrupt. The depression continued into the next year, and panic ensued. Most of the city's banks closed their doors. Adams & Co. Express and Page, Bacon & Co., two of the West's major banks, became insolvent.

In the midst of this economic crisis, a scandal was revealed when a prominent and prosperous lumber merchant by the name of Henry Meiggs fled San Francisco just before it was discovered that he had stolen bond books with unissued bonds from the city treasurer's office and had fraudulently sold the bonds after forging signatures.

Meiggs had been a member of the city council, and because he had often voted in the public interest, had become known as Honest Henry. He had become involved in a major speculation venture by buying a great deal of land in North Beach — land he bought on credit and which plummeted in value during the depression of 1854–55. The fraudulent sale of bonds was an attempt to keep him from going bankrupt.

Meiggs' flight to the South Seas and subsequently to South America uncovered the massive political and business corruption in San Francisco and the alliance between corrupt politicians and criminals. The mercantile community became increasingly outraged.

Lotta Crabtree (opposite) and Lola Montez (below) were popular entertainers during San Francisco's Gold Rush days. Montez was known for her version of the tarantella, called the Spider Dance. Crabtree, Montez's protégée, was an accomplished dancer and singer who developed a national reputation. She donated Lotta's Fountain, which is located at Market and Kearny streets, to the city.

(SAN FRANCISCO HISTORY CENTER, SAN FRANCISCO PUBLIC LIBRARY)

Lola Montez

The economic and financial collapse of the mid-1850s and the continuing corruption finally became too much for the business community to swallow. In May 1856, an incident occurred that triggered yet another extra-legal seizure of power by San Francisco's business class. A twice-bankrupt banker by the name of James King had begun a newspaper that excoriated all the moral lapses in San Francisco in very intemperate language. One of his targets was a young New Yorker by the name of James Casey, who had been elected to the Board of Supervisors through blatant fraud. King revealed a little-known fact about Casey: He had been a prisoner in Sing Sing Prison for beating up his mistress and stealing her furniture.

King refused to listen to the infuriated expostulations of Casey, and shortly thereafter, Casey shot King on Montgomery Street. King would die within a few days. In the meantime, the remnants of the 1851 Committee of Vigilance were summoned. They recruited additional members, fortified a warehouse belonging to one of its members on Sacramento Street (called Fort Gunnybags because of the sacks of merchandise placed around the warehouse to protect it) as its headquarters, and proceeded to force the sheriff to release Casey into their custody.

In addition to Casey, the vigilantes also took into custody an Italian gambler by the name of Charles Cora, who had killed the federal marshal in San Francisco and was in jail awaiting a second trial. The two men were tried by the Committee of Vigilance, found guilty and, on the day of King William's funeral, were hanged from the second floor of Fort Gunnybags.

Despite strong opposition from a group called the Law and Order Party, which was against the assumption of judicial powers by the Committee of Vigilance, from California Governor J. Neely Johnson, and from the alliance of criminals, politicians and corrupt businesspeople, the committee thwarted all efforts to disband. Having dealt capital punishment to two additional malefactors, deported others and warned still others to leave the state, the committee decided that the crime and corruption in San Francisco would end only with the assumption of political power by a group of reformers. It put together such a reform political party, which swept the municipal elections in late 1856 and successfully governed the city for almost two decades.

The City of the Argonauts

San Francisco's emergence during the Gold Rush as one of the busiest cities in the world resulted in a unique, energetic, largely male-driven culture. The hallmarks of the San Francisco lifestyle quickly became a habit of eating out, an important role for prostitutes in the social and economic fabric of the city, and a particularly rambunctious energy.

The political structure of the city was an adaptation of the de facto Mexican system that had prevailed before the American conquest. In May 1850, the Legislature, which was elected as a result of the constitutional convention held in Monterey before California was admitted to the Union, began the political organization of the state. The city of San Francisco, with its boundary at Larkin Street, and the county of San Francisco, with its boundary in present-day Palo Alto, were chartered in May 1850. This political situation lasted until 1856, when the Legislature passed the Consolidation Act, creating a coterminous city and county of San Francisco and a new county to the south, named San Mateo.

Real estate — as it is in any rapidly expanding city — was a key feature in the city's development. Wharves thrust out into the Yerba Buena Cove, which was filled in between 1849 and 1855 to the present Embarcadero. Stockton Street became the first premier residential section of the city. Then the city's magnates began to build on Rincon Hill, in the northeast area of San Francisco. (Rincon Hill was the city's posh residential area until the late 1860s.) In the mid-1850s, George Gordon, a multifaceted English-born entrepreneur, developed South Park, on the edge of Rincon Hill, as another exclusive enclave for the city's nabobs.

Early in the 1850s, the city's harum-scarum construction — adobes, wooden shacks, canvas structures, salvaged ships that had been abandoned in the cove — had given way

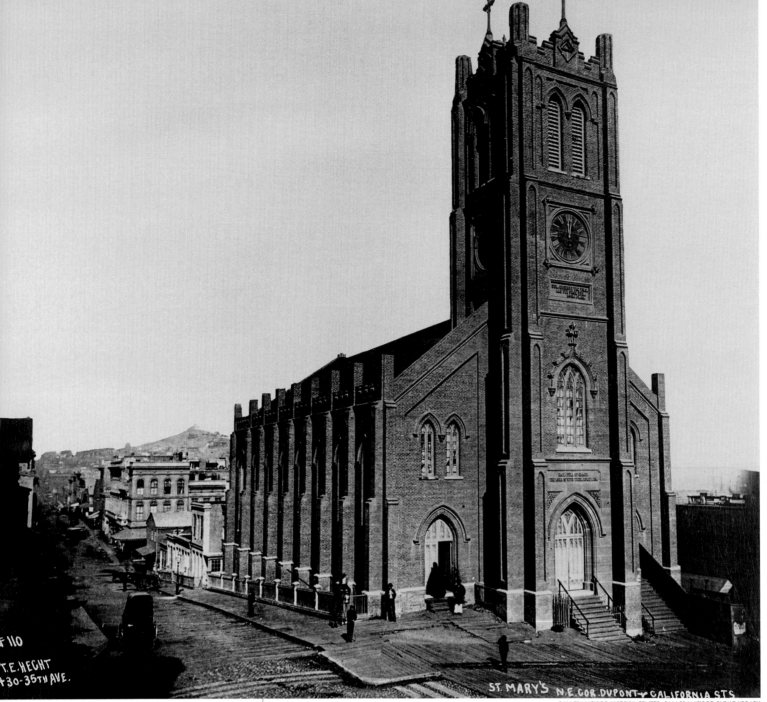

ST. MARY'S N.E.COR.DUPONT + CALIFORNIA STS.

Two of the city's first houses of worship: Old St. Mary's Catholic Church (above) has stood at the corner of California and Grant since 1854. Founded in 1851, the original Temple Emanu-El (opposite) was erected in the 1860s at 450 Post Street.

In 1852, the city purchased the Jenny Lind Theater, at the corner of Kearny and Washington streets, to use as its first city hall.

to the brick-and-stone construction of commercial buildings (residences continued to be built of wood). The constant grading and regrading of the streets on the city's hills caused great inconvenience and consternation among the city's residents.

All was in flux as the city's businesses struggled to meet the ever-changing conditions in the economic maelstrom of San Francisco and Northern California.

Such unsettled conditions were exacerbated by yet another set of circumstances: that of the uncertainty of California's land titles. The huge ranchos granted during the Mexican period had come under assault by the Anglo-Saxon settlers in California after the discovery of gold. Squads of squatters seized lands belonging to the rancheros or their assignees, claiming such grants were invalid and therefore part of the public domain, or maintaining that the US conquest rendered such huge grants of land against the customs of the conquering country.

The Congress attempted to settle this instability by passing legislation in 1851 providing for a land commission appointed by the president to adjudicate the question of the validity of land titles issued prior to July 8, 1846. These land grant cases, even after adjudication by the land commission, trickled through the federal courts well into the 1860s.

San Francisco's cases provide some of the most complicated land-grant issues in the state. The Santillan and the Limantour cases both claimed the bulk of the city. The former was ruled invalid; the latter was shown (after approval by the Land Commission) to have been a massive fraud. But the unsettlement of the titles to land had the effect of establishing mortgage rates at between 3 percent and 10 percent per month.

1848–1859

The turmoil did not deter the cultural life of the city, though. Two newspapers were started just after the conquest of California, and in 1847 the first book was published. In 1855, there were 20 daily newspapers in San Francisco — most were published in English, but there were also French, German, Chinese and Italian papers — and scores of weeklies, biweeklies and monthlies.

The first theatrical performance took place in 1849, and by the early 1850s, there were numerous well-appointed theaters in San Francisco, producing plays in English, French, Italian and Chinese. Because of the affluence of Northern California and because of the vociferous admiration of its entertainment-loving inhabitants, San Francisco became a magnet for theatrical troupes and entertainers from Europe and the eastern states.

Gambling casinos, some quite modest and others splendidly decorated, and brothels, from cheap "cribs" to lavishly appointed houses, were also part of the city's complex of entertainment.

This raffish element was offset by San Francisco's entertainment gardens, established for the city's extensive German enclave, where concerts of both choral and symphonic music were performed and, amazingly, opera, which was first presented in 1851.

Amusement areas — such as Russ' Gardens, south of Market, The Willows in the Mission district, the Cliff House at Land's End — provided additional opportunities for San Franciscans and visitors to the city to while away their time away from work.

Trivia

Lillie Coit arrived in San Francisco in 1851, at the age of eight, and began chasing fire engines soon after. She eventually became an honorary member of Fire Engine Company No. 5, and when she died, she left $100,000 to the city, which was used to build Coit Tower, a replica of a fire hose nozzle.

SAN FRANCISCO HISTORY CENTER, SAN FRANCISCO PUBLIC LIBRARY

Trivia

The Jewish high holy days were first celebrated in the city by 50 pioneers in 1849. By April 1850, several of the congregants had gone on to found Sherith Israel, but it was not incorporated until after the city's second synagogue, Temple Emanu-El.

The original St. Francis Hotel stood at the corner of Clay and Dupont (now Grant) streets. The stylish (by 1849's standards) hotel was the site of the state's first polling place.

The Gold Rush also sparked an upsurge in transportation, with the city becoming the commercial nexus for the entire West. There had been transportation connecting San Francisco with other parts of the area, of course, even before the discovery of gold. Small ships had plied between San Francisco and Sutter's Fort; the town had been the port for trading vessels; horses and mules had been used for both individuals to travel and for the transportation of goods.

With the discovery of gold, however, came a skyrocketing of population in Northern California and a quickening of economic activities. Hundreds of ocean-going vessels were coming into San Francisco Bay, bringing both passengers and goods from every part of the world. Both people and goods would then continue on into the interior by water transportation to Stockton, Sacramento and Marysville.

Stagecoach lines soon linked the mining towns and the principal market towns of California with San Francisco. Ferries crisscrossed San Francisco Bay on a regularly scheduled basis. And by the end of the 1850s, stagecoach lines from the Midwest to California were supplanting the overland wagon trains that had brought many thousands to California at the beginning of the Gold Rush.

The first recorded intra-urban transportation line was established in 1851, when an omnibus line was chartered from Portsmouth Plaza to Mission. It was operated by a conductor and a driver, and pulled by two horses along wooden tracks. The fare was $1.00 on weekends, 50 cents on weekdays.

The growth of transportation was largely at the behest of the growing number of businesses in San Francisco and the rest of Northern California. As early as 1852, two easterners founded Wells, Fargo & Co. as both a bank and an express company — just one of many such companies started during the Gold Rush.

Mining during these days — both the prospecting of the surface placers, as well as quartz and hydraulic mining — was the driving force of the economy. It was gold from the mines that stimulated the diverse economy. Fledgling manufacturing companies sprouted to produce needed equipment for the mining industry, as well as for the many mercantile pursuits that had grown up in San Francisco. Warehouses to store goods both for the city and for communities throughout the West proliferated. Retail establishments dotted every block. The very earliest directories show as diverse a business structure as the older cities of the East and Midwest.

It was not long after the discovery of gold that the extraordinary possibilities for agriculture were discovered. Soon, the Central Valley was growing large amounts of wheat. Fruit orchards, vineyards, nut trees and a wide variety of vegetables began to be grown. Growth of this industry over the decades turned California into one of the most productive agricultural areas in the world. The Hungarian-born Agoston Harazsthy pioneered the growing of grapes and the production of wine as a major industry; the English-born George Gordon was the first to grow sugar beets and refine them into sugar.

Thus, as the production of gold began to decline in the mid-1850s, far from becoming a ghost town, as some had predicted, San Francisco instead became the central point for the growing financial, commercial and mercantile industries in the West.

Founded in 1856, Lowell High School is the oldest public high school in California. Among its distinguished alumni are Albert Michelson (class of 1868), the first American to win the Nobel Prize in physics; Carole Channing (1938), star of stage and screen; US Supreme Court Justice Stephen Breyer (1955); and business leaders Walter Haas of Levi Strauss; William Hewlett, cofounder of Hewlett Packard; and Gap founder Donald Fisher.

CHAPTER 3

The Silver Age
1860–1879

The Silver Age

The year 1859, in many ways, symbolized the end of California's Golden Age and the beginning of its Silver Age.

During that year, one the most notable of the argonauts, David Broderick, died in a duel. Broderick, a New York City saloon-keeper who had run unsuccessfully for the US House of Representatives, came to California in 1849, intent on fulfilling his dream of becoming a US senator. He and a partner began a private assay firm, buying gold and coining it. This business made them a great deal of money, and Broderick invested his in San Francisco real estate, enabling him to enjoy an independent income and to pursue his political dreams.

Broderick was elected to the state Senate from San Francisco in 1850, and became one of the city's most powerful politicians, as well as a statewide political leader. His roller-coaster political career, thwarted at every turn by his principal rival, US Sen. William Gwin, finally yielded to him the coveted US senatorship, where he became aligned with the Douglas faction of the Democratic Party.

An incautious remark by Broderick led to the challenge to a duel by hot-blooded southerner David Terry, who was the chief justice of the California Supreme Court. Broderick was mortally wounded and died a few days later in great agony at the home of a banker friend on the shore of what is today called Aquatic Park.

The death of this colorful and dynamic pioneer who had arrived in San Francisco in 1849 and who had seized the economic and political opportunities that the Gold Rush offered, seemed to close an era of great excitement, great opportunity and great upheaval.

The changes that had occurred were observed in that same year by a prosperous and influential Bostonian lawyer and writer by the name of Richard Henry Dana. Dana, as a very young man, had been on a New England trading ship in the Yerba Buena Cove in the winter of 1835–36 and had described his voyage from New England to the ports of California in one of the classics of American literature, *Two Years Before the Mast*. His message on his stay in the Yerba Buena Cove commented on the ruinous state of the mission and the Presidio, on Richardson's trading shack on the bank of the cove, and wild animals drinking the waters of the cove from the beach.

A quarter-century later he returned. In an article published after he went back to Boston, he wrote:

> When I awoke in the morning and looked from my window over the city of San Francisco, with its storehouses, towers and steeples; its courthouses, theaters and hospitals, its daily journals; its well-filled learned professions; its fortresses and lighthouses; its wharves and harbor, with their thousand-ton clipper ships, more in number than London or Liverpool sheltered that day, itself one of the capitals of the American Republic, and the sole emporium of a new world, the awakened Pacific; when I looked across the bay to the eastward, and beheld a beautiful town on the fertile, wooded shores

PREVIOUS SPREAD: The Big Four — Leland Stanford, Charles Crocker, Collis P. Huntington and Mark Hopkins — built their railroad monopoly through duplicity, bribery and corruption, as depicted in this political cartoon.

The San Francisco Stock and Exchange Board, the first in the West, was founded in 1862. Speculation in the Comstock mines was rampant, but by the time this photograph was taken, in 1928, the silver boom had given way to other financial interests.

of the Contra Costa, and steamers, large and small, the ferryboats to the Contra Costa, and capacious freighters and passenger carriers to all parts of the great bay and its tributaries, with lines of their smoke in the horizon — when I saw all those things, and reflected on what I once was and saw here, and what now surround me, I could scarcely keep my hold on reality at all, or the geniuses of anything and seemed to myself like one who had moved in "worlds not realized."

The rapid changes wrought by the Gold Rush, and so well-contrasted by Dana, were to be drastically expanded by another event that took place in 1859.

Prospectors on the eastern slopes of the Sierra Nevada, just on the other side of California's border with the territory of Nevada, had long cursed the bluish-white clay that had clogged their rockers. But when someone thought to send a sample of this clay to Ott's Assay House in Nevada City, Calif., it was revealed to have a very light content of silver — another rush was on.

But the Comstock Lode — as this discovery was named — was different from the gold discovery in California. The latter was spread over a very wide area and had rich surface placers, while the Comstock was a narrow ravine on a mountain and almost immediately necessitated burrowing into the mountain. Thus, the discovery of silver needed large amounts of capital to dig the mines and tunnels deep beneath the surface, to ventilate and drain the mines and to hire miners to dig out the ore. It was to the business leaders of San

1860–1879

Francisco, custodians of substantial amounts of capital, that the early Comstock entrepreneurs turned to finance the development of the Comstock mines.

During the next 20 years, hundred of millions of dollars of silver would fill the pockets of San Franciscans, expanding the population of the city and thrusting its development toward every point of the compass.

The Comstock and San Francisco

The Comstock mines very early had become companies with publicly traded securities, and in 1862, the first stock exchange in the West, the San Francisco Stock and Exchange Board (many years later named the San Francisco Mining Exchange), was founded. Speculation was rampant, new fortunes were quickly made and lost.

The mines themselves swung from bonanza to bust, and the stocks of the mining companies rose and fell. One such mine, the Crown Point, would soar from $3 per share to $6,000 within eight months. Needless to say, such upward movements in the Comstock provided enticement for San Franciscans of every class to speculate.

The town of Virginia City, Nev., became the Comstock metropolis, with a bustling population that was involved in the nearby mines. Virginia City businesses supplied the numerous prospectors who had fanned out throughout Nevada hoping to find a similar bonanza.

The Comstock mines tended to be operated in an inefficient manner. The San Francisco capitalists who controlled them were novices to the world of deep-rock mining, and it was only slowly that experts from Europe, parts of Latin America and the eastern United States would bring to Nevada improved techniques for the mining and refinement of the silver ore.

Furthermore, the sudden discovery that a mine was in *borrasca* (meaning without silver ore) could send the shares of a company plummeting, and if the company had borrowed money, the lack of ore could mean it was bankrupt.

Into this uncertainty entered two men who would dominate the Comstock until the mid-1870s: William C. Ralston and William Sharon.

The Age of Ralston

Ralston had had success in some Comstock mining speculations and had great confidence in the future of the lode. When he began an agency of the Bank of California in Virginia City, he sent a man recommended by his father-in-law to head it: William Sharon.

The two men combined to control virtually all the mines on the Comstock and formed a separate refining company, to which all the ore on the Comstock was sent. They owned timberlands in the Sierra Nevada and constructed the Virginia & Truckee Railroad. Millions of dollars flowed into their pockets and into those of a few associates.

But Ralston's success in Comstock investments was marred by some spectacular failures or, more correctly, missed opportunities. A habit of Ralston and Sharon was to sell their stake in a mine when it no longer produced ore and to reacquire the stake when the mining superintendent notified them that he had once again found profitable silver ore.

Trivia

Before the Civil War, Thomas Starr King, minister of the First Unitarian Church, gave speeches in the public square near his church urging Californians to remain loyal to the Union. This plaza became known as Union Square.

San Francisco was still pastoral in 1865, as this scene from 15th and Market streets attests.

FROM THE GOLD RUSH TO CYBERSPACE

Trivia

The oldest continuously operating bar in San Francisco is The Saloon, which opened as Wagner's Beer Hall in 1861. It's at 1232 Grant Ave.

(John P. Jones, the superintendent of one mine, contacted instead an associate of Ralston's and the two of them obtained control of the mine, which then produced a huge bonanza — one of the few bonanzas that eluded Ralston and Sharon.)

Two mines that had been thought played-out — the California and the Consolidated Virginia — were purchased in the early 1870s by a quartet of Irish Americans: James Fair and John Mackey were mining men, William O'Brien and James Flood were bartenders. After the partnership had acquired two mines, the largest bonanza ever on the Comstock was discovered. The four became the Bonanza Kings, multimillionaires from their strike.

The actual flow of ore from the Comstock was marked by wild speculation. Between January and May 1872, for example, the market value of the stocks traded on the San Francisco Stock & Exchange Board rose from $17 million to $81 million — a fivefold increase in as many months.

Then, during 10 days in June, some $60 million was wiped out. The stock market eventually recovered, and between October 1874 and January 1875, there was yet another upsurge before prices retreated once more in February 1875. The stock market rallied, but collapsed again in August. This was to be the end of the euphoric speculation that had marked San Francisco and the West since the beginning of the 1860s.

In the wake of the August 1875 stock-market collapse came the collapse of William Ralston. The sanguine financier had made unauthorized loans to himself to shore up his own commitments. Further, the bank's own investments had become increasingly illiquid. In late August, a rumor began to circulate that the stock market's collapse was due to the Bank of California's need to raise funds. Withdrawals became substantial, and at 2 pm on Aug. 26, Ralston ordered the doors closed. The Bank of California had suspended operations.

The bank's board of directors met the next day and stripped Ralston of his position as a director and president. He left the bank and walked out to Aquatic Park (then called Black Point) to take a customary swim. Shortly thereafter a body was seen struggling in the waters of the bay. A rowboat brought to shore the body of William Ralston, dead of either a stroke or a heart attack.

Thus died the titan of San Francisco's Silver Age. His funeral was one of the largest in the city's history, attended by San Francisco's business and social elite, as well as by thousands of common laborers. The latter recognized that Ralston, despite his desperate financial gambits, had elected not to close money-losing businesses because he did not wish to lay off workers, and that he truly loved San Francisco.

Less than two months after his death, Ralston's associates re-opened the bank (it is today called the Union Bank of California). Also in October 1875, the Palace Hotel, in which Ralston had been a heavy investor, opened its doors. It would be San Francisco's premier hostelry for more than a quarter-century.

Tracks and Rails

Transportation is key to any civilization, and efficient transportation is essential for a thriving economy. It was sluggish during Spain's rule of California; somewhat improved during that of Mexico. The Gold Rush utilized every form and conveyance of transportation in order to facilitate the movement of individuals and goods to California — and from California to all parts of the United States and the world.

Numerous ocean-going vessels entering and leaving San Francisco Bay made the port one of the busiest in the United States. River steamers and bay ferries connected San Francisco with towns and cities throughout Northern California. Stagecoach lines crisscrossed the state and, from the beginnings of the Gold Rush, plank toll roads and omnibus lines traversed the rapidly expanding city. The first railroad in the West — the Sacramento Valley Railroad, which went from Sacramento to Folsom — began in 1855, but its difficulties did not inspire many entrepreneurs to construct additional railroads.

It was only the need for San Francisco banker and financier Francois Pioche to provide transportation from downtown San Francisco to his large real-estate development in the Inner Mission that prompted him to finance, in the early 1860s, the first steam railroad in

The Silver Titan

William Chapman Ralston was the dominant San Franciscan during most of the Silver Age. His creative mind and energy focused on the economic opportunities that began during the Gold Rush, extended during the period of the Comstock Lode and expanded San Francisco's role as the Queen of the Pacific.

Ralston was born and raised in Ohio, where he was preoccupied with the boats that plied the rivers of the Midwest. Eventually, after a move to New Orleans, he was employed by various transportation companies, including one owned by Commodore Cornelius Vanderbilt. During the Gold Rush, numerous transportation companies vied for the traffic from the United States to Central America.

Ralston came to San Francisco in the early 1850s and became a banker — a junior partner with associates from his shipping days. His verve, imagination and daring made him a success, and he successively became a more important — and wealthy — financier in San Francisco. A succession of banking partnerships culminated in 1864 with his founding the Bank of California — the first banking corporation chartered in the West under new federal legislation. It was also one of the most highly capitalized banks in the country.

Banks in the 19th and early 20th centuries operated both as commercial and investment banking firms, and Ralston was therefore able to function as a venture capitalist or equity investor for the bank and for his personal funds. Thus, Ralston's financial involvements present a bewildering array of businesses during the Silver Age.

He heavily invested in water transportation companies that connected San Francisco with other parts of the country and the world, including the California–Oregon Steamship Co. Because of his many successes, he is often overlooked as a pioneer in California agriculture, leading a group that purchased Agoston Haraszthy's Buena Vista winery, financing the planting and export of wheat from the Central Valley, and attempting to raise tobacco and to start a silk-making industry. Nor did he overlook manufacturing: A watch company, a carriage-making company and a textile company were all part of his portfolio.

Ralston sought the reconfiguration of San Francisco for both his own real-estate profits, as well as for what he considered the best interests of the city. The creation of Columbus Avenue (originally called Montgomery Avenue) to create a wider thoroughfare from North Beach to the Financial District and the creation of New Montgomery Street (an abortive attempt to better connect the financial district with the docks South of Market), are both a testament to Ralston's imagination and vitality.

He also constructed two hotels, the second of which — the Palace — was the second-largest and most luxurious in the world when it was completed in 1875. Unfortunately, Ralston died shortly before the opening.

This partial list of Ralston's many business ventures testifies to the financier's optimism about the business possibilities in California. His optimism extended to Nevada, where he would impose order on the chaotic conditions of the Comstock.

Banker William Ralston (above) was an investor in all sorts of businesses, not the least of which was the Palace Hotel (left).

the West, which provided commuter services for those buying lots in Pioche's development to go to their jobs downtown.

The unsuccessful Sacramento Valley Railroad did bring to California an engineer by the name of Theodore Judah. Judah's dream was to participate in the building of a transcontinental railroad. Such a railroad had been talked about since the 1840s, but the sectional rivalry between North and South in the Congress during the aftermath of the Mexican-American War had paralyzed any action on the part of the federal government, and the undertaking of building a transcontinental railroad was seen as beyond the capacity of a merely private venture.

That didn't stop Judah, however. He tried to interest California capitalists in setting up a company that would be ready to construct the western portion of the railroad when the US government authorized a route, and to help financially with the building of the railroad.

No San Francisco financier was interested in such a venture, but finally such a company was incorporated when Judah was able to get a quartet of Sacramento businesspeople to invest collectively a few thousand dollars with which to begin. The four were Leland

Lillie Coit was a fan of firefighters, especially those of Knickerbocker Company No. 5. When she died, funds from her estate were used to build Coit Tower atop Telegraph Hill, as well as the monument to firefighters that still stands in Washington Square.

OVERLEAF: The crowds at this pro-North rally at Post and Market streets in May 1861 belie the lukewarm support for California's adherence to the union during the Civil War.

Stanford, who would shortly be elected the first Republican governor of California; Charles Crocker; Collis P. Huntington; and Mark Hopkins.

Soon the Civil War broke out, and Congress passed legislation authorizing the building a transcontinental railroad to be constructed over a northern route. The contract was given in the early 1860s to the Union Pacific Co. to build from east to west and to the Central Pacific Railroad — Judah and his associates' company — to build from west to east. Congress decided to provide the wherewithal and incentive for the building of the railroad: It would guarantee bonds to be issued by the railroads, it would make outright cash subsidies (a specific amount for each mile of track laid with a bonus for building over mountains), and it would grant alternate sections (a section is 640 acres) along the right-of-way.

Each of the five men had his task: Judah was the engineer, Stanford was both the political operative and the public-relations front person, Hopkins the accountant, Hungtington the lobbyist in Washington, DC, and Crocker the construction boss.

Almost immediately the Sacramentans and Judah were at odds. The latter was appalled by the chicanery of his business partners. The Sacramento quartet would lie to the federal government about where tracks were being laid in order to obtain the higher subsidies for doing so in the mountains. They engaged in extortion from towns and counties for assurance that the railroad would pass through their territory. Those towns and counties that refused the subsidy were bypassed, no matter how logical and efficient a route through them may have been.

The argument soon split the four against Judah, but Judah was allowed to buy out his partners. On a trip to New York to raise capital to do so, he died, and his equity interest in the railroad was essentially expropriated by the men who would soon become known as the Big Four. The Sacramentans, now sole owners, continued their devious methods.

The Big Four

Once the last spike was driven at Promontory, Utah, and the transcontinental railroad was complete, the Big Four — Charles Crocker, Leland Stanford, Collis P. Huntington and Mark Hopkins — got busy extending its reach.

They continued the railroad to Oakland and built or bought up other lines in the state, north to Oregon and south through the San Joaquin Valley. As trade with Asia and Europe stepped up, with goods making their way through the ports of Oakland and San Francisco, the Central Pacific (later renamed the Southern Pacific) set about controlling the waterfronts. Soon the company owned the ferries and riverboats, setting fares as high as they wished. The railroad company also enticed easterners to develop the vast land parcels the federal government had set aside for the company as part of its deal for building the transcontinental railroad (and then repossessed it once these farmers had irrigated the land and it was producing). And it built the Del Monte Lodge in Pebble Beach in an effort to up its ridership on its line to the Monterey Peninsula.

As single-minded as the Big Four were — motivated simply by the desire to extend their wealth and power — their personal styles were quite different. This can be seen in their reported draws from the railroad's treasury during one four-month period. Crocker took $31,000, Huntington $57,000, Stanford $276,000 and Hopkins $800.

To say Hopkins was frugal is an understatement. A vegetarian who grew his own food, he was the last of the four to purchase Nob Hill property — and then he left the details of building their mansion to his wife. Huntington, too, was austere, insisting that the company's offices tend toward simplicity.

Crocker's lifestyle was more lavish. He owned two acres on Nob Hill, as well as a horse-breeding farm in Palo Alto and vineyards. He also financed coal mining, banking and cattle-ranching enterprises.

Leland Stanford, president of the railroad, was the most grandiose. The politician of the group, he founded the California Republican Party and held office as both governor and US senator. When he was turned down for an appointment to the University of California board of regents, he went on to found Stanford University.

Despite the feuds and in-fighting that are naturally bred among men of such different characters, the empire they created was one of the largest of its time. Their heirs sold the railroad in 1901, and it remained a major presence in San Francisco until late in the century, when it was acquired by the Pennsylvania-based Union Pacific.

THE BIG FOUR: (clockwise from top right) Leland Stanford, Charles Crocker, Mark Hopkins and Collis P. Huntington.

Cable-car creator Andrew Hallidie sits in front of car No. 10 for a run of the Clay Street Hill Railroad Co. The line ran a distance of only 2,880 feet, but soon the city was crisscrossed with similar rail lines.

CALIFORNIA HISTORICAL SOCIETY

One of the problems with building the railroad was labor. Many of those working on the railroad left their jobs to work in the Comstock mines, and others agitated for higher wages. The choleric Crocker, furious at these demands, contracted with the Chinese Six Companies, a San Francisco–based organization that dominated the affairs of the Chinese communities in the West, to provide Chinese laborers for him. All Caucasian workers were fired and replaced by new immigrants from China. They became known as Crocker's Pets and labored diligently, chiseling the road-bed on the granite cliffs of the Sierra Nevada, laying track across the arid plains of Nevada and Utah, hauling materials to the construction sites and never asking for more than they initially had been offered.

In 1869, at Promontory Point, Utah, the converging railroads met. The transcontinental railroad had been built. The Big Four, as a result (and from the subsequent development and acquisitions of the railroad), amassed massive fortunes, and from their homes atop Nob Hill and the Central Pacific's (subsequently renamed the Southern Pacific) headquarters in San Francisco, would dominate the political and economic life of the West for many years.

Shortly after the railroad was completed, San Francisco's intra-urban transportation received a new form of conveyance. In August 1873, Andrew Hallidie, a Scotland-born wire-rope manufacturer, drove the first cable car down Nob Hill along Clay Street to Portsmouth Plaza.

Hallidie had witnessed a troubling incident one foggy evening when a team of horses pulling a heavy wagon had slid backwards on the slippery cobblestones on a hill, and had been mangled. He purchased the invention of a man named Brooke, which used a continuous wire-rope beneath the street to pull a vehicle up and down a hill. He then obtained financing and constructed the Clay Street Cable Car Co., the city's first cable-car company.

Soon San Francisco's streets were being traversed by cable-car lines, replacing most of the horse-drawn omnibus lines. The marvel of San Francisco's intra-urban transportation system was born.

1860–1879

A quarter of a century after Hallidie's first use of the cable car, the cars began to be replaced by electric trolleys, and in the aftermath of World War II, the cable cars were deemed inefficient and archaic. They were to be totally replaced by electric trolleys and buses. However, a diminutive doctor's wife named Frieda Klussman galvanized a battalion of San Francisco matrons to put a proposition on the ballot to save the existing cable cars. The ballot measures was successful, but six subsequent ballot measures continued to affect the embattled cable cars, and a clever publicity campaign enabled the authorities to further reduce their numbers.

Finally, however, the city's residents definitively voted to save the remaining three cable-car lines, and today they are an icon of San Francisco, used and beloved by residents and visitors alike.

The Civil War and San Francisco

If one goes to Massachusetts or Indiana, to Mississippi or Virginia, the rending experience of the Civil War is all too obvious. It is there in monuments, in battlefield sites, in the family memories of residents.

In California, it is as if this watershed experience of US history had never occurred.

OVERLEAF: The Conservatory of Flowers is a feature of Golden Gate Park, which was begun in the 1870s.

(CLIFF CROSS)

Norton I, self-proclaimed emperor of the United States and protector of Mexico, was perhaps the first eccentric to capture San Francisco's fancy. Joshua Abraham Norton had been a successful shipper, but business reversals sent him into bankruptcy and a precarious mental state. Residents of the city embraced him as he wandered the streets in full uniform, accompanied by his dogs, Bummer and Lazarus.

HOUSEWORTH/CALIFORNIA HISTORICAL SOCIETY

FROM THE GOLD RUSH TO CYBERSPACE

In 1879, the California Electric Light Co. was formed to sell electrical service, perhaps the first company in the world to do so.

Actually, an influential percentage of California's population sympathized with the South as the country came nearer to conflict in 1860–61. Many more were in favor of California becoming an independent republic should the North and South resort to warfare. But the election of Sacramento businessperson Leland Stanford as the first Republican governor of California, the state's plurality vote for Lincoln in 1860, and the strenuous efforts of San Francisco lawyer Colonel Edward Bakar and Thomas Starr King, pastor of the city's Unitarian Church, for the Union cause combined to keep California loyal to the North when the Civil War erupted.

A fort was built at the entrance to the Golden Gate — the presently existing Fort Point. Fort Mason and Alcatraz were fortified to protect the harbor from Confederate raiding ships; an iron-clad ship was sent in parts to San Francisco. (The vessel sank in the harbor.) That was the extent of California's participation in the Civil War.

California's tepid adherence to the Union and its detachment from the bloody four-year conflict removed it from the economic, political and social scars that resulted from the internecine struggle. California was exempt from the compulsory draft and was, therefore, free from the casualties that saw a half-million dead (on both sides) from the war.

The City Expands

San Francisco grew rapidly in the 1860s and '70s as the result of the increased wealth from the Comstock and other economic enterprises. In 1861, the city's population was 83,223; six years later it had risen to 131,000. In 1870, it was 149,743; and in 1880, it was 233,959.

A financial district developed along Montgomery Street, centering on Pine and California streets. Kearny Street was the center of the retail district, which from there expanded up Post and Sutter streets to Union Square.

The city directory for 1864–65 stated there were 15,518 buildings in the city, of which 12,268 were of wood and 3,250 were of brick or stone.

During the mid-1860s and again in the 1870s, the streets and sidewalks were repaved, and wooden plank or cobblestone streets were replaced with basalt blocks. Streets were graded; buildings grew taller and displayed more decoration, schools and colleges were begun or grew from their 1850s origins, among them St. Mary's College, St. Ignatius College (now the University of San Francisco), and the beginnings of what was to become the University of California, Berkeley. Numerous theaters, private libraries, hotels, restaurants and shops were added to those that had been in existence since the Gold Rush.

As the population grew and as the city's business expanded, San Francisco also grew physically. The manufacturing sector solidified its presence South of Market, and residential areas sprang up in the Mission district and in the Western Addition (a term that, at the time, included Pacific Heights). Homestead associations, 19th century tract developments, fueled the subdivision of large areas of the city and the mass production of the long, narrow wooden houses that continue to be part of the city's landscape.

A municipal center, with a city hall to be built in the French Renaissance manner, was begun in 1871 on a triangular plot of land bounded by Market, Larkin and McAllister streets. The city hall would not be finished until 1901.

The prosperity of the Silver Age also bought forth a park system. Only three small parks existed — Portsmouth Plaza, Washington Square and Union Square — when the city laid out an extensive number of large parks in the late 1800s. In 1871, there commenced the development of the jewel of the chain of parks: Golden Gate Park.

A thousand acres of sand dunes, running from the center of the city out to the ocean, were set aside, and an engineer named William Hammond Hall was selected to be the first superintendent of parks.

Hall faced a daunting task. Those 1,000 acres of sand were daily whipped by San Francisco's prevailing west winds, but, though his achievements were eclipsed by those of one of his successors, John McLaren, Hall succeeded in taming the arid wilderness and creating the beginning of the beautiful park.

1860–1879

CLIFF CROSS

McLaren would serve San Francisco's parks from 1887 until his death in 1943, when he was in his mid-'90s. This legendary horticulturist and park superintendent not only expanded what Hall had begun, but was to be the zealous custodian of what he considered to be the purpose of the parks.

When he felt Golden Gate Park was threatened by the depredations of private interest abetted by venal or obtuse politicians — whether a trolley line through the park, placing statues therein or hosting a world's fair — the canny Scotsman would use any device his imagination could conjure to defeat what he considered to be despoliation of the park.

Some battles he lost; others he won. But McLaren's vision for the city's parks and his love for Golden Gate Park were able to create and maintain beautiful oases in San Francisco that remain much-used and much-beloved by residents and visitors.

Depression and Anti-Chinese Racism

The prosperity of the Silver Age began to diminish during the late 1870s, as the production of silver precipitously declined. San Francisco did not soon recover from the burst of the speculative bubble in 1875, and by late in the decade, the city was caught up in the nationwide depression that had begun in 1873.

The economic malaise brought unemployment and hard times. The situation was inflamed by an Irish-born former drayage businessperson who had gone bankrupt in 1877. Dennis

The Music Concourse is but another feature of Golden Gate Park.

OVERLEAF: Arnold Genthe photographed day-to-day scenes of Chinatown, including this one of a vegetable peddler, circa 1882.

(CALIFORNIA HISTORICAL SOCIETY)

The waterfront in 1860 harbored sidewheelers and schooners.

Kearney, made furious by his personal financial disaster, turned his natural oratorical gifts to haranguing crowds on the two evils he felt were responsible for the economic hardships: big business and the Chinese.

The corruption of American big business was already a theme emerging on the national political scene. Kearney localized this theme, pointing out, most notably, the monopolistic practices and the political control of the Southern Pacific Railroad and the railroad's preference for hiring Chinese laborers.

The Chinese, Kearney maintained, took jobs properly belonging to Caucasian workers. His diatribe against the Chinese contained an amalgam of the racism toward them that had existed since the Gold Rush. He made much of the fact that they had no concept of union solidarity and would work for less and take jobs from striking workers.

He would regularly conclude his weekly harangue on the sand lots adjoining the spot where City Hall was being built with the injunction, "The Chinese Must Go!" Kearney would then lead the crowds up Nob Hill, where they would demonstrate in front of the home of Charles Crocker (occupying the block where Grace Cathedral now stands). For Kearney and his followers, Crocker was the perfect symbol for their anger: He was one of the Big Four; his arrogance was seen in the 30-foot "spite-fence" he had built to harass the one person on the block who had refused to sell his property to him, and he had himself brought to California the last large immigration of Chinese.

From Crocker's home atop Nob Hill, the demonstrators marched down the hill into Chinatown, where their attempts to destroy property and harm the Chinese were thwarted by the police.

This ferment would culminate in 1879, when the elements in California that agreed with Kearney's assessments formed the Workingman's Party, which assembled a state constitutional convention whose purpose was to incorporate the reforms advanced by them into a new constitution.

A new constitution was approved by the voters, but the rivalries among various components of the Workingman's Party diluted its effectiveness in reforming the abuses that Kearney and his followers had descried.

Three years after the constitutional convention of 1879, the US Congress passed the Chinese Exclusion Act, which was sealed by a treaty between the United States and China. It stated that no immigrants from China would be allowed into the United States, with the exception of immediate family members of those Chinese already residing here. The legislation and treaty would remain in effect until 1943.

Hunters Point dry-dock facilities were kept busy with repairs and ship building in the 1860s.

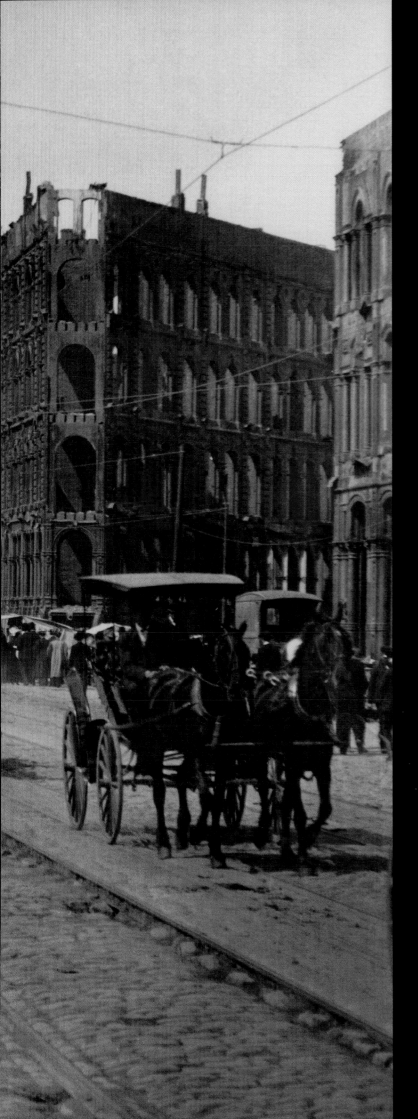

CHAPTER 4

Corruption, Disaster and Reconstruction

1880–1915

HUNTING FOR RELICS

Corruption, Disaster and Reconstruction

By the mid-1870s, the political-reform movement that had been initiated by the 1856 Committee of Vigilance began to wane. In 1880 began the reign of a political boss who would dominate the decade: Christopher Buckley, known as "the Blind Boss of San Francisco." Buckley was the first of a long series of political bosses who formed effective coalitions that would result in domination of political offices for their own benefit and for that of certain interests, notably the Southern Pacific railroad.

The Irish-born Buckley, who in 1880 captured the city's Democratic Party machinery, kept his power by keeping the city's tax rate down to a bare minimum. This resulted in a paucity of municipal amenities, even by the standard of the late 19th century, but the voters seemingly approved the governmental parsimony of Buckley and his adherents.

Such boss-rule was endemic in American cities during the latter part of the 19th and early 20th centuries. During his decade of power, Buckley was able to make ad hoc adjustments to the chaotic and anachronistic municipal constitutional process, which had been rendered obsolete in the wake of the urbanization and industrialization of the post–Civil War era.

By 1890, Buckley's power had diminished, but for the next decade and a half, he would be succeeded by other bosses — some Democrats, some Republicans. There would be occasional periods of reform, but political boss control of municipal government would be endemic in San Francisco's politics for a long period to come.

Gold and War

In the mid- and late-1890s, two events that occurred long distances from San Francisco both had a major impact on the city. The first of these was the discovery of gold in Alaska's Yukon in late 1896. By the summer of the following year, San Francisco was in the grip of yet another gold fever.

Thousands made the trip to Alaska to prospect for gold, and San Francisco's merchants increased their profits substantially by providing supplies and services to them. By 1898, however, it became apparent that the discovery had been greatly exaggerated, and the prospectors drifted out of Alaska and back to their homes. Among them was a San Francisco–born drifter by the name of Jack London, who would subsequently mine his gold-seeking experiences for some of the best fiction in American literature.

The second event began in April 1898, when war was declared between Spain and the United States in the Spanish-held Philippine Islands. San Francisco became the depot for men and materials to be sent to fight this sector of the war. Tent encampments for soldiers were set up in the Presidio and in the sand dunes of what was to

PREVIOUS SPREAD: People strolled Market Street surveying the damage in the aftermath of the earthquake and fire. The 18-story Call Building (center left), the city's tallest at the time, was ruined.

(SAN FRANCISCO HISTORY CENTER, SAN FRANCISCO PUBLIC LIBRARY)

James Phelan was responsible for bringing the Midwinter Fair of 1894 to Golden Gate Park. Later, as mayor, he worked to stem the tide of corruption in the city government.

(SAN FRANCISCO HISTORY CENTER, SAN FRANCISCO PUBLIC LIBRARY)

Adolph Sutro built the Sutro Baths for the enjoyment of San Franciscans such as those pictured here.

become the Richmond district. The port was crowded with ships; industries in San Francisco and the Bay Area hummed with activity. It was the first war in which San Francisco was an active participant, and the city reveled in news of the quick victories.

A more permanent effect of the Spanish-American War was to tie San Francisco's destiny more closely to the Far East. The conquest and subsequent absorption of the Philippine Islands made the United States a power in Asia, and boosted San Francisco's growing interest in the trade, cultural and political affairs of the region.

Attempts to Root Out Corruption

In 1894, the fiery, rambunctious and wealthy Adolph Sutro won election as mayor of San Francisco on a reform platform that included lessening the power of the Southern Pacific in the city's politics.

Sutro had made a fortune in constructing the Comstock Tunnel, which solved many of the technical problems in the silver mines. When Sutro subsequently sold, he invested his profits in San Francisco real estate. He became an avid book, manuscript and art collector, and a notable philanthropist. His estate at Land's End overlooked the new Cliff House, which he had built, and the Sutro Museum and the Sutro Baths, which he had had constructed as a benefit for San Francisco.

But Sutro's paternalistic and irascible personality put him at odds with the Board of Supervisors, and his two-year term was unsuccessful. Already lapsing into senility, he could not stem the tide of corruption.

More successful was his successor, James Duval Phelan. Urbane, cultivated, politically astute, young and reform-minded, Phelan, a Democrat, was the son of a wealthy Gold Rush pioneer, who held interests in liquor distribution, banking and real estate. He had a classical education at St. Ignatius College (today's University of San Francisco) and toured

California Midwinter Fair

It was a world's fair in Chicago in 1893 that inspired two of California's commissioners to that fair, Michael de Young and James Phelan — the former the owner of the *San Francisco Chronicle*, the latter a young, wealthy banker and real-estate owner — to promote a similar event in San Francisco.

Such a fair would provide employment to San Franciscans amid the depression of that time, they reasoned. They also felt it would promote tourism and immigration to San Francisco and California; staging the fair in winter would showcase the state's comparatively mild weather.

Many exhibits from Chicago's fair were shipped to San Francisco, and the fair, located in Golden Gate Park, opened on Jan. 1, 1894. During the next six months it drew 2.5 million visitors.

The principal attractions were in what is today the Music Concourse. They included a tall tower with a restaurant on the top, a large wooden structure resembling an Egyptian temple that housed the fair's art (and that became the beginning of today's de Young Museum), and the Japanese Tea Garden, still one of the park's most popular attractions.

The tea house in the Japanese Tea Garden, built for the Midwinter Fair, is still a popular park attraction.

Achille Philion, "the marvelous equilibrist," atop his spiral tower was a popular attraction at the California Midwinter Fair in Golden Gate Park.

Today's de Young Museum housed the fair's art. It was named for Michael de Young, the owner of the San Francisco Chronicle and one of the promoters of the fair.

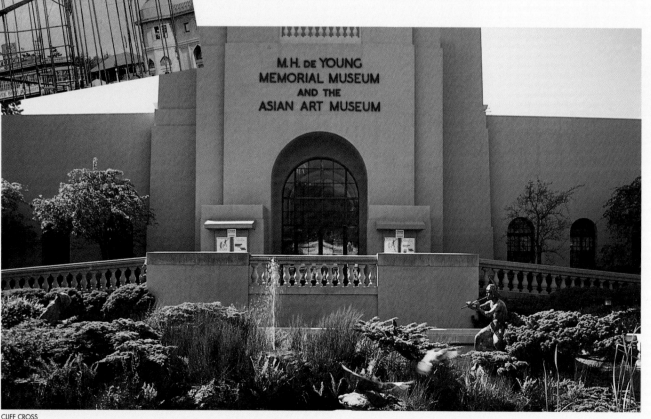

M.H. DE YOUNG
MEMORIAL MUSEUM
AND THE
ASIAN ART MUSEUM

Europe. Phelan's charisma was largely responsible for the city's voters adopting a new charter in 1898, shortly after his election, which strengthened his hand in rooting out the corrupt practices of the previous quarter-century.

Because the city's artificially low tax rate had not allowed for long-overdue improvements, San Francisco's need for municipal services was extraordinary by the time Phelan came to power. Phelan's bond issues for a new sewer system, city hospitals, City Hall completion, park expansions, schools and port improvements raised the city's indebtedness from $186,000 to $11 million.

The mayor's programs appealed to the city's business community, and his being an Irish-Catholic made him attractive to the city's workers, a majority of whom were Irish. But toward the end of his last term — in the summer of 1901 — Phelan's labor support evaporated.

A bitter strike had pitted a militantly anti-union Employers' Association against the City Front Federation, which represented 16,000 teamsters and waterfront workers. Phelan attempted to arbitrate, but the owners would not cooperate; his use of the police to prevent striking workers from destroying private property or using violence to keep replacement workers from taking their places made him anathema to the city's labor class.

The Republican governor stepped in with the state militia and declared martial law, and the strike ended. San Francisco's workers now turned to a hastily assembled political party that would represent their interest.

Steam beer, like sourdough bread, is a San Francisco invention, necessitated because the ice used in the fermenting process was so expensive during Gold Rush days. Creative brewmasters fermented their beer in shallow pans and took advantage of San Francisco's cool temperatures. Only one steam brewer exists today: Anchor Brewing Co., founded in 1896.

Ocean Beach and the Cliff House were popular day-trip destinations.

The Union Labor Party

The unions knew they needed a local political party that would be favorable toward them and, just before the municipal elections of 1901, formed the Union Labor Party.

The genius behind the party's platform, which was dedicated to union principals, but also declared the party's aims to be of a conservative nature, was a canny and ambitious lawyer, Abe Ruef, who had been impressed by Phelan's success in forging coalitions for his political candidacy and his programs.

The Union Labor Party elected three members of the Board of Supervisors and, as mayor, Eugene Schmitz, a handsome and charming Catholic of Irish-German parentage, a businessperson and employer, and the president of the Musicians Union. These victories were extended in 1903, and in 1905 all city elected officials had run on the Union Labor Party ticket.

From the beginning of the party's electoral triumph, Ruef orchestrated a massive program of corruption that had not been experienced in San Francisco since Gold Rush days. Through carefully appointed commissioners, Ruef, Schmitz and the Board of Supervisors were able to obtain money from businesses seeking governmental favors. Someone seeking a franchise for a transportation line or an exemption from a provision of the building code, someone seeking to install trolley lines overhead instead of underground, someone seeking to increase gas rates — all would go to Ruef and pay an "attorney's fee" commensurate with the favor; this sum would be shared with the politicians in office. In addition, the police could be held back from arresting gamblers and prostitutes in return for graft money from gambling houses and brothels.

Trivia

Following the Spanish-American War, soldiers who returned from the Philippines with tropical ailments were sent to Alcatraz to recuperate, but the damp weather did little to heal them.

From his modest office in North Beach, Ruef was able to control the relationships of virtually every business in San Francisco to city government. But after 1905's Union Labor sweep of political offices, he began to lose control of the graft process, as the supervisors began to go their ways independently, making their own deals without the precautions Ruef had taken to make them appear legal.

The worsening corruption aroused the ire of reformers. A crusading editor named Fremont Older, former Mayor James Phelan and the scion of a sugar fortune, Rudolph Spreckels, allied themselves to try to root out those responsible for San Francisco's municipal corruption. Older went to Washington, DC, to seek President Theodore Roosevelt's cooperation in ending the Union Labor Party's stranglehold on San Francisco. The president offered to aid his crusade in any way that he could.

An event in the spring of 1906 would momentarily forestall the investigation, but Older's persistence paid off later in that year and during the following year. The Union Labor Party's days of graft and corruption were numbered.

City Beautiful

San Francisco had developed into an instantaneous city at the time of the Gold Rush, had expanded during the Silver Age and had continued to grow during the quarter-century subsequent to the end of the silver boom. But its physical development had been without plan or aesthetic considerations.

Toward the end of the 19th century, both European and American cities sought to recreate themselves according to classical architectural and urban planning dictates. The urbane and well-educated Phelan led the way in San Francisco during his term as mayor by appointing a committee to consider proposals for beautifying the city. The

plan that came from the committee deliberations went nowhere, but in 1904, under
Phelan's leadership, the Association for the Improvement and Adornment of San Francisco was founded. Shortly thereafter, the group hired architect and city planner Daniel
H. Burnham to produce a plan to transform San Francisco into the perfect Beaux Arts
city — a Paris of the Western United States.

Burnham came to San Francisco, where he lived in a cottage on top of Twin Peaks.
By the fall of 1905, he and his assistant, Edward Bennett, had developed their plan
for San Francisco.

The Burnham Plan, as it was called, envisioned a magnificent civic center as the nexus
of the city, from which broad boulevards would radiate out, like the spokes of a wheel.
A grand boulevard would traverse the perimeter of the city, taking advantage of the bay
and ocean views. A large cultural complex was slated for Upper Haight Ashbury. The
hills of San Francisco would be made to appear something like Athens' Acropolis. And
Burnham's plan for the large undeveloped tracts that have become the Richmond and
the Sunset — had it been realized — would have been very different from the banal,
box-like rigidity of the present grid.

Burnham foresaw the problem of vehicular congestion in San Francisco, and provided for some streets on steep hillsides to be rerouted in order to conform to the con-
tours of the land. Heavily traveled streets would be widened, and new streets would be
laid in order to improve access to downtown. He also provided that all the downtown
areas would be closed to vehicular traffic except for deliveries (and those only during
certain hours).

Little did Phelan and his associates or Burnham realize in the spring of 1906, when
the printed copies of the report were given to the Board of Supervisors, how close the
city was to a major opportunity to easily implement Burnham's plan for rebuilding.

 *Trivia*

With limited space for the city to grow, in 1912 the Board of Supervisors decreed that all cemeteries be removed from San Francisco. Graves were moved to Colma.

Lateen-rigged boats, crewed mostly by Italians and Dalmations, filled Fisherman's Wharf early in the century. Today the wharf is the No. 1 tourist attraction in the city.

Disaster at Dawn

The city of San Francisco was changing dramatically in 1906 from the city photographed in a dramatic panorama taken from the tower of Mark Hopkins' home at the very crest of Nob Hill at the end of the Silver Age by Edward Muybridge. Tall buildings were being constructed in the downtown core: Rudolph Spreckels' newly built Call Building at Third and Market streets was the city's highest at 18 stories. There had been 10 years of national prosperity — a relief after the almost constant depression of the 1870s, '80s and '90s. Business was booming.

On the balmy spring day of Tuesday, April 17, 1906, a generally happy citizenry of San Francisco was well-employed, the port was bustling and that evening offered numerous choices for entertainment: Caruso and Fremsted in Bizet's *Carmen*, John Barrymore in Richard Harding Davis' *The Dictator*, Victor Herbert's *Babes in Toyland* at the Columbia Theater on Powell Street or a score of vaudeville theaters, among them the Orpheum, scattered throughout the city.

Visitors to San Francisco might be staying at the city's dowager hotel — the Palace, completed some 31 years before — or at the new St. Francis Hotel, which had been open only two years. And within a few days, a new hostelry, the Fairmont Hotel, situated among the mansions of Nob Hill, would be having its grand opening.

Everyone in San Francisco — its 400,000 residents and its thousands of visitors — awoke the next morning, Wednesday, April 18, at precisely 5:13, just as the violet, predawn streaks were appearing over the East Bay hills, as an earthquake along the 200-mile San Andreas Fault shook the city. A major jolt was followed by a secondary one and then by aftershocks throughout the day.

SAN FRANCISCO HISTORY CENTER, SAN FRANCISCO PUBLIC LIBRARY

As people poured forth from their homes to see what had happened, they left rooms strewn with broken glass and shards of crockery. They stood on the streets, which had fissures in them, rips showing gaps along the cobblestones. Damage to buildings caused by the earthquake was greatest in those areas of the city that had been built on filled land: Yerba Buena Cove and those parts south of Market that had been built on the bay or on lagoons.

No one will ever know the death toll in San Francisco from the earthquake and the subsequent fire. The official figure was 456, but a recent revisionist historian has come up with a figure of 3,000. One of the most notable among the dead was San Francisco Fire Chief Dennis Sullivan. Sullivan had been awakened by the earthquake and had run to his wife's bedroom to see to her safety just as the chimney of an adjoining building toppled through the Sullivan residence, taking him and his wife down two stories to the basement. Mrs. Sullivan's landing was cushioned by a mattress; her husband landed on the concrete floor and died a couple of days later.

Although the catastrophe is known as the San Francisco Earthquake, its impact was felt in scores of communities along the San Andreas fault, from Fort Bragg to Salinas. Santa Rosa, 55 miles to the north, was almost entirely destroyed by earthquake and fire. Severe damage was done to Palo Alto and Stanford University. At Agnew State Insane Asylum, near San José, more than 100 inmates and staff were killed, redwood trees in the Santa Cruz Mountains were splintered into kindling.

The Goddess of Progress remained atop City Hall through the earthquake and fire. When it was finally removed in 1909 as reconstruction got under way, the statue fell off the wagon that was carrying it, and the 700-pound head broke off.

FROM THE GOLD RUSH TO CYBERSPACE

The city was first lighted by electricity in 1902. By 1905, Pacific Gas and Electric Co. controlled all the power companies in the region.

OPPOSITE: Residents searched for relics among all the debris left by the earthquake.

(SAN FRANCISCO HISTORY CENTER, SAN FRANCISCO PUBLIC LIBRARY)

Although the damage to San Francisco as a result of the earthquake was substantial — the physical damage to buildings, the city's fire-alarm system, the knocking out of the city's transportation and telephone facilities, the destruction of much glass and furnishings within homes — it is probable that such damage could have been repaired within a few weeks were it not for the fires that broke out just after the earthquake.

Ominous plumes of smoke began to rise from the dust- and rubble-strewn streets of the city just after the earthquake. Most of the fires were easily put out. One — on Stuart Street, south of Market near the waterfront — could not be doused, and Engine Company 38 was sent for. The firefighters attached the hoses of their fire wagon to a nearby hydrant. No water came out. They went to another fire hydrant — still no water. It began to occur to the desperate firefighters that the water mains that brought the city's water from Crystal Springs Reservoir, located in San Mateo County, had been broken. There would be no water to fight the fires in San Francisco.

By 9 am, it had become apparent that San Francisco faced a fiery holocaust. Mayor Eugene Schmitz hastily convened a meeting of city leaders at the Hall of Justice on Kearny Street. A Committee of Safety, headed by former Mayor James Phelan, was called into being. Saloons were ordered to be closed, and the mayor issued a proclamation announcing that all looters would be shot.

General Frederick Funston, temporarily in charge of US troops in the area, realized the danger to the city and its citizens. He offered the use of the army troops to the civilian authorities. They would be indispensable to the maintenance of order in San Francisco and to the subsequent care of the refugees. (Martial law was never declared during the emergency.)

By mid-morning, the fires that had started near the waterfront had coalesced. Along Market Street, the Emporium, the Hearst Building and the Call Building had been destroyed; the Grand Opera House on Mission Street between Third and Fourth streets had collapsed from the flames; Rincon Hill and South Park, those premier residential districts of the 1850s and '60s, were destroyed. Only the railroad tracks along Townsend Street would contain the conflagration south of Market Street.

A second fire, north of Market, roared through the wholesale and produce districts adjacent to the waterfront and then through the financial district. It was hoped that this fire might be stopped at Sansome Street, but this was not to be.

At mid-morning, the fire's venue expanded, when on Hayes Street in Hayes Valley — an area bordered by Van Ness, Octavia, McAllister and Market streets — a woman began to prepare breakfast. She did not know that her stove's chimney had been damaged, and soon her two-story frame dwelling was engulfed in flames. The fire, henceforth to be known as the Ham-and-Eggs Fire, spread, raging though the area around the collapsed City Hall and destroying St. Ignatius Church and College.

As the fire spread, businesspeople, residents and those responsible for various institutions valiantly attempted to save their possessions. Bankers, such as William Crocker of the Crocker Bank (which later became part of Wells Fargo) and A.P. Giannini of the recently founded Bank of Italy (which would become the Bank of America), were able to save their cash: Crocker placed his bank's on a tugboat in the bay, Giannini drove his in a buckboard to his home in San Mateo.

Curator Alice Eastwood was able to save a substantial portion of the botanical collection of the California Academy of Sciences, but virtually the entire collection of the Society of California Pioneers was lost, and the studios of painter William Keith and of photographer Arnold Genthe were destroyed.

Meanwhile, San Francisco's citizens removed whatever possessions they could carry and left their homes for the parks and open spaces to the south and the west.

By midnight on Wednesday, Chinatown and the retail district around Union Square were in flames. The pernicious Ham-and-Eggs Fire had crossed Market Street at Ninth and at 12th streets to join the South of Market fire, and the conflagration roared into the Mission district.

But the desperate efforts of firefighters and citizens helping to fight the fires were beginning to have results. By dawn of Thursday, April 19, the western part of the Ham-and-

San Franciscans watched as their city burned for three days following the earthquake.

Eggs Fire was contained along Octavia Street and Golden Gate Avenue. Early on Friday morning, the fire that had been threatening the Mission District was stopped at 20th and Church streets. The bulk of the Mission district — San Francisco's most extensive residential neighborhood — had been saved.

At 3 am on Thursday the fire jumped yet another hurdle — Powell Street, which the firefighters had hoped would be an effective barrier. Soon the mansions atop Nob Hill were engulfed in flames. The newly constructed Fairmont Hotel, awaiting its grand opening, was gutted, as was silver king James Flood's brownstone mansion (today the Pacific Union Club).

The next line of defense was Van Ness Avenue. At 6 pm on Thursday, however, Claus Spreckels' estate on the west side of Van Ness Avenue began to burn. The exhausted firefighters were horrified but continued their efforts. Only six blocks west of Van Ness Avenue were to burn before the fire was contained on the west.

But it was not yet the end. Both at Green Street and at Washington Street, along Van Ness, fires began, and as a result of the wind shifting to the west, began to sweep eastward back toward the waterfront and the northeastern portion of the city. Russian Hill was destroyed, and at Columbus Avenue, the two fires joined and swept throughout North Beach and over Telegraph Hill.

By Friday night and Saturday morning, when the fire reached the waterfront, fire-fighters fought the fire from both land and fireboats. They succeeded in saving the docks and the warehouses at the water's edge — an important aspect of the city's ability to reconstruct.

By Saturday morning, the fire had run its course, and that evening rain began to fall on San Francisco.

The Aftermath

A stunned city assessed the damage. Some 490 city blocks had been destroyed — 2,831 acres. All municipal buildings, the libraries, the courts and jails, theaters, most restaurants had burned. Some 30 schools; 80 churches, convents and synagogues; the entire business district; and the homes of a quarter-million San Franciscans were gone. Vast stores of business inventories, art and book collections, and many of the historic documents and artifacts of the city's and the state's past were wiped out.

OVERLEAF: The entire downtown was devastated by the earthquake and fire that followed.

Tent camps sprang up in the city's parks and in the Presidio. Families lived in tents such as this one until they were replaced by wooden cottages.

On Nob Hill, only the Fairmont Hotel, which was not yet open, and the James Flood mansion were left standing, though both were gutted. Refugee tents soon sprouted on the former site of the Crocker mansion, the land on which Grace Cathedral now stands.

OPPOSITE, TOP: Alice Eastwood was the botany curator of the California Academy of Sciences at the time of the earthquake and was able to save most of the collection of specimens.

OPPOSITE, BOTTOM: Reconstruction was well under way on Market Street when these workers laid new track in 1907.

It was the greatest urban conflagration ever: six times the area burned by the famous London Fire of 1666 and half again as large as the Chicago Fire of 1871. Not until the Allied bombing of German and Japanese cities during World War II would such devastation be seen again.

Aid poured in from the state, the country and the world, and as San Franciscans resolved to rebuild, sentimentalizing of the stricken city began.

Will Irwin, a Stanford graduate and a writer in San Francisco before he left for a journalism career in New York, wrote an eloquent tribute — called *The City That Was* — to the destroyed city. It begins:

The old San Francisco is dead. The gayest, lightest hearted, most pleasure loving city of the western continent, and in many ways the most interesting and romantic, is a horde of refugees living among ruins. It may rebuild; it probably will, but those who have known that peculiar city by the Golden Gate, have caught its flavor of the Arabian Nights, feel that it can never be the same. It is as though a pretty, frivolous woman had passed through a great tragedy. She survives, but she is sobered and different. If it rises out of the ashes it must be a modern city, and without its old atmosphere.

Many of those who had been burned out in San Francisco decided not to participate in its rebuilding; instead, they moved to the city's suburbs. The communities of the peninsula, Oakland and Alameda were the most popular venues for the migrants.

Some had gone to the homes of friends or relatives in suburban communities during the fire or in its immediate aftermath. The great bulk of homeless who remained in San Francisco had to be housed, fed and clothed. In the parks throughout San Francisco and in the Presidio, tent cities mushroomed. In time they became replaced by wooden refugee cottages. Communal dining facilities fed the dispossessed population, and the Red Cross and the US Army supervised the building of sanitation facilities.

Those who had retained their homes could not cook in their kitchens until the city inspected the homes for any problems that may have led to other fires. Thus along the streets of San Francisco, residents cooked over makeshift campfires.

Reconstruction

A Committee of Forty on the Reconstruction of San Francisco (actually, the committee was composed of as many as 200 people), was formed to rebuild the city. The group was faced with numerous problems and challenges: questions of establishing titles to lands, street widening, whether to implement the Burnham Plan, revenue and taxation, assessments and medical care. The allocation of resources and the orchestration of the technological problems of making these resources available were enormous problems facing the committee and others responsible for San Francisco's reconstruction.

The rubble and the remaining walls of buildings on more than 2,800 acres had to be removed; property owners then had to decide what kind of buildings they wished to build on the sites. Institutions had to determine whether to rebuild on the site of destruction or to move to some other location.

San Francisco surged with vitality during the three years following the April 1906 disaster: The city was largely rebuilt by the end of 1909, and was indeed "a modern city," as Will Irwin had predicted. Much of the city was to be totally transformed: Nob Hill, for example, would be largely composed of hotels, a cathedral and apartment houses; gone were the mansions of San Francisco's nabobs.

Alice Eastwood
SAN FRANCISCO HISTORY CENTER, SAN FRANCISCO PUBLIC LIBRARY

The desire to rebuild quickly, a desire voiced by everyone from a real-estate magnate such as M.H. de Young to the humblest landlord, led to a debunking of the Burnham Plan. People wanted to rebuild immediately on the same pattern as had previously existed. Only the idea of an enhanced civic center was to emerge from Burnham's ambitious plan.

Woes and Sorrows

Earthquake and fire — with its disastrous results — were not the only problems facing San Francisco during the first decade of the 20th century.

In 1900, while Phelan was mayor, several deaths from the bubonic plague had occurred. In 1907, the plague broke out again in the city. Edward Robeson Taylor, an attorney and physician (and poet), had become mayor, and it was his vigorous attempts to eradicate the plague that brought in federal help. Taylor advanced a vast rat-catching project and established medical help for the infected.

By the end of 1908, when the plague was declared eradicated, 160 San Franciscans had been infected, of whom 77 had died. As a result, the city authorities passed legislation that forced property owners to "rat-proof" buildings. (A bacillus in an infected flea that lives on a rat is the cause of the bubonic plague.)

Earthquake. Fire. Plague. What else could happen? The answer came directly on the heals of the destruction of the city: six years of graft trials.

Almost as soon as the April catastrophe was ended, Older, Phelan and Spreckels swung into action to end the Ruef/Schmitz rule of San Francisco. An attorney for the US government, Francis Heney, and a detective working with him, William Burns, were loaned to the reformers to pursue Ruef and his minions. Soon the corrupt cadres of politicians were facing hard evidence of their larceny. Indictments followed immediately, not only of the politicians who had taken bribes, but also of the businesspeople who had given the bribes. A veritable Who's Who of San Francisco now faced trail for bribery.

Trivia

The *Bulletin* newspaper named Virginia Barstow its city editor in 1897. She was the first woman in the country to hold such a position.

The corner of Eighth and Market streets boasted a wide array of San Francisco's shops.

OPPOSITE: By the time this photograph was taken, reconstruction was nearly complete and residents were shopping on Union Square again.

The Buena Vista, at the corner of Hyde and Beach streets, as it looked in 1909. While the establishment continues to serve its famed Irish coffee, the building had to be replaced after a runaway cable car slammed into it.

OPPOSITE: The Emporium on Market Street was topped by a glass dome.

The business community fought back, complaining that such publicity was bad for San Francisco business. Increasingly, San Franciscans tired of the efforts of the reformers, and the last of the trials took place in 1912.

Although Ruef and his cronies were removed from political power by late 1906, the trials achieved little. Eugene Schmitz was convicted of corruption, but his conviction was overturned on appeals over a technicality. Abe Ruef was convicted and sent to San Quentin for five years — the only one to go to prison as a result of the graft trials. He was later pardoned.

The Rolph Years

In the 1909 municipal election, a member of the Union Labor party, P.H. McCarthy, a conservative union leader, was elected mayor: It was a sign that the reform movement that had prompted the graft trials had lost momentum.

But in 1911, McCarthy was defeated by a self-made millionaire who had been born in a poor area south of Market and raised in the Mission District: James Rolph, better know as "Sunny Jim" Rolph.

As mayor, Rolph presided over numerous municipal programs that marked the years after the rebuilding of San Francisco. One of the most notable of these was the building of

Sunny Jim

James Rolph was born to be mayor of San Francisco. His abundant energy, his flamboyance and his congeniality were qualities well-suited to the reborn city. He served 20 years as mayor and then was elected governor of California.

Rolph was a ubiquitous presence in the city. He would don a variety of uniforms to preside over various civic functions: a motorman's hat and uniform to drive the first trolley through the Twin Peaks Tunnel, a baseball cap and uniform to throw out the first ball at the beginning of a season. His smiling, cheerful personality was seen at numerous gatherings and events, both civic and private, and the citizens responded with affection and admiration to Rolph's palpable love of the city.

The two decades of Rolph's administration, sandwiched between the reconstruction of the burnt city and the beginning of the Great Depression, was, in many ways, a golden age for San Francisco. They were largely prosperous years with a minimum of tensions between workers and employers, between business and labor. Rolph was an effective mediator between the various interests in the diverse city, and San Franciscans responded to his constant urgings to enhance the city he so loved.

SAN FRANCISCO HISTORY CENTER, SAN FRANCISCO PUBLIC LIBRARY

Sunny Jim Rolph served the city as mayor for 20 years before he was elected governor. He oversaw some major municipal improvements, from the post–earthquake and fire reconstruction to the beginning of the Hetch Hectchy water project.

a new city hall and the development of a civic center around it. The superb City Hall — a masterpiece of Beaux Arts architecture and arguably the finest municipal building in the United States — was completed in 1913, as was the nearby Civic Center Auditorium. Two years later, the classical Main Library (now the Asian Art Museum), across the handsome plaza from City Hall, was finished, and in the mid-1920s another classical building, the State Building, rounded off the Civic Center. (In the early '30s, when Rolph was no longer mayor, the Opera House and the Veterans Building were constructed across Van Ness Avenue from City Hall.)

Rolph both loved and had pride in City Hall. As he ascended or descended the grand staircase of the rotunda, a string orchestra sedately hidden by palm trees would play his theme song, "Smiles." He delighted in showing visitors to the city around the building.

Yet another of the feats accomplished during Rolph's tenure was the beginning of a municipally owned intra-urban transit system. In the November 1911 mayoral election, the voters approved a bond issue to buy the busy Geary Street Railroad. San Francisco was the first city in the United States to own its own transportation system, and during the 40 years subsequent to the purchase of the Geary Street line would acquire all the city's privately owned transportation companies and forge them into a city-owned system.

It was also in the early years of the Rolph administration that another municipal project — that of securing a water source for San Francisco — was begun. In the aftermath of the earthquake and fire, engineering studies were undertaken to determine a source for such a water supply. It was decided to utilize the waters of the Tuolumne watershed in the Sierra Nevada. Since the watershed was on federal property, San Francisco had to get the permission of the US government, which was formally granted by the Raker Act, which was passed in 1913. World War I caused a delay, but construction on what is called the Hetch Hetchy water system began in 1919. The huge project, a stupendous engineering feat, was completed in 1934 — the year Rolph died.

A Fair for San Francisco

The idea for expositions or world's fairs began in Europe during the mid-19th century. They became symbols of economic and scientific progress, opportunities to showcase new inventions and provide entertainment for visitors.

The first car was driven in San Francisco by J.W. Stanford in 1889.

OPPOSITE: San Francisco City Hall is a masterpiece of Beaux Arts architecture. Completed in 1913 under Sunny Jim Rolph, the building was restored to its original splendor in 1998.

(GARY STRENG)

1880–1915

CALIFORNIA HISTORICAL SOCIETY

Ferries from Oakland and Marin put in at the old Ferry House at the foot of Market Street, shown here a few years before it was replaced by what we now call the Ferry Building. Carriages were available for hire at the dock.

OPPOSITE: The 435-foot Tower of Jewels was the centerpiece of the Panama Pacific International Exhibition of 1915. It glowed when its million pieces of glass were illuminated by searchlights.

(SAN FRANCISCO HISTORY CENTER,
SAN FRANCISCO PUBLIC LIBRARY)

The California Midwinter Fair of 1894 in San Francisco had been a middling affair, almost an offshoot of Chicago's world fair of the previous year. But San Francisco's business community began to make plans for yet another exposition during the early years of the 20th century.

These plans were laid aside after the April 1906 disaster, but early in 1907 a group of San Francisco business leaders formed a nonprofit corporation in order to put on a world's fair. In 1910, the city passed a bond issue for such an event (the sum being matched the following year by the state), and in 1911, Congress gave San Francisco the coveted distinction of being able to hold an official world's fair in 1915.

The city selected as the site for its world's fair an area of unimproved tidelands between Van Ness Avenue and the Presidio, an area now known as the Marina district. A seawall was constructed and a 635-acre area was filled with sand and covered with three feet of topsoil.

Meanwhile, a large array of architects (led by Willis Polk), engineers, landscape gardeners (led by John McLaren), painters and sculptors began to make plans for the fair. They designed a huge rectangle opening into a series of courtyards, which contained the 10 main exhibit places. Beyond were agricultural and livestock exhibits, a racetrack, a stadium and an airfield (from whence aviator Lincoln Beechey flew and lost his life performing aerial stunts over the bay). An amusement area or boardwalk extended along Lombard Street from Van Ness Avenue to Fillmore Street.

In the midst of the exhibit rectangle stood the 435-foot Tower of Jewels, whose millions of pieces of glass provided a dazzling glow when struck by the sun during the day or by searchlights at night. Machinery Hall, an eight-acre exhibit hall, anchored one end of the rectangle, and Bernard Maybeck's dauntingly beautiful Palace of Fine Arts was built at its western end. (The Palace was the only building not to be destroyed at the end of the fair; in the 1960s it was reconstructed in concrete.)

John Alpegene, shown here in 1910 with his bride, Minnie Sola, was typical of the Italian immigrants who found their first San Francisco lodging in the rooms above the Fior d'Italia. Founded in North Beach in 1886, the Fior is still serving traditional Italian cuisine.

CALIFORNIA HISTORICAL SOCIETY

The Panama Pacific International Exposition was home to exhibit buildings from 29 states and 25 foreign countries. Its exhibits looked back to the 19th century and forward to the technological marvels of the 20th.

During the eight and a half months the fair was open, almost 19 million visitors passed through its gates — a huge increase over the 2.5 million that had visited the California Midwinter Fair less than a quarter-century before.

Thus, nine years after San Francisco had been shaken down by an earthquake and burned by fire, and only a few years after it had rebuilt its residences and replaced its commercial and municipal infrastructure, the city showcased itself and its indomitable spirit by producing a spectacular world's fair. The Panama Pacific International Exposition proclaimed to the world that San Francisco had indeed risen from ashes.

ABOVE: A.P. Giannini opened the Bank of Italy in 1904 to serve small depositors. By 1909, he had expanded beyond the city boundaries and opened his first out-of-town branch in San José (pictured). Giannini's bank, later renamed Bank of America, went on to become the biggest in the world. It was bought out in 1998 by NationsBank, headquartered in Charlotte, NC.

RIGHT: Buckboards shared space with cable cars along Market Street near Kearny. Lotte's Fountain, a gift to the city from entertainer Lotta Crabtree, is in the foreground. The fountain survived the 1906 earthquake, and some believe it was used as a message center in the days following that disaster. Over the years, survivors of the quake have convened at the fountain at 5:13 am every April 18.

OPPOSITE: The Palace of Fine Arts, designed by Bernard Maybeck, is the only building from the Panama Pacific International Exhibition that still stands. Today, it houses the Exploratorium science museum.

(COURTESY OF GARY STRENG)

Trivia

The Palace of Fine Arts, built for the 1915 Panama Pacific International Exposition, was meant to be temporary, so it was built using chicken wire, burlap and sprayed-on fake travertine.

SAN FRANCISCO HISTORY CENTER, SAN FRANCISCO PUBLIC LIBRARY

THE VOICE OF BUSINESS

A History of the
San Francisco
Chamber of Commerce
1850–2000

by Thomas Stauffer

The Voice of Business for 150 Years

I t is unlikely that in 1849 any of the 19 citizens of San Francisco who proposed "formation here of a Chamber of Commerce similar to those existing in the great Atlantic cities" could have predicted the scope of influence the Chamber would have on the social and economic development of San Francisco.

The founding of the San Francisco Chamber of Commerce occurred as a consequence of an economic boom heard around the world: the California Gold Rush. The discovery of gold in January 1848 and the huge influx of fortune seekers off hundreds of ships entering San Francisco Bay in the following few years gathered economic strength that resounds to this very day. The Chamber of Commerce, since that time, has been a constant presence and guiding hand in the development of one of the greatest of global cities: San Francisco.

The news that gold was discovered at Sutter's Mill spread slowly in the beginning. On April 3, 1848, San Francisco's first school opened and a teacher from Yale University was hired at $1,000 per year, but when the meaning of the gold strike sank in, school trustees abandoned the project and ran off to the gold fields. The *California Star,* the area's first newspaper, itself ceased publication for a time for the same reason, after Sam Brannan, the publisher, touted the strike's magnitude.

On Aug. 19, 1848, the *New York Herald* carried news about the discovery. Appearance of California gold dust in Washington, DC, and President James Polk's confirmation of the find 10 months after the fact, brought on the dash to find the metal. Meanwhile, serious business got underway. The *Star* and a second paper, the *Californian,* merged to form *Alta California.* In November 1849, the Merchants Exchange and Reading Room was opened by E.E. Dunbar, and both the *California Exchange* and the *Journal of Commerce,* a business newspaper, commenced two months later.

Gold changed everything, and did it quickly. It was not surprising that a chamber of businesspeople would form in this environment, attempting to bring some order to the chaos that was commerce in early San Francisco. Various dates can be claimed for inception of the Chamber of Commerce, ranging from Aug. 6, 1849, to Nov. 1, 1911, though the best evidence from primary sources in the archives of the California Historical Society and secondary sources at offices of the San Francisco Chamber of Commerce, the San Francisco Public Library and elsewhere, points to May 9, 1850.

During a 38-day period in August and September 1849, three identical notices were published in *Alta California* calling a meeting to discuss the formation of a Chamber of Commerce. Though sponsored by 19 "citizens and merchants of San Francisco," the notices "to elect the members of such a chamber, and board of arbitration, if it shall be considered expedient" did not draw sufficient interest to succeed at that moment. But organizers went ahead with exploratory meetings that were held at the schoolhouse on the plaza, soon to be called Portsmouth Square.

Things were just too hectic, at that moment, to get a chamber organized. A state, a county and a city had to be formed amid the chaos of the Gold Rush, a military presence, frequent fires, general lawlessness, mud, rats and several epidemics. By the spring of 1850, the impulse to form a chamber was re-established. Like the Committee on Vigilance initiated by Sam Brannan in 1851 to bring civic order and end crime, the Chamber's founders wanted to bring order to trade, shipping and business, and to end commercial disputes. *Alta California* reported on a meeting held on April 10, 1850, "in the fine room in Ward's Court...to take into consideration the propriety of establishing a Board of Trade. It was numerously attended. Capt. H.M. Naglee presided... The chairman stated the objects of the meeting to decide as to the necessity existing for the establishment of a Chamber of Commerce in San Francisco."

The result was adoption of a resolution to form a 12-person committee charged with drafting a constitution and bylaws for a Chamber, because, as the resolution stated, "our commerce, though of short duration, has already reached that of older and more populous cities, and as where there is a large amount of shipping, there is risk in the lightering of merchandise from vessels to the beach or wharves and with other incidental difficulties" with the hope that "as many of these difficulties can be amicably settled by the establishment of certain rules and usage by the Chamber of Commerce." Committee members included Talbot H. Green, who later ran for mayor; J.W. Orborn, the first fruit-grower in the Napa Valley; and William Cooper, who had come to San Francisco in 1846 after failing in a sugar plantation scheme in the Sandwich Islands, later named Hawaii.

Six meetings in all were held between April 10 and May 9, 1850, to establish the Chamber. At the April 17 meeting, 200 copies of the draft constitution and bylaws were ordered printed after it was decided that 100 copies would be insufficient. On May 7, three men from the drafting committee were elected officers, including William Hooper as president *(see list of all heads of the Chamber board of directors, 1850–2000, page 107),* and three more were elected to the six-member Committee of Appeals, the first committee established. The appeals process related to the Chamber's initial primary purpose: arbitration of business disputes. Indeed, the Chamber's stated purpose was "to diminish litigation and to establish uniform and equitable charges." The first arbitration case in 1851 involved breakage of four jugs of linseed oil out of a 110-jug shipment from London; a claim on owners of the ship *Lady Amherst* to pay the damage cost was denied.

Chamber and City Share an Anniversary

According to Colville's Directory of 1856, the city of San Francisco and the Chamber of Commerce were "organized" on the same day: May 9, 1850. This was exactly four months before California was admitted to the United States — word did not reach San Francisco for 39 days — though the county of San Francisco was established April 1, 1850, and the city of San Francisco was incorporated 20 days before the Chamber's founding. San Francisco's first mayor, John White Geary, was elected on May 1, 1850. The "Constitution and ByeLaws of the San Francisco Chamber of Commerce" were published in seven pages at the *Journal of Commerce* office on Clay Street.

PREVIOUS SPREAD: The second annual banquet of the newly reorganized San Francisco Chamber of Commerce was held on Dec. 8, 1912, in the Garden Court of the Palace Hotel.

CALIFORNIA HISTORICAL SOCIETY

The bylaws contained 15 rules. One established the meeting place and time as the first Monday each month at 8 pm at the Merchants Exchange, on Portsmouth Square on the east side of Battery Street, opposite the Customs House. (Later, the Chamber moved to the Merchants Exchange Building at California and Leidesdorff streets with an Assembly Room occupying the second floor.) Members who were more than a half-hour late, unless excused, were fined $2. That was a substantial penalty for its time (all dollar amounts in this history are not translated into current values). Annual dues were $10; $20 was crossed out in the text as a rejected thought. All motions had to be in writing, and no member could speak more than twice on any one issue. A Standing Committee of Arbitration was established for the "purpose of awarding, deciding, arbitrating and settling all disputes, accounts and other matters which may be submitted" peacefully. Members of this committee who failed to show up for a meeting were charged $5. The Chamber was incorporated in California on Nov. 3, 1851, with the proviso that the "duration of the said Association shall be for 50 years." It was re-incorporated in 1868. The budget for the first year of operation was $2,139.21.

The business leaders and merchants of the city needed a reason to be optimistic. In 1851, commodity prices fell drastically, and between May 1850 and June 1851, five major fires raked the city. The worst was in early May 1851, when a fire started at an upholstery firm and, whipped by a high wind, destroyed the 16 blocks that housed the center of trade and business. To top that off, crime was rampant, and Sam Brannan's first group of vigilantes was formed in June, one day before the fourth big fire.

Gold literally raised all ships, and business, even under these conditions, was stirring. The 1850 City Directory carried advertise-

An artist's rendition of the original Merchants' Exchange Building on Portsmouth Square on the east side of Battery Street, opposite the Customs House, where the Chamber of Commerce first took up residence in 1850.

ments for 13 firms under the heading of Commercial, two firms under Books and Stationery, one under Legal, four under Medical, three under Hotels and Restaurants, one under Livery Stable and two under Mechanical. Among these 26 establishments were Turner, Fish and Co. Shipping and General Commission Merchants; Bellnap, White & Co., Dealers in Provisions, Wines, Liquors, Teas and Groceries of Every Description; Mohler, Cadve & Co., Lightermen, Ships Discharged, Supplied with Water and Ballasted at the Shortest Notice; Cooke & Lecount, Booksellers and Stationers, Publishers of Cheap Publications and Periodicals, Agents for American and Foreign Newspapers; Pratt & Cole, Attorneys and Counselors at Law; Benjamin H. West, MD, Physician & Surgeon, Office over the Eagle Saloon; Mrs. Shannon, Midwife; Dr. May's Dysentery and Diarrhea Syrup; O.N. & H. Bush, Proprietors of the Well Known Bush House; and Economy is Wealth? — The Model — the Cheapest Eating House in Town.

Although gold shipments to points east for 1851 of $34,492,000 and for 1854 of $51,429,101 were reported, chaotic business conditions were the norm. Feb. 27, 1855, was dubbed Black Friday when several banks failed, including Wells, Fargo & Co. In 1857, the nation experienced a stock-market panic. Heavy rainstorms and several severe earthquakes, including one in 1858 that damaged the Merchants Exchange Building and a bigger one in 1868 that caused the president of the Chamber to telegraph a message of the calamity to chambers on the East Coast and in Europe, added to the excitement. In 1862, the San Francisco Stock and Exchange Board was founded without deference to the American Civil War then raging. Although a free Union state, California's isolation from the rest of the nation was the primary message.

The Old Merchants Exchange

Initially, as noted, the Chamber met in the Merchants Exchange, which also served as a courthouse, jail, school and church, and from which the San Francisco Vigilance Committee executed one misfortunate, John Jenkins. On June 10, 1851, at 2:10 in the morning, the vigilantes hanged Jenkins out of a second-story window after he stole a small safe from a merchant and then rowed with it out into the harbor. An alarm was sounded, and Jenkins threw the safe overboard. He was caught by vigilantes and taken for a speedy "trial" at a building on the corner of Pine and Sansome streets. The hanging was in front of a crowd on the plaza.

Early Chamber activity centered on arbitration of disputes, but members quickly became involved in other causes. These included constructing harbor fortifications, promoting the idea of a railroad across the United States, simplifying the Bankruptcy Act, dealing with public access to the waterfront and building the Point Lobos and Pigeon Point lighthouses. (The first electric telegraph in the city was between Point Lobos and the Merchants Exchange Building in 1853.) Later in the 19th century, the Chamber supported annexation of Hawaii to the United States, expansion of the US Navy, survey of Alaska's coast, access improvements to the Sacramento River, and growth of the sugar-beet industry.

In 1857, the bylaws and rules of the Chamber were amended in a 19-page document. Ninety members were listed and 17 were crossed out; all names designated males. A seal was adopted, a circle "with the words: 'Chamber of Commerce' around the edge and 'San Francisco, 1850' with the figure of a steamboat in the center." Dues were set at $5, paid twice yearly "in advance," and new provisions were added for expulsion of a member and for a table of commission and brokerage fees. By 1857, the Chamber was directly involved in facilitating business transactions involving the "sale of stocks, bonds and all kinds of securities…on purchase or sale of specie, gold dust or bullion," "purchase and shipment of merchandise," "purchase or sales of vessels" and "landing and reshipping goods from vessels in distress."

Increasing Influence

In all the Chamber's early dealings, one thing was obvious: San Francisco's business leaders acted only if they had a direct commercial interest in the outcome of events. For example, starting in 1861, California's fabled Big Four — Collis Huntington, Leland Stanford, Charles Crocker and Mark Hopkins — were instrumental in building the Central Pacific Railroad, later becoming part of the Southern Pacific. They financed construction of the western half of the Transcontinental Railroad, which was lobbied by the Chamber, based on Theodore D. Judah's 1857 plan. The Big Four were celebrated when the eastern and western roadbeds met at Promontory, Utah, in 1869. Likewise, San Francisco business leaders, not lacking for ambition, assumed general responsibility for economic and infrastructure development of the West Coast and saw the potential of Hawaii and Alaska as suppliers of raw materials for trade.

In 1905, Second Street, in the South of Market area, bustled with commerce.

Apparently, early members of the Chamber were satisfied with their work. The 1858 annual report of the Chamber, for instance, states: "We have encouragement in the fact which presents itself in the increasing influence our Association has been the means of bringing to bear upon our commercial relations at home and abroad. This is the eighth year of our organization, and we have had a period of great indifference to the general interests of the influence of the combined representation of the different mercantile classes upon our city, and state, as well as the Congress of the United States." That year, the Arbitration Committee settled two more cases, one involving a bill of lading and the other the quality of a shipment of Chilean coal. The committee also made proclamations about rocks in the bay, taxation, sugar from China and postal rates. With a positive year-end cash balance of $33.70, the report declared "our finances…in a healthy condition" with "some $40 to $50 of dues considered good."

Members had begun to feel their importance as merchants in a great seaport. They made more pronouncements on national issues. To take a stand on the treatment of sailors in New Orleans, the Chamber passed a resolution in 1858, and on Christmas Eve 1861, it petitioned the "Honorable Congress of the United States" concerning the Tariff Act, the first national income-tax and tariff bill, passed in August of that year to pay for Union troops in the Civil War. The Chamber's resolution said that while the legislation might make sense for Atlantic ports, it made no sense for San Francisco because "of [its] isolated geographical position [and] remoteness of the great markets of supply." The Chamber wanted an exemption from the law because "San Francisco, favored by position and by acquired resources, has given sure promise of becoming the great warehousing and distributing port of the Pacific."

Most annual reports of the Chamber of Commerce and transactional documents do not survive, but those that are available glimpse at what was happening. The 1871 annual report said, "Business…flowed in its accustomed channels with unusual regularity" and "nothing has occurred to seriously challenge the anxiety of [Chamber] members." The biggest event of 1871 was a visit paid to the West Coast by the Boston Board of Trade, similar to a visit then by a 1998 San Francisco Chamber delegation to Boston, albeit then by plane rather than train. By 1871, there were 246 Chamber members operating within a program budget of $3,376.06, with a $216.75 cash balance at year's end.

Special committees in that year included the mundane, such as Wharfage and Dockage, in addition to standing committees on Finance, Library, Membership, Arbitration and Arbitration Appeals, while others had a more distant California or international flair, signifying larger ambitions: the Committee on the San Diego and Fort Yuma Turnpike Road, concerning conveyance through the Southern California desert on land acquired by the Gadsden Purchase in 1853; the Committee on French Relief, relating to the Franco-Prussian War and the birth of the Third French Republic; and the Committee on the Fiji Islands, referring to trade and events leading up to its becoming a British Crown Colony in 1874. In 1875, the Pacific Stock Exchange formally opened.

Recession

The 1870s, for the most part, were a time of economic recession, widespread unemployment and bank failures, including an anti-Chinese riot in San Francisco in 1877 relating to job scarcity, while the 1880s witnessed statewide population increases brought on by a publicity campaign in the eastern states; generally, agriculture and industry flourished. Yet the Chamber's 1885 annual report expressed a darker picture and this lament: "The past year has not been one of prosperity to the commercial interests of this city for we have shared the great depression which has prevailed in business circles all over the world." In 1885, a Joint Committee on Depression in Business was appointed to address "extreme dullness" in commerce by issuing study reports on eight topics. Committee members complained about Portland and Los Angeles, the railroads and eastern interests siphoning business from San Francisco.

The Chamber in 1885 tackled an eclectic agenda, including warehousing, harbor security and water safety, anchored by the Presidio Military Reservation, a new harbor survey, the Odd Fellows Temple, the territorial government in Alaska, Australian mail service, a US–Nicaragua treaty concerning a scheme to build an oceanic canal, a signal station on Mount Tamalpais for ships at sea, bankruptcy law and international bills of lading. Activity also centered on petitioning Washington for "completion of the iron-clad Monadnock, as necessary for the safety of our harbor." The annual report was utilitarian to members by including a table of rainfall amounts since 1849 (these data demonstrate that weather patterns have not changed much over time), along with railroad traffic, export and import volumes, production levels of various goods, taxation amounts, holdings of savings banks, and real-estate sales in the city ($13,374,207 volume on 3,874 transactions). Membership stood at 169 for the year.

Chamber Responds to Earthquake and Fire

All the while, San Francisco grew and grew. At the Chamber's 50th anniversary, the population of the city was 342,782, an increase of 422 times since 1848. The economy grew as well, subject to the same business cycles as the rest of the nation.

The seminal event around the turn of the century, of course, was San Francisco's Great Earthquake and Fire of April 18–21, 1906, one of the worst disasters in US history. Five square miles, 514 city blocks and 28,188 buildings were devastated. Damage was estimated at the time in the range of $350 million to $500 million with probable insurance coverage of $235 million from 117 companies. When talking to the press, business leaders emphasized damage caused by the fire — the rate was $6 million in property lost per hour — rather than the earthquake, which started it all, fearing that shaky ground sent a more negative business message.

A sign erected in the ruins of the city expressed the spirit to rebuild: "Don't talk earthquake, talk business." The Chamber of Commerce convened a banquet open to the sky in the ruined Fairmont Hotel a few months after the fire to underscore that determination, but the Chamber's principal response was highly practical: circulation of a "blank insurance form" to members and non-members alike to learn about their levels of coverage and identify their insurance carriers.

It was called the Fire Insurance Inquiry, and its purpose was to collect information for a report on the treatment accorded San Francisco property owners. From the Chamber's relocated offices in the Ferry Building, Professor A.W. Whitney, an "insurance expert of the University of California," was hired to conduct the study of "the greatest conflagration in the history of insurance," actually the seventh huge fire to strike the city in 58 years. While many Chamber records were destroyed in 1906, enough other records were saved for Whitney to reconstruct the property history. With his report, which is a precise catalog of fire losses and insurance payments, the Chamber put pressure on the carriers to pay up by publicizing which ones paid in full or failed to do so.

Whitney reported that the general ratio of insurance to value was 70 percent and that only 5 percent of damaged or gutted property carried no insurance, acknowledging that the "situation that the companies had before them…was the most difficult in the whole history of fire insurance." The report named the companies that settled their obligations at 100 percent and those that settled at 75 percent, 30 percent or other levels. It concluded that "unquestionably, taken all in all, the companies have done remarkably well… The companies will finally have paid undoubtedly in the neighborhood of 80 percent of the amount of insurance involved." Final words were these: "May there never be another such fire!"

The cooperative spirit, manifest in the earthquake recovery drive, energized planning for a world's fair in the Marina district, the Panama-Pacific International Exposition of 1915 to honor the opening of the Panama Canal the previous year. Though the fair was state-sponsored, like another one in San Diego, a Chamber committee was active on its behalf. This constructive mood also sparked an idea to merge four San Francisco business organizations under one banner in 1911, to be called the San Francisco Chamber of Commerce, the name that has survived since.

United were the Chamber of Commerce of San Francisco (the original name), the Merchants Association, the Merchants Exchange and the Down Town Association. The Chamber at the time mostly addressed foreign and domestic commerce, the Port of San Francisco, and national and international affairs of interest to businesspeople. The Merchants Exchange handled shipping and maritime affairs, including a grain-and-produce trading floor and commodity-inspection service. The Merchants Association worked on civic improvements, better city government and expansion of wholesale and retail trade. The Down Town Association was established after the earthquake to aid reconstruction. Two other active business organizations of the time, the Board of Trade, which concerned itself with wholesale and jobbing commerce, and the Manufacturers and Producers Association, evolved into statewide bodies and were thought to be too specialized for inclusion in the new Chamber.

These organizations provided elements that altered the agenda pursued by the old Chamber. The Merchants Association was founded in 1894, first to improve the sweeping and lighting of San Francisco's streets and to promote the "Bituminizing," or paving, of Montgomery Street from California to Market streets. Heavy rains in 1849 and 1851, for example, had turned Montgomery Street into a brush-laden muddy grave for some animals, and its condition had long been a civic problem The Merchants Exchange grew from the Ship Exchange, which was founded in 1865 to signal the arrival of vessels in the harbor, and introduced the telegraph and telephone to San Francisco for this purpose. The Produce Exchange merged with the Merchants Exchange in 1903, and elements later became the Grain Trade Association (GTA) division of the Chamber. Relations with GTA soured in 1938, however, after Chamber offices were moved to a five-story structure at 333 Pine St. and GTA members decided to stay put at the Merchants Exchange Building, thus resigning from the Chamber. Later in 1938, the Merchants Exchange designation was re-established to include importers, exporters and shipping interests, and in a further compromise, a new Marine Exchange became part of the Chamber.

A New Chamber

On June 9, 1911, after months of negotiation among representatives of the four organizations, including a lengthy debate about the name of the consolidated structure, the San Francisco Chamber of Commerce was incorporated. Operations began on Nov. 1. The Merchants Exchange, which kept ownership of the Merchants Exchange Building, offered it to the new Chamber for $1.75 million, but the new group pulled back from taking on that obligation. Members from the four previous organizations were invited to join the new Chamber, under three dues categories ranging from $12 to $60 per year. Staff members from all the organizations were employed by the new Chamber, but in 1913, a departmental organization was adopted, the first vice president and general manager, Robert Newton Lynch, was hired, and staff levels were reconfigured.

The consolidated Chamber drew 2,500 members — more than the four previous organizations combined. Demand for more income, moreover, led to a membership drive in 1915 that yielded 3,500 additional members, for 6,000 total. Soon various trade bodies, includ-

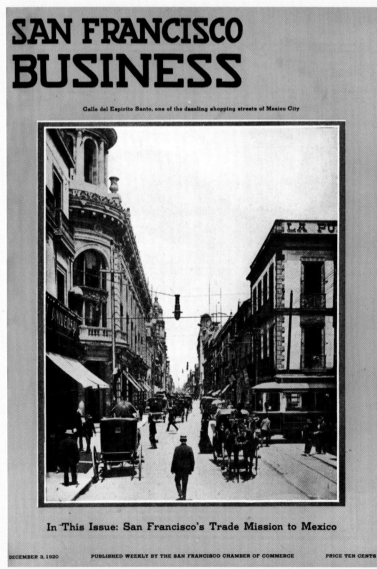

SAN FRANCISCO BUSINESS

Calle del Espirito Santo, one of the dazzling shopping streets of Mexico City

In This Issue: San Francisco's Trade Mission to Mexico

DECEMBER 3, 1920   PUBLISHED WEEKLY BY THE SAN FRANCISCO CHAMBER OF COMMERCE   PRICE TEN CENTS

ing the previously mentioned Grain Trade Association, plus the Green Coffee Association, the Rice Brokers' Association and others, joined for the purpose of doing business deals on the Chamber's Trading Floor, where commodity prices were set between buyer and seller. The exchange function became a major regional business focus. The Retail Merchants' Association also came on board, though a newly renamed Downtown Association re-established itself outside the Chamber's jurisdiction.

Overall, the complexity of the Chamber's work increased greatly and included 10 standing and 11 special committees. Chamber departments included Publicity, Foreign Trade, Transportation, Exchange and Maritime, Marine, Grain Inspection, Municipal Affairs, Industrial, and federal government liaison.

The newly revitalized San Francisco Chamber mirrored the upbeat mood of the city, especially in the 1920s. During the '20s and '30s, at any given time, the Civic Center, the Hetch Hetchy Water System, the two great bridges or the first municipal public-transit system in the United States were either being advocated, planned, financed or constructed, and the Chamber weighed in on each project from its commercial perspective, often with a formal committee.

Still, there were always those members who were discontent. By the time of the Wall Street crash in 1929, enough members were unhappy with the Chamber's work that they demanded action. They believed the city and county of San Francisco was lagging behind the overall growth of California's economy. Miner Chipman, an industrial expert from Boston who had advised the Chamber previously on labor matters, was called upon as a consultant to examine "the effectiveness of the organization." Although Miner's report was later labeled "caustic," and did not result in major changes, he stated that the Chamber was "a faulty organization…a defective tool unable…efficiently to accomplish its purpose." The Great Depression had slammed the economy hard by the time of the report's issuance, and internal bickering suddenly became a minor cause célèbre.

Depression and Labor Unrest

The 1930s meant tough times for the Chamber, and its membership suffered, though a can-do spirit remained discernable, probably because San Francisco was not hurt by economic collapse to the extent other parts of the country were damaged. Chamber President J.W. Howell, in his 1937 annual report, offered "no apologies, although there was a lot that could have been done that wasn't." He went on: "Three thousand people cannot be expected to solve all of the problems of a city of 700,000, and where…[the Chamber] failed, the blame belongs to the crowd on the sidelines and not the workers."

"[Only] one out of 10 [businesspeople] belongs to the Chamber of Commerce," Howell concluded.

That year, 27 committees operated, including one for the Junior Chamber of Commerce, established in 1927 "to give young men between the ages of 21 and 35 an opportunity to become familiarized with civic problems and assume leadership." The Junior Chamber eventually grew to a membership of 1,600 in 1954, though it faded, in turn, to 125 by 1977, when it was abandoned. However, the Junior Chamber served as the forerunner to the successful Leadership San Francisco, a program founded by the Chamber in 1985 to involve younger civic and business leaders in the affairs of the community.

Initiative to improve business conditions in San Francisco was the Chamber's principal work. The Chamber provided a venue for gathering the collective political clout of its members to advocate many infrastructure projects that are taken for granted today. Before

Crowds turned out for the dedication of the Hetch Hetchy water project in 1934. The plan for a publicly owned water system was first proposed in 1900, but since it called for the damming of the Tuolomne River in Yosemite National Park, the project required federal permission. Opposed to the project were conservationists, led by John Muir, as well as Pacific Gas and Electric Co., which lobbied against the project because, in addition to water, it was also intended to provide hydroelectric power to the city. Proponents of Hetch Hetchy finally prevailed, and Congress granted permission for the water project to move forward. PG&E, the largest power company in the country, was, however, able to halt the creation of a public-sector power distribution system in the city.

SAN FRANCISCO BUSINESS

Washington street, main artery of the whole-sale produce district, which keeps San Francisco's cupboard stocked with the most diversified food supply on the continent, as described in this number.

Published Weekly by the San Francisco Chamber of Commerce.

looked mostly to Europe, and the Chamber did play a historic role in helping develop the concept of what is now called multi-national or global business. International consciousness is striking throughout the Chamber's archives. This was, of course, driven by the importance of the Port of San Francisco to the city's economy. In the 1930s and before, the Chamber had its own launch, the *Jerry Daily*, to meet and greet all ships entering the harbor; Chamber staff members helped sea captains with their paperwork. This had been a function of the Merchants Exchange, a separate organization before its 1911 merger with the Chamber, when great stress was placed on first sightings of ships nearing Golden Gate Straits.

The Port of San Francisco was both the city's economic and emotional bellwether, and a good portion of the history of the San Francisco Chamber of Commerce turns on the history of labor in the city. Union membership in private-sector firms declined in the latter part of the 20th century — this was countered by increases in public-sector unionism encouraged by President John F. Kennedy's decision to permit federal employees to join unions — and, hence, labor issues all but dropped off the Chamber's agenda in the 1980s and 1990s, something dramatically opposite agendas for more than 125 years.

Labor actions in the city began in 1852 when Chinese laborers, working on a granite building, walked off their jobs for higher wages and, in 1864, when stable grooms struck for the same reason. Then in 1865, some 2,000 workers swamped Market Street to demand an eight-hour working day; the norm was then 12 hours. Business owners formed a Ten Hour Association to counter the protests, but the state Legislature enacted an eight-hour law in 1868, only to see it become moot amid a heavy influx of unemployed workers after the Civil War and upon completion of the Transcontinental Railroad.

Working conditions declined anew. This was articulated in labor organizer Dennis Kearney's fiery rhetoric and the founding of his Workingman's Party of California in 1877, a movement that left behind a strong labor voting tradition in San Francisco. In the 1880s, local brewery workers struck to protest their 16- to 18-hour workdays, but they did not succeed. Later, Union Labor Party activity, from 1901 to 1912, with its ties to the most notorious of San Francisco's political bosses, attorney Abraham Ruef, helped create an environment that brought on a series of strikes between 1902 and 1908, culminating in Bloody Tuesday, May 7, 1907, a large strike during which two were killed. Socialist activists called upon workers to "Tie Up the Town," while the pro-business *Argonaut* lamented the tepid response by the "jellyfish of our capitalistic and mercantile community." The same year brought a sharp Wall Street panic that ended with J.P. Morgan's intervention.

The Chamber's contentious mood on labor issues was most succinctly articulated by its president, Frederick J. Koster, in a 1918 address that was printed and widely disseminated, entitled "Law and Order and the San Francisco Chamber Commerce." It related to finding "a rational solution [to San Francisco's] grave industrial problem…labor unionism." Labor unrest, especially on the waterfront, had long been part of the city's history, and the Chamber played its natural role in opposition. The Chamber passed an anti-union resolution in 1916 that Koster said "could not be misunderstood. It resolves itself down to the one thing — the maintenance

1925, the Chamber helped locate US Route 40 from Salt Lake City to San Francisco, establish public gardens in Golden Gate Park, retain Mare Island as an active Navy yard and develop the Bayshore Highway to San Jose. From 1925 to 1950, the Chamber played important catalytic roles in pushing political leaders to construct the Golden Gate and Bay bridges, build a federal office building in the city, develop the Islais Creek area for industrial purposes, lay out state parks, bring new highways and military bases to the Bay Area, and establish what became San Francisco International Airport (SFO) at Mills Field in San Mateo County. In the case of the Bay Bridge, the Chamber sent a delegation to Washington, DC, headed by its president, Leland Cutler, to seek money from the Reconstruction Finance Corp., and, thanks to a crucial nod from President Franklin D. Roosevelt that was requested by Cutler, came away with $62,400,000 for construction.

Among notable Chamber activities in the first half of the 20th century was its hosting of a delegation in 1915 from the Republic of China, which sought commercial ties with California. Then, in a reciprocal move in 1921, the Chamber organized its own three-month grand tour by San Francisco business leaders who traveled first-class on the SS Empire State to Hawaii, Japan and China, as well as to the "Straits Settlements, Java, French Indo-China and the Philippines."

The Chamber really was a leader in bringing the potential of Pacific commerce to the nation's attention, while the eastern establishment

of law and order. That is all, in the ultimate, the maintenance of the principle of the open shop amounts to." He went on to say that the Chamber was not opposed to collective bargaining or "unions as such," though the Chamber's Law and Order Committee strongly opposed strikes and other labor actions and organized a rally, attended by 6,000, following a bombing at Stewart and Market streets where nine died on Preparedness Day, July 22, 1916.

Still, the Chamber did try on occasion to be constructive. In 1921, its Industrial Committee published "The San Francisco Program" to advance economic development and labor peace. Prepared by Dr. B.M. Rastall, the plan received editorial support from all the major newspapers in the city. *The Daily Commercial News* called it "the most carefully worked out that has been presented in the history of the city." Rastall said the Chamber was "engaged in the most…painstaking endeavor…to find those things…essential…for winning the contest for Pacific Coast supremacy." The plan boils down to advocating a host of improvements in government, business, infrastructure, living conditions and region that would be good for workers and employers alike, something around which "all citizens can unite." The general exuberance of the 1920s apparently overtook the government intervention necessary to enact such ambitions, but many of the ideas were eventually realized.

Like in the rest of the nation, prosperity tended to dampen union unrest; economic depression encouraged it. The 1920s were relatively quiet for labor actions as a result, while the 1930s saw city unemployment of 25 percent by the middle of the decade and armed conflict resulting in two deaths in the general strike of 1934. It got bad enough during the Great Depression, with thousands of jobless people arriving in California, that the state passed laws to close its borders to poor people; the laws were declared unconstitutional by the US Supreme Court.

The May 9, 1934, strike followed a period of union decline coincident with deteriorating workers' living standards. The Chamber attacked unionism, starting around 1915, and ship owners defeated a 1919 strike. By 1933, half the longshore workers in the city were on relief rolls. Union schisms and New Deal labor legislation, not to mention the waterfront's charismatic labor leader, Harry Bridges, emboldened stevedores and sailors to strike the port.

The 1934 strike closed the docks for 84 days, and the Industrial Association, consisting of employers and business interests encouraged by the Chamber, employed strike breakers to move goods.

From 1806, when the schooner Juno initiated commerce off Yerba Buena, to 1933, when it was said that goods worth more than a half-billion dollars crossed the docks, shipping had been the cornerstone of San Francisco's prosperity. In the 1930s, dozens of steamship companies did business in the city, including 20 American lines that called San Francisco their home port.

An October 14, 1935, supplement to the *San Francisco Examiner*, likely sponsored by the Industrial Association but labeled from "public spirited citizens," called the previous year's strike an effort to foment "strife along Pacific Coast ports, in conformity with a general Communistic program to Sovietize first the seaports of America and then the entire United States." The "facts," from the business perspective listed in the supplement, were that "half of our commercial life comes [from the port] and from which half of our people make their livings [and] it faces the growing menace of a handful of radicals bent on destroying San Francisco's water-borne trade to their own selfish ends."

When IBM President Thomas G. Watson visited the Golden Gate International Exposition, he was greeted by winners of the Outdoor Girl Contest, sponsored by the San Francisco Chamber of Commerce.

Chamber of Commerce members check out the dry-docked USS Boxer *at a 1952 Coastal Days celebration.*

By the late 1930s, the Chamber's tone became more conciliatory. The Chamber's 1937 board appointed a Committee of Forty-three under its Committee on Labor Relations that adopted seven principles "to formulate a long-range program to bring about industrial peace in San Francisco." These principles included law and order, but also fair wages for workers. The Chamber even became a collective bargaining agency when a special association of wholesale and distribution businesses negotiated with their workers under Chamber auspices.

Chamber President Howell said in 1937 that he was not prepared to draw "the red herring of Communism across the path of every labor activity." "The day of 'union buster' is over. Organization, under existing laws and conditions, is inevitable. I find here [that] the average employer is quite willing to meet with any true representative of labor and reach an agreement that is fair, but we cannot permit ourselves to be at the mercy of those groups who have assumed leadership often by forceful means and whose objective is social revolution." That statement marked a rapprochement with labor compared with President Roster's rhetoric 19 years earlier.

In 1939, a summit meeting of sorts, consisting of the city's business and labor leaders, took place to facilitate business-labor harmony. Though war clouds were readily evident in the world, the summit meeting signaled a mood of general hopefulness in the city that was also home to the successful Golden Gate International Exposition, held in 1939 and 1940, on Treasure Island in San Francisco Bay, the last worldwide celebration until the end of World War II.

War...and the United Nations is Founded

Depression Era issues, not to mention hope, were overtaken by world events surrounding the war and Holocaust. The San Francisco Chamber had an inkling of trouble to come, and in 1934 took significant action by convening the Military Committee of the Chambers of Commerce of the Pacific Coast in Los Angeles, requesting that "each body make a survey of the defensive requirements…and…formulate a consolidated Military Defense Program for the entire Pacific Coast." Chamber representatives believed that this could all be accomplished for $5 million.

Although patriotic events were commonplace in the last few years of peace before the Japanese attack on Pearl Harbor, San Francisco–area troops were each issued 40 rounds of small-arms ammunition on Dec. 5, 1941, and mine-laying in the bay began one hour after the Japanese air attack on Oahu on Dec. 7. The following day, at 6:15 pm, saw the first blackout drill, the importance being underscored nine days later when Japanese submarine 1-15 surfaced to charge its batteries off the Farallon Islands. Even if Chamber reports in the early 1940s hardly mention the war, the Bay Area was a focal point in support of the Pacific theater, with more than $6.5 billion in war contracts pouring into the area and thousands of new residents who came to work in war-related plants.

SAN FRANCISCO
CHAMBER OF COMMERCE

Amid all the hubbub, the Chamber remained concentrated on representing its members' business interests, and in 1943, the Chamber invited the Chamber of Commerce of the United States to do a survey of the San Francisco Chamber's work. The report, in contrast to Miner Chipman's earlier blast, was effusive in its praise, saying, "It is doubtful whether there is a better Chamber of Commerce anywhere in the terms of morale and personnel." Membership expanded by 500 in 1943 to 4,127; the Junior Chamber of Commerce grew from 403 to 1,013 members. A "Road Map" of projects, including highways, parks, the waterfront and other capital improvements, was developed to chart San Francisco's future, "ready to start the day the war is over." (The Road Map presaged attention in the 1950s to citywide decay that had become all too evident. Urban renewal projects replaced slum housing in Hunters Point and the Western Addition, added business-district office towers, built downtown automobile garages and wiped out tawdry elements near the Embarcadero with an ambitious project: the large residential and commercial complex known as the Golden Gateway.)

In 1944, the Chamber formed a Victory Day Committee to help organize celebrations to mark the war's 1945 end in Europe and then Japan. Unfortunately, the celebrations deteriorated into "peace riots" that resulted in some deaths. Also that year, the Chamber encouraged the San Francisco Conference where 50 nations approved the United Nations World Charter of Security. Coincidentally, a Western Conference of Chambers from 11 Western states was initiated at the Chamber's behest.

Membership in the Chamber stood at 6,083 in 1945, and for the first time, a woman's name appeared in the leadership record: Marie A. Harlan, a Chamber employee, was named secretary of the Chamber, a post she held for many years. The history of the involvement of women in the Chamber's work began in 1921 when the bylaws were amended in a move related to the women's suffrage movement in the United States. Qualifications in draft form read, "Any man, firm or corporation of good standing, and residing doing business, owning property in or interested in the advancement of San Francisco, and any responsible business woman who is the proprietor or active manager of her own business, shall be eligible." As finally adopted, the word *man* was struck in favor of *person* as was the section on businesswomen. Women did become Chamber members, but for the next 50 years, they were largely excluded from leadership positions.

Women in Leadership

If involvement of women was a slow process, participation by businesspeople who were also minority-group members was even slower. Virtually all Chamber boards and committees consisted of white males — some of whom enjoyed cigar-smoking at board meetings —

Regina Phelps, president of Health Plus, in 1990 was the first woman in the Chamber's history to chair the board of directors.

Eunice Azzani, managing director of Korn/Ferry International, in 1999 was only the second woman in 149 years to serve as board chair.

until 1987, when on a board of directors of 49, names of four women appeared along with one Asian surname. In 1988, seven women and three minorities were found on the board roster of 50. In 1990, 10 women were counted, including the chairelect Regina R. Phelps, president of Health Plus, who became the first female board president in 140 years; the second woman to serve as board chair was Eunice Azzani, a principal with the executive search firm Korn/Ferry International, who was chair in 1999. In 1990 also, five names of minority-group members appeared on the board's roster, signaling gradual inclusion of all segments of the San Francisco business community, a trend that continued throughout the 1990s. Representatives of the gay business community were welcomed, as well.

The year 1950 marked the 100th anniversary of the San Francisco Chamber of Commerce, the oldest chamber in the Western United States. A gala banquet at the Palace Hotel culminated a series of celebratory events. Stuart Symington, chair of the National Security Resources Board and soon to become US senator from Missouri, was the speaker of the evening. He was greeted by California Gov. Earl Warren, later to be named chief justice of the US Supreme Court by President Dwight D. Eishenhower. Symington warned of the "necessity for military preparedness by this country." This call echoed earlier Chamber work. In the 1930s, there was a Chamber Committee to Combat Communism, though that pointed mostly to labor unrest, citing "alien radicals." After World War II, San Francisco joined the nation in wanting to return quickly to peaceful pursuits. The Chamber promoted commercial air service and the location of headquarters for the United Nations in the city. Walter Haas, head of Levi Strauss and Co., chaired a committee for this latter purpose, and though Mayor Lapham pronounced the prospect "good," the outcome was negative.

Although the UN was ultimately headquartered in New York, on June 26, 1995, San Francisco commemorated the 50th anniversary of the signing of its charter. In ceremonies at the War Memorial Opera House, President Bill Clinton delivered the keynote address. Speakers included David Brinkley, ABC News anchor; Desmond Tutu, bishop of the Anglican Church of South Africa; Amara Essy, president of the United Nations General Assembly; Boutros Boutros-Ghali, United Nations secretary-general; Madeleine Korbel Albright, permanent representative to the United Nations from the United States; Warren Christopher, secretary of state of the United States; and Maya Angelou, poet. The major sponsor of the event was San Francisco real-estate mogul Walter H. Shorenstein.

The upbeat mood was such in the 1950s that the Chamber declared itself the senior commercial body of the Pacific Coast. It

sponsored a supplement to *Newsweek* in 1954 to brag about the commercial greatness of the Bay Area. Entitled "Boom With Sense: Making Dreams Come True in Golden Gate Area," the text compared the city favorably with New York, Chicago, Paris, Rio de Janeiro and Hong Kong, while touting its economic base in financial and managerial know-how, distribution, petroleum and chemicals, and the food-processing and metals industries. By recalling great San Francisco business names such as Lick, Flood, Hearst, Ralston, Giannini, Sutro, Strauss, Ghirardelli and others, the Chamber ensured that a conservative busi-

Cyril Magnin (center), owner of Joseph Magnin and known as Mr. San Francisco, was presented with a portrait at the Chamber's 118th annual dinner meeting. Magnin was honored for serving the Chamber as president for three terms. David Sachs, general manager of KGO-TV, made the presentation, while Mayor Joseph Alioto looked on.

ness spirit in the city was alive and well and offered great opportunities for investment and corporate headquarters. Yet, the *Newsweek* piece did not get it all correct from the perspective of 45 years later:

The Port of San Francisco was said to be the key to the city's economic future, as were heavy industry and nuclear power. The 1957 annual report of the Chamber listed a budget of almost $350,000 in pursuit of 146 activities during the year.

Toward Professionalism

In the 1960s, a trend toward professionalization began that continued through the end of the century. William E. Dauer was appointed Chamber executive officer in 1963, a post he held for 18 years. He was followed, in turn, by John H. Jacobs, Gerald E. Newfarmer, Donald D. Doyle and G. Rhea Serpan, the latter being named in 1993. In 1999, a chief operating officer was also named. An article in *San Francisco Business*, the Chamber's magazine from 1965 to 1994, summed up the new way of working: "No longer slap-you-on-the-back, booster organizations, effective Chambers must rely on action-motivated leadership and specialized staffs to solve community problems."

The decade of the '60s was a time of social dislocation in San Francisco, notably represented by anti–Vietnam War protests, the Summer of Love, American Indians' seizure of Alcatraz Island and the Beatles' last live concert at Candlestick Park. The Bay Area was national epicenter of counterculture clamor. More conservative Chamber members tried to understand what was happening, and the Chamber made efforts to adapt. Articles early in the decade in *San Francisco Business*, such as "Men Worth Watching," "The Feminine Scene on Montgomery Street" and "Jobs and the Negro" changed later in the decade to "Executives on the Move," "What Happened to Topless?" and "Black Business in the City."

Being a conservative organization in a liberal city, the Chamber tried to articulate a voice of business amid the hullabaloo, though the task was not simple. In the early 1970s, environmental pollution and policy were among the top national issues, and the Chamber's president in 1974 declared that his principal agenda was finding balance between environmental controls and economic development. When the Chamber strayed from issues that were not strictly business-related, ambiguity about its image resulted. A 1976 survey of 450 businesspeople in the city uncovered confusion about the Chamber's nature. For example, they thought the Chamber was only dedicated to big business, that it was supported by tax dollars and that its job was mostly to promote tourism. In fact, the bulk of the Chamber's membership was small businesses, the organization received no tax dollars and the job of promoting tourism was the purvue of the Convention and Visitors Bureau. Most of the Chamber's agenda concerned crime control, parking, clean streets, taxes, government efficiency, optimal commercial environment and the like. Meanwhile, the city advanced with a downtown building boom, notably the Transamerica Pyramid in 1972, and with opening of the transbay tube in 1974 as part of the Bay Area Rapid Transit system.

William Dauer was a reflection of the Chamber's orientation in the 1960s and '70s. Labeled "Conservative, Constructive (and) Controversial" by *San Francisco Business*, his years of service were thusly summarized. Dauer's major accomplishments involved achieving financial stability for the Chamber, encouraging international business by constant exchanges with foreign executives, and increasing the institutional profile for business. Until he arrived from the Kansas City Chamber, the city of San Francisco funded 20 percent of the Chamber's budget, but Dauer dropped that practice quickly, citing the Chamber's need for political independence. At the end of his term, he said his major accomplishment was the "Chamber's ability to stop well over $200 million dollars in taxation on business," though he admitted his biggest challenge was being a fiscal conservative in nonconservative political surroundings.

It was also under Dauer's leadership in 1979 that the Chamber's Sports Committee first had dreams of a Bay Area Sports Hall of Fame (BASHOF) to honor the area's athletic legends. Dauer engaged Lou Spadia, former president of the San Francisco 49ers, to guide the effort, and it was Spadia who first came up with the notion of a "hall without a hall." It would be better, he reasoned, to put the money that could be raised into a fund to benefit-youth recreation programs in San Francisco and the Bay Area. From its modest beginnings, BASHOF grew in stature and in 1999, the BASHOF Youth Fund exceeded the $1.5 million mark in grants made during its 20-year history.

Two sharp economic recessions struck the city in the early '80s and again in the early '90s. In the early '80s, 40 San Francisco corporations with 1,000 local employees or more left the city or expanded elsewhere, for a net job loss by 1985 of 17,000. This was all related to expansion of the service economy, influx of technical and professional jobs, competition from abroad generally and especially from Japan, growth of tourism as an economic mainstay and the shift of shipping activity from San Francisco to Oakland, Long Beach and the Pacific Northwest. The old industrial base faded while information- and biologically based technology companies took over. The decade ended with the Oct. 17, 1989, earthquake of 7.1 magnitude, that did damage in the Bay Area of $3 billion.

San Francisco emerged favorably from this era of fundamental change with a population that was at once the best-educated and best-paid of any large American city. A *Fortune* magazine survey in the mid-1990s rated the city and adjacent Silicon Valley as "the best place to do business in the nation now and in the future." San Francisco was also rated the top tourist destination on the planet with its restaurants being ranked as the best anywhere by *Condé Nast Traveler*. *Money*, another national magazine, in 1999 touted San Francisco as the best big city in the United States in which to live. The Chamber did not hold back its euphoria.

The second recession was the most significant, resulting from the end of the Cold War upon the demise of the Soviet Union and the consequent decline in defense industries where California had great economic exposure. Membership in the Chamber declined, and there was much talk that the institution had lost its way. Economic development emerged as the rallying theme.

Focus on Economic Development

The story of the Chamber in the late 1980s and throughout the '90s, as a result, is one of a continuing focus on economic development. In 1983, the city was suffering the effects of Proposition 13, which heralded an ongoing taxpayers' revolt against costly and inefficient government, and an economic downturn. Like other municipalities, San Francisco was faced with making radical cuts to cover budget deficits. The Chamber, under the leadership of President John Jacobs and Chair James Harvey of Transamerica, and the San Francisco business community undertook the development of a $600,000 Strategic Plan for San Francisco.

The Strategic Plan identified four closely related issues facing the city: housing, transportation, city finances, and job and business opportunities. The plan reported that the city lost substantial ground during the 1970s as inflation eroded revenues and raised the cost of municipal goods and services — all exacerbated by the limits placed on property-tax revenues by Prop 13.

Robert Kemper, vice chair of Wells Fargo Bank and chair of the Strategic Plan's Finance Task Force, warned, "Prudent financial management is essential if the city is to successfully weather its uncertain fiscal condition over the next five years." Kemper predicted that even under the best of circumstances the city was headed toward a deficit situation at the latest in 1988, or earlier in 1984.

Kemper's predications proved correct. By 1985, the city was facing a potential $76 million deficit for 1986, brought on by spending a $152 million surplus on new city employees, public-works projects and upgrading public buildings.

The Chamber spent much of 1985 updating the 1983 Strategic Plan. Edward Stokes of Bechtel and John Greene of Arthur Andersen & Co. co-chaired the effort. Because of declining economic conditions, the plan was revised to include a new focus on international business, the visitor industry and the retention and diversification of jobs and business in San Francisco. The Chamber began work on a new series of economic strategies, focusing on the expansion of Moscone Convention Center, documenting the economic impact of the city's visitor industry, forming a San Francisco Bay Area Biosciences Center and retaining the Federal Home Loan Bank.

A major Chamber-supported battle was lost when the business community was unsuccessful in stopping the passage of Proposition M in November 1986. Prop M placed strict limits on the construction of new commercial and office space in the city, and in some minds seriously curtailed the city's ability to grow and expand. It was a harbinger of San Francisco's reputation for being unfriendly to business and was a setback that caused the Chamber's "clout and credibility" to be called into question.

In 1987, James Edgar, principal in the strategic management firm of Edgar, Dunn & Conover and a member of the Chamber's board of directors, surveyed San Francisco employers to help determine how best to market the city to business. The survey covered 1,000 companies representative of San Francisco employment by organization size.

The results confirmed the Chamber's thinking: While employers rated the city "slightly positive as a 'place to operate your business,'" San Francisco did not compare well to five years prior or to other areas within or outside the Bay Area. Employers said the best thing San Francisco had to offer was "image and prestige of location." On the downside, cost and the political environment were the biggest detractors. The problem was no single ordinance, piece of legislation or tax that was particularly onerous, but a perception of an anti-business climate that grew from an accumulation of regulations and added business costs.

The Edgar study served as an important precursor to the Chamber's efforts to establish an economic-development corporation that could stem the tide of dissatisfaction — and retain businesses in San Francisco.

On Nov. 29, 1988, a news conference was called to announce the inauguration of the newly formed San Francisco Economic Development Corporation (EDC), sponsored by a broad cross-section of public and private interests in the city, which dubbed them "The Partnership for San Francisco." Participants included Mayor Art Agnos, EDC President Kent Sims and prominent business, labor and community leaders. The stated aim was to address "an erosion of the city's economic base that threatens employment, public revenue and major sources of support for nonprofit social and cultural programs."

The EDC claimed a crucial element missing in past efforts to improve the city's image as a business location was the lack of consensus, so it billed the new effort as "a virtual 'rainbow coalition' of San Francisco business and politics."

Statements made by supporters seemed to concur:

"Labor supports the EDC because only by working together can we retain and attract responsible employers to San Francisco," said Walter Johnson, secretary-treasurer of the San Francisco Labor Council.

"The Chamber supports the EDC because we share its vision for San Francisco," said David Chamberlain, president of Shaklee Corp. and chair of the San Francisco Chamber of Commerce.

"We support the EDC because it recognizes the vital role neighborhood businesses play in the city's economy," said Malcolm Thornley, president of the Council of District Merchants.

"The economic vitality of San Francisco is critical to the progress of our city in the years to come," said Mayor Art Agnos. "A healthy business climate is essential to all San Franciscans."

Ironically, it may have been the weight of its diverse makeup that eventually tilted the EDC away from its roots in the Chamber organization. By 1990, the organization had declared its independence and moved its offices out of the Chamber.

Unfortunately, the EDC did little to stem the tide of companies leaving the city. From 1991 to 1993, the city lost 37,000 jobs. Some of that loss could be blamed on perceived anti-business policies, but much of it was the result of general economic conditions: a sluggish national economy, downsizing, increasing local regulations, escalating taxes and a perception on the part of business that residents failed "to equate a vibrant economy with quality of life."

Gorbachev Visits Chamber

One of the most dramatic events in the history of San Francisco and the Chamber occurred on Monday, June 4, 1990, when the Chamber arranged a visit of then-President of the Union of Soviet Socialist Republics Mikhail S. Gorbachev to San Francisco. Preparations for the historic visit began a scant three weeks prior, when the Chamber's director of international programs, Harry Orbelian, excused himself for being late to a board of directors' meeting, saying, "I was just on the phone with Moscow. Gorbachev wants to come to San Francisco, and he wants the Chamber to arrange the visit."

The visit was the first of a Soviet leader to California in more than 30 years, since Nikita Krushchev had come to visit Disneyland and stargaze in Hollywood. The luncheon was held in the Venetian Room of the Fairmont Hotel and was cohosted by the governor of California, George Deukmejian, and the mayor of the city and county of San Francisco, Art Agnos. Welcoming remarks were made by Chamber Chair G. Rhea Serpan, at the time an AT&T vice president .

Gorbachev's visit was a sweet victory for Orbelian, himself an Armenian-born former Russian soldier who had spent two and a half years in a Nazi concentration camp before immigrating to the United States in 1949. Orbelian worked on the idea for five years. It was at a state dinner in Moscow in December 1985 with then–San Francisco Mayor Dianne Feinstein that Orbelian first posed the question of inviting the then–general secretary of the Communist Party to visit San Francisco, the birthplace of the United Nations and home to corporations eager to make inroads to the Soviet market. For the next five years, Orbelian never missed an opportunity to remind his Soviet contacts that San Francisco's invitation was still open.

No sooner was the announcement made public than the Chamber was deluged with requests — and demands — for tickets from all over the country. But officials in the Soviet embassy insisted that the luncheon event be held to no more than 150 invited guests and

San Francisco Chamber of Commerce Chair G. Rhea Serpan (left) presented an original oil painting by famed Russian painter Anatolio Sokoloff showing native Californians attending a feast with Russian fur traders to Mikhail Gorbachev, president of the Union of Soviet Socialist Republics (right). California Governor George Deukmejian (center) co-hosted the historic visit of the the Soviet leader.

that they have final approval of the guest list: Their top priority were CEOs in a position to make business deals.

Press and media from all over the globe covered the event. In the best traditions of *perestroika*, Gorbachev declared, "The Cold War is now behind us," and called on West Coast business leaders to help him rescue the Soviet economy as he moved to make it easier for foreign businesses to form operations in the USSR.

The visit to San Francisco ended with a historic summit meeting between Gorbachev and South Korean President Roh Tae Woo. Roh hailed the meeting as "an epoch-making event," officially ending 42 years of silence between the two ideological and military foes. He predicted their dialogue would lead to vast changes in political and economic relations among competing nations throughout Asia.

Attract, Develop and Retain Business in San Francisco

Also in June 1990, the Chamber's board of directors held a mid-year planning conference that laid the foundation for profound change within the organization and for the Chamber's future in the community. Perhaps most significantly, the directors wrote a new mission statement. 1990 Chair Rhea Serpan declared it "perhaps the most important piece of work we did that day." Gone were the references to a "healthy business climate" and enhancing the quality of life. The new mission of the Chamber was simply and unambiguously stated: "To attract, develop and retain business in San Francisco."

The emphasis on economic development illustrated the Chamber's frustration with the EDC. The Chamber had been struggling with the EDC since soon after its inception. Differences arose as to appropriate action steps and the ability of the EDC to deliver on its promises. The Chamber was coming to the conclusion that it needed to take back control of the effort to attract new business to San Francisco — and hold on to the companies at risk of leaving town. In addition to the refocusing of the mission, the other significant decision to come out of the 1990 mid-year meeting was a resolve to create economic-development functions within the Chamber. On the agenda for that year's annual fall planning conference was an item to "resolve (issues pertaining to the EDC) by either bringing the current EDC into the Chamber or starting a new department."

While the Chamber was questioning the effectiveness of the EDC it had helped to create, it felt a need to increase its own ability to fulfill the new mission statement.

In 1991, following on a spate of articles critical about San Francisco's business climate in such publications as *Forbes, Fortune, The Wall Street Journal* and the city's own *San Francisco Chronicle*, a group of CEOs from a dozen of San Francisco's largest and most prominent

San Francisco Chamber of Commerce

Mission Statement

The Mission of the San Francisco Chamber of Commerce is to Attract, Develop and Retain Business in San Francisco.

The Chamber is dedicated to ensuring that San Francisco is a great international city in which to live and work, and an attractive, nurturing place to do business.

The Chamber ensures that San Francisco is economically strong and viable by serving as a bridge to businesses and economic development efforts and uniting them to solve the economic challenges facing the City. This is accomplished by taking a leadership position in setting direction and pace for economic development and serving as a catalyst and facilitator to the City.

The Chamber acts to create an environment in which business is understood, welcomed and supported in San Francisco, by educating the public, its agencies and its officials about the vital tie between quality of life and economic vitality. This is accomplished in a facilitative style that earns respect and support for business.

The Chamber acts as the recognized spokesman for business in matters of economic and business development within San Francisco by ensuring that the business viewpoint is clear, understood, and respected by all in the City.

The Chamber serves as an essential contact point for businesses wishing to locate in San Francisco by providing personalized information, advice, resources and follow-up work to ease the process of locating a business here.

The Chamber actively supports local government and its agencies by supplying business skills to assist in problem solving.

The Chamber helps make doing business in San Francisco attractive, by serving as an ombudsman and facilitator for businesses working through issues with City Hall and government agencies.

companies, including the chair and president of the Chamber, formed the Committee on Jobs. Their aim was to flex their collective political might to reverse business flight and improve the quality of life in the city. Their efforts continue to the present in the form of public-education campaigns, lobbying and political action on behalf of business issues and business-friendly candidates for office.

In the summer of 1991, the Chamber embarked on a long-range planning process to "set the future direction for the Chamber and assure that the Chamber is focused on its mission." The effort was led by Regina Phelps, president of Health Plus and the first woman chair of the board of directors in the history of the organization. The work begun that summer led to a restructuring of the board of directors and staff responsibilities. The shift was from an internal focus to a more city-focused operation. The big emphasis was on economic development and marketing San Francisco, with a push toward building community partnerships and alliances that would help "win over the people of San Francisco."

At the 1991 fall planning conference, the board adopted a long-range business plan that set forth three external goals: economic vitality, to "support economic development projects, marketing of San Francisco and direct assistance to businesses"; outreach to create "a receptive environment for our economic vitality efforts"; and education, which was to be addressed in subsequent planning phases. Internal goals were to create an Economic Vitality department, design a new membership-development approach "with a strong focus on more mid-size companies and change the Chamber into a planning organization."

Jay Cahill, president of Cahill Contractors Inc., chaired the new Marketing San Francisco Committee. The committee hired Jessie Knight, formerly the marketing director for the San Francisco Newspaper Agency, as senior vice president to head up the newly formed Economic Vitality department. In addition to the work associated with fulfilling the Chamber's mission, the committee was charged with raising funds to support the effort.

By the time of the annual 1992 fall meeting, incoming 1993 Chair James Altman, president of Johnson & Higgins of California, was able to report the Chamber had "left behind the negative thinking that in the past has clouded the business climate, and we have begun to create a growing new attitude, a new belief in the future of San Francisco and in the important mission and vision of the Chamber."

In 1993, Donald Doyle, an emeritus director who had been recruited as president at a time of internal upheaval, retired, signaling that the job of rebuilding stability and credibility was done, and the directors selected G. Rhea Serpan, vice president of international services operations for AT&T, to lead the Chamber into the future. In the fall of that year, Altman cited such Economic Vitality successes as the passage of tax-incentive legislation authored by Supervisor Barbara Kaufman, job retention in the city and "the maturation of Economic Vitality from direct assistance to marketing and attraction."

When James Edgar became chair in 1994, he noted the important contributions of a cadre of more than 300 volunteers whose work was essential to the ongoing functions of the Economic Vitality Department. Knight had resigned the year before to accept an appointment to the California Public Utilities Commission, leaving much of the direction up to the committee now headed by Michaela Cassidy, president of Aspen Affiliates management consultants.

The emphasis in 1994 was on the Economic Vitality fund-raising effort. The Chamber brought in the Suddes Group, a pre-eminent national firm specializing in economic-development projects, to do an initial feasibility study. The prospects were good, and the board, led by Serpan, Cahill and John Larson, a partner in Brobeck Phlegar & Harrison, began fund-raising in earnest.

In 1995, at the Chamber's annual luncheon, Chair Jay Cahill announced the formation of the Marketing San Francisco Partnership (MSFP), a successor to the defunct Economic Development Corp. On July 25, 1995, a news conference was held at Gap headquarters, hosted by MSFP Chair Donald Fisher, chair and CEO of Gap Inc. Joining Fisher was Mayor Frank Jordan, Chamber Chair Jay Cahill and other city and business leaders. They announced that individual businesses had pledged $815,000 a year for five years to support the partnership in attracting and retaining business and jobs in the city. Later that year, the name was changed to the San Francisco Partnership and Mara Brazer, a public-relations executive, was brought in as managing partner.

The 1996 fall conference was a time for reflection and review. Serpan's opening remarks summed up the first half of the decade, saying: "Beginning in 1990, the Chamber was in a state of disrepair and suffering from a lack of focus. We built a five-year plan based on a vision and focused on a mission to attract, develop and retain business in San Francisco. That mission became our rallying cry, against which we tested everything going forward."

New Majority for Sound Economic Policy

With the San Francisco Partnership laying claim to economic development, the Chamber shifted to the public-policy arena. In his inaugural address to the 1997 annual lunch, Chair Lawrence Stupski, vice chair of the Charles Schwab Corp., enumerated the ways in which the city's economy had turned around, but also pointed out that "there are significant challenges on the horizon that we must pay attention to."

Stupski was specifically referring to the coming changes in welfare reform and the need to provide young people with school-to-work experience. Stupski's comments attracted the attention of Roberta Achtenberg, former city supervisor and assistant secretary of HUD for the Clinton administration. Soon after, Achtenberg joined the Chamber as senior vice president/public policy and initiated two programs aimed at correcting the "access gap" Stupski had referred to in his speech. Those initiatives were San Francisco Works, formed in collaboration with the Committee on Jobs and United Way of the Bay Area, and the School-to-Career Partnership between the Chamber, the unified school district, City College of San Francisco and the mayor's office.

Also in 1997, the Chamber engaged the help of Art Cimento, principal in McKinsey & Co. Inc. and the 1998 chair-elect, to assess how the Chamber could increase its value to its members. The McKinsey work identified two main groups of Chamber members: those who joined to build their business and those who were mainly interested in being an advocate for sound public policy. This focus on what members wanted indicated somewhat of a shift to an internal focus that had been overshadowed through much of the '90s by the need to attend to the city's economic recovery.

One of the measures of the Chamber's increased effectiveness in the last three years of the 1990s was the degree to which the electorate was swayed by the Chamber's recommendations on ballot measures. For three years running, polling of city voters showed a strong identification with the Chamber's message that sound economic policies contribute to the city's overall quality of life. At one time in the late '80s and early '90s, politicos avoided attaching the Chamber's recommendations to issues for fear the liberal San Francisco electorate would shy away from those positions. By 1998, political consultants recognized the value of the Chamber's endorsement and actively sought out its seal of approval. It seemed that the organization had fulfilled one of the early tenets of its long-range plan to better connect with the community.

In 1999, the Chamber elected as chair the second woman in its history, Eunice Azani, managing director of Korn/Ferry International. Azzani brought with her a passionate interest in promoting diversity — of women, of people of color, of a broad representation of the many people who make up the richness of San Francisco. She insisted the organization look beyond its traditional base and reach out to new audiences, both to increase and diversify the membership and to broaden the base of political support in the community.

As the San Francisco Chamber of Commerce began its 150th anniversary year, incoming Chair A. Lee Blitch, regional vice president with AT&T, was able to stand on a platform that became the theme for the Chamber's celebration's of its history and future: The Chamber had truly been a part of San Francisco's history from the Gold Rush to the new age of cyberspace.

Throughout its history, the San Francisco Chamber of Commerce has served in a capacity like all other strong chambers: a vehicle for informal communication among the commercial power brokers on civic, business and political propositions. Although only a minority of city businesses have ever been members of the San Francisco Chamber of Commerce, the commercial elite of San Francisco has been heavily involved, directly or indirectly, in the Chamber's work, and though their support has waxed or waned with mercantile and leadership cycles, there is no doubt that the Chamber, at least since 1911, has been at the center of representing the city's business interests before the political and economic establishment, whether locally or externally.

If the Chamber had not been founded, it would have had to be invented. Much of the Chamber's work, arguably the most important part, does not appear in the historical record through such formalities as committees. The Chamber is a meeting point for opinion leaders, and the thousands of decisions, large and small, that have resulted, albeit mostly lost over time, have shaped the city and its lifestyle in myriad ways. The record of the Chamber's accomplishments has depended on this operational convergence dynamic. Informal contacts, among Chamber members, board leaders and staff people, whether about agreements or disagreements, have left their fingerprints on most venues of the city's life.

For example, in June 1987, the San Francisco Chamber of Commerce was the first major business organization in the country to adopt a set of guidelines to enable employers and their employees to cope with concerns of AIDS in the workplace. In a preface, the Chamber called on society as a whole, and businesses in particular, to respond in a rational manner to what was becoming a epidemic of enormous proportions: "Any sensible and humane response to the epidemic must be based on accurate information, not irrational fear and discrimination."

The pioneering workplace guidelines were developed in consultation with the San Francisco AIDS Foundation and written for the Chamber by Dr. Julius Krevans, then-chancellor of the University of California, San Francisco, and a member of the Chamber's board of directors.

The guidelines were widely disseminated to businesses, policy makers and organizations across the United States and abroad. They stressed the need to treat employees suffering from AIDS with compassion and sensitivity and to offer them the right to continue working as long as they are able to continue to perform their job satisfactorily and do not pose a health or safety threat to themselves or others. The guidelines also call upon employers and co-workers to treat all medical information obtained from employees with strict confidentiality.

The Chamber did not stop there, but in consecutive years on lobbying trips to Washington, DC, the Chamber brought the voice of business to national policy makers, urging increased funding for research, education and prevention. The significance of this work was that for many national lawmakers, accustomed to being approached by health and social-service groups, it was the first time they had heard these concerns expressed by business leaders.

And the work is ongoing. In the 150 years of the San Francisco Chamber's service to its members, the city and the Bay Area, the institution has responded to social and economic dislocations. It is the trick to see the forces coalescing and adapt in advance, however, and the Chamber's results there have not been perfect. The 21st century will pose new challenges and opportunities for the organization, including the growing gap between rich and poor, an aging population base, transportation, business cycles, reliance on the service sector, demographic and transnational exposures and inevitable major earthquakes. Even the economic development theme of the 1990s will transmogrify sometime later, because one lesson of the San Francisco Chamber's history is clear: Everything will eventually change. Future leaders will have to measure up in the third millennium to the heritage of success left by their forebears ever since the days of the Gold Rush to the celebration of the Chamber of Commerce's sesquicentennial. ■

A HISTORY OF THE SAN FRANCISCO CHAMBER OF COMMERCE

While the title has variously alternated over the years among president, chairman, chairperson and chair, the duties of the top volunteer leadership have remained similar: to direct the activities of the board of directors of the Chamber of Commerce.

SAN FRANCISCO
CHAMBER OF COMMERCE

1850–1851 William Hooper	**1887–1889** William L. Merry	**1923–1925** Colbert Coldwell	**1952** W.P. Fuller III	**1979** Thomas C. Paton
1851–1853 Beverly C. Sanders	**1889–1890** Ira P. Sankin	**1925–1927** H. Clay Miller	**1953** J.W. Mailliard III	**1980** Arthur V. Toupin
1853–1854 D.L. Ross	**1890–1891** George C. Perkins	**1927–1929** Philip J. Fay	**1954** John N. Watson	**1981–1982** J. Gary Shansby
1854–1856 J.B. Thomas	**1891–1892** C.L. Taylor	**1929–1930** Almer M. Newhall	**1955** Thomas J. Mellon	**1983** James R. Harvey
1856–1857 F.W. Macondray	**1892–1894** E.B. Pond	**1930–1933** Leland W. Cutler	**1956** E.W. Littlefield	**1984** Robert A. Fox
1857–1859 Daniel Gibb	**1894–1896** W.H. Dimond	**1933–1934** J.W. Mailliard Jr.	**1957** E.D. Maloney	**1985** Gordon B. Swanson
1859–1861 Albert Dibblee	**1896–1999** Hugh Craig	**1935–1936** B. R. Funsten	**1958** Alan K Browne	**1986** Ross J. Turner
1861–1863 George H. Kellogg	**1899–1901** Charles Nelson	**1936–1937** Raymond M. Alvord	**1959** Jack H. How	**1987** James T. Clarke
1863–1865 James De Fremery	**1901–1906** George Newhall	**1937–1938** J.W. Howell	**1960** Dan E. London	**1988** David M. Chamberlain
1865–1866 J.A. Donohoe	**1906–1907** W.H. Martson	**1938–1940** Marshall Dill	**1961** O.R. Doerr	**1989** Richard L Barkhurst
1866–1868 R.G. Sneath	**1907–1908** C.H. Bentley	**1940–1941** Walter A. Haas	**1962–1963** Harry A. Lee	**1990** G. Rhea Serpan
1868–1870 James Otis	**1908–1909** Charles C. Moore	**1942 (to 8/27/42)** Dwight L. Merriman	**1964–1965** William J. Bird	**1991** Regina R. Phelps
1870–1872 Robert B. Swain	**1909–1910** James McNab	**1942 (to 12/31/42)** Russell G. Smith	**1966–1968** Cyril Magnin	**1992** Leland Gustafson
1872–1873 C. Adolphe Low	**1910–1911** W.L. Gerstle	**1943** Ernest Ingold	**1969–1970** Samuel B. Stewart	**1993** James Altman
1873–1874 William T. Coleman	**1911–1912** William Matson	**1944** Adrien J. Falk	**1971** Louis W. Niggeman	**1994** James M. Edgar
1874–1876 William F. Babcock	**1912–1913** M.H. Robbins	**1945** Henry F. Grady	**1972** James E. Stretch	**1995** John E Cahill Jr.
1876–1878 L. Friedlander	**1913–1914** William T. Sesnon	**1946** Brayton Wilbur	**1973** John A. Sutro	**1996** John W. Larson
1878–1879 James C. Patrick	**1914–1915** C.F. Michaels	**1947** Carl J. Eastman	**1974** William M. Witter	**1997** Lawrence J. Stupski
1879–1880 George C. Perkins	**1915–1916** W.N. Moore	**1948** W.P.F. Brawner	**1975** Donald D. Doyle	**1998** Arthur P. Cimento
1880–1883 William F. Babcock	**1916–1919** Frederick l. Koster	**1949** Henry E. North	**1976** Walter H. Shorenstein	**1999** Eunice Azzani
1883–1885 Horace Davis	**1919–1921** Atholl McBean	**1950** Paul A. Bissinger	**1977** Ross F. Anderson	**2000** A. Lee Blitch
1885–1887 Henry I. Dodge	**1921–1923** Wallace M. Alexander	**1951** Alan J. Lowrey	**1978** William W. Morrison	

CHAPTER 5

The **Tumult** of the Times
1915–1960

The Tumult of the Times

During the next four and a half decades — approximately the same amount of time as Spanish rule and colonization had extended over San Francisco — the city participated in two world wars and the Korean War. It also enjoyed two periods of great prosperity: the 1920s and the decade and a half following World War II. It also suffered during the Great Depression of the 1930s. This latter decade also saw San Francisco as the venue of a bitter maritime strike, which then led to one of the only general strikes ever called in American history.

In the immortal words of Charles Dickens, "It was the best of times, it was the worst of times."

PREVIOUS SPREAD: Spanning the Golden Gate took six years, $3.5 million and 10 lives.

(SAN FRANCISCO HISTORY CENTER, SAN FRANCISCO PUBLIC LIBRARY)

A Fatal Preparedness Day Parade

The euphoria produced by the Panama Pacific International Exposition was followed by a sharp rise in labor unrest in San Francisco. In response, business groups formed a Law and Order Committee in an attempt to impose an open-shop policy in those trades where workers were on strike.

That, combined with the planning of what was called a Preparedness Day Parade by those who wished to see the United States participate on the side of the Allies in World War I, caused feelings to run high. The labor movement of the time harbored strong pacifist convictions. There were rumors that the parade might be disrupted, but its backers refused to postpone it.

On July 22, 1916, as the parade progressed up Market Street, a bomb exploded in the crowd near the Ferry Building. The death toll was nine; 50 more were injured.

Fury against the perpetrators erupted, and the authorities, under intense pressure to arrest the culprits, did arrest two men: Thomas J. Mooney and Warren K. Billings.

In what was a bitter and patently unfair trial, both men, militant members of the labor movement who had previously been tried for some labor-related bombings, were convicted. Mooney was sentenced to death, Billings to life imprisonment. For more than 20 years, the two men were a cause célèbre in the international labor movement. Mooney's death sentence was eventually commuted to life imprisonment, and both men were released from prison in 1939.

War and Revolution

When the United States entered World War I in April 1917, military-industrial activity in San Francisco took off. Shipyards and factories were enlarged and worked around the clock to produce the ships, commodities and supplies to fuel the war effort. While thousands of San Franciscans were drafted and thousands more volunteered for service, there was a tremendous influx of workers to the city. There was an acute shortage of housing; every public facility in the city was overcrowded.

FROM THE GOLD RUSH TO CYBERSPACE

SAN FRANCISCO HISTORY, CENTER SAN FRANCISCO PUBLIC LIBRARY

ABOVE: San Franciscans flocked to Fleishhaker Pool, the largest in the world, until it closed in the 1960s.

RIGHT: An early version of television was developed in San Francisco by Philo Farnsworth with backing from W.W. Crocker. Fransworth, pictured here, submitted his first television patent in 1927.

SAN FRANCISCO HISTORY, CENTER SAN FRANCISCO PUBLIC LIBRARY

Trivia

President Warren G. Harding passed away in 1923 while staying at the Palace Hotel. Some historians believe he was poisoned by his wife and doctor.

Although San Francisco was no longer the most populous city in the West — it had been surpassed by Los Angeles in 1910 — the city's population stood at a bit more than a half-million by 1920.

The increasing population pushed the physical development of San Francisco west and south. Building increased in the Richmond district, the Sunset district, and the Outer Mission and Potrero areas. A building boom transformed the business district, and in Pacific Heights, many of the huge wooden mansions from the Victorian era were torn down and replaced with apartment houses, flats and modern single-family homes.

But the prosperity and post-war optimism were not to last. In October 1929, the stock market crashed, sending the nation into the Great Depression. A grim decade would now be faced by San Franciscans and the rest of the world. Long lines of people at soup kitchens and in front of the few businesses still hiring were common, California's unemployment rate climbed to 20 percent, and the calm labor situation that had prevailed in the United States during the 1920s came to an end. As the economy of the 1930s grew more dire, unions began to demand better pay and benefits and better working conditions, and the workers became more aggressive in their demands and won substantial victories.

This new world of union militancy coalesced in San Francisco during the mid-1930s. The explosion of a bitter strike of the maritime unions of San Francisco's waterfront workers took place in 1933 against the Matson Line. Then on May 9, 1934, the unions struck against all shipping companies on the West Coast. Soon all related unions joined the strike.

The major issues were wages and benefits and the shipping companies' support and exclusive use of unions controlled by them. The strikers demanded that such unions be independent and controlled by the workers. They also refused to tolerate the shippers' refusal to hire militant union men or the practice of providing kickbacks to the men in charge of hiring.

But the shipping companies refused to compromise. This led to the rise of one of the most controversial labor leaders of the 20th century, Australian-born Harry Bridges, who became head of the longshoremen's union and who galvanized the workers in support of the strike.

Tensions began to increase during the early summer of 1934, as the striking workers watched strike-breakers, under police protection, fill maritime jobs. On July 5, a day that would come to be known as Bloody Thursday, a melee occurred on the waterfront, where police and strikers had been confronting each other for some time. At one point, the police opened fire, killing two strikers and injuring scores of strikers and bystanders.

California's governor sent in the National Guard, and several days later the unions called for a general strike. The general strike paralyzed San Francisco. The streets were empty of vehicles (there was no gasoline for autos, and transit employees had joined the strike), shops saw their inventories dwindle, and there were great fears of food shortages.

The general strike was called off after a few days, and through the mediation of a conservative lawyer named John Francis Neylan, the shipping companies agreed to submit the dispute to the Federal Arbitration Board.

Trivia

It's-Its, which were invented in 1928 by George Whitney and sold at Playland-at-the-Beach, consist of vanilla ice cream between two oatmeal cookies dipped in chocolate.

Not yet Manhattanized, the cityscape of 1930 showed a burgeoning skyline.

The strikers returned to work on July 31, and a little more than two months later the board awarded the International Longshore and Warehouse Union (ILWU) its primary demand: control of all hiring through its own halls.

The maritime strike and the general strike had struck fear in many of those who, in the midst of the Great Depression, worried about a general uprising against the capitalist system in the United States. Neylan, who can be credited with forcing an end to the strike, was no doubt motivated by his concern that the strike could have led to violent revolutionary activity. San Francisco's business leaders and the workers in the city's businesses would in the future be less intransigent.

A Party in the City

Depression, labor unrest, the rise of dictatorships around the world and the increasing threat of war cast a gloomy pall over San Francisco. In answer, the city decided to host another fair, just as it had in another time of economic depression, the 1890s. After all, backers of the idea argued, an exposition would provide jobs and an economic stimulus.

When the Golden Gate International Exposition opened in February 1939, it was located on Treasure Island, the world's largest human-made island, created especially for the fair by the Army Corps of Engineers. The fair truly was international in flavor, drawing on Mayan, Incan, Malay and Cambodian architecture for its inspiration. But even its carnival strip, called the Gayway, didn't draw enough visitors, and by the end of the year the exposition was slated to close.

Labor strife reached a climax in May 1934, when unions struck against maritime companies to protest open shops and the taking of kickbacks by the companies' hiring men. When the shippers tried to reopen the port using strike-breakers, the scene turned violent. On July 5, police fired tear gas into the crowd and ended up killing two strikers, leading the workers to call a general strike.

Trivia

Sts. Peter and Paul Church, on Washington Square in North Beach, was featured in Cecil B. DeMille's *The Ten Commandments.*

Precursor of the Blue Angels: Army maneuvers (opposite) thrilled the crowds at Mills Field in 1930. In 1937, Mills officially became San Francisco Airport (right).

(SAN FRANCISCO HISTORY CENTER, SAN FRANCISCO PUBLIC LIBRARY)

SAN FRANCISCO HISTORY CENTER, SAN FRANCISCO PUBLIC LIBRARY

A group of promoters talked the fair's officials into reopening it four months later, this time with "Fun in '40" as its theme. With Sally Rand's Nude Ranch, big-band concerts, comedians and Billy Rose's Aquacade starring swimmers Johnny Weismuller and Esther Williams, attendance increased.

By the time the Golden Gate International Exposition closed in Sept. 1940, there were signs of an improving economy. But all was not well on the international front. In Europe, France had fallen to Nazi Germany, and England was mounting a desperate defense; Japan was expanding in Asia.

San Francisco Goes to War

The neutrality of the United States ended on Dec. 7, 1941, when the Japanese bombed the US naval base at Pearl Harbor in the Hawaiian Islands. For more than three and a half years the country would be locked in mortal combat in Europe, North Africa and the Far East.

San Franciscans, like other Americans, were outraged by the bombing. The surprise attack also fueled the flames of anti-Asian feelings throughout the West. Politicians, newspapers and organizations, including the California State Chamber of Commerce, the American Legion and the Native Sons of the Golden West, were soon calling for all people of Japanese descent, whether they were citizens or not, to be rounded up.

With Executive Order 9066, President Franklin Roosevelt authorized the removal of Japanese-Americans from their homes and businesses. San Francisco's Fillmore District, the principal Japanese-American neighborhood, was cordoned off, and residents were given but a few hours to pack up whatever they could carry. They were taken by trucks to the Tanforan Race Track in San Bruno and transported to various camps around the West.

Trivia

In 1944, San Francisco ranked second in the nation as a banking center.

The slips are full at the Ferry Building, circa 1929–30. Before the Golden Gate and Bay bridges were built, the ferryboat system took riders to Oakland, Alameda, Point Richmond and Marin County.

The forced internment of Japanese-American citizens was one of the least justified and most shameful episodes in US history.

San Francisco was forever changed by the war. As some 1.65 million military personnel passed through the Golden Gate, many of their wives and families stayed on in the city. Workers flooded the area to staff factories and shipyards. Between 1941 and 1943, the number of wage-earners more than doubled, from 101,000 to 269,000. These workers produced 23.4 million tons of war material.

The skyrocketing population strained the area's supply of housing and schools. With most resources allocated to the war effort, there were severe shortages of many products. Food, gasoline and other commodities were rationed, but San Franciscans gladly made the sacrifices required of them.

When it was all over — after victory had been won over Nazi Germany, after the United States had dropped two atomic bombs and Japan had capitulated — the city went wild. On the evening of Aug. 16, 1945, thousands of San Franciscans took to Market Street in a giant celebration Unfortunately, the joyous public party got out of hand, and rioters broke windows and street lights and looted stores.

Even as the war was raging, the Allies had begun thinking about a worldwide peace-keeping organization. San Francisco was chosen as the location for the founding of what was to become the United Nations, and on April 25, 1945, delegates from 50 countries — including Georges Bidault from newly liberated France; Jan Christion Smuts of South Africa; V.M. Molotov of the Soviet Union; Lord Halifax, Clement Attlee and Anthony Eden of Great Britain; and US Secretary of State Edward Stettinius — descended on Civic Center to begin deliberations on the charter for the new organization. By the end of May, a

draft was complete, and on June 26, the delegates unanimously approved the United Nations' world charter. After the signing, President Harry S. Truman addressed the delegates. San Franciscans felt proud that such an organization — an organization that would promote peace — was born in their city.

The Kisen Co. was just one of the Japanese-American businesses that had to shut its doors when the owners were interned at the beginning of World War II.

Post-War Transformation

By 1948, San Francisco's population peaked at 850,000. Again the city pushed against its borders; new homes and apartment buildings went up, especially on the west side of town, giving San Francisco such large-scale developments as Diamond Heights.

Shortly thereafter, though, the city began to feel the effects of post-war affluence and the growing reliance on the automobile in another way. San Franciscans began leaving the city, drawn to suburbs that offered lots of space and warmer weather. The population would decline by about 200,000 during the next 20 years.

Even as the population dwindled, the city undertook several major projects. In 1952, for example, the Broadway Tunnel was completed, providing a major artery to the Financial District. The Stonestown Shopping Center, in the western portion of the city, opened in 1953. (Though successful, this early mall did not kill downtown business as was the case in so many other American cities.) In 1958, San Francisco business and political leaders successfully lobbied Horace Stoneham, the owner of the New York Giants, to move his baseball team to the West Coast.

But the entity that got its start in the fifties and has had perhaps the greatest impact on the region is the Bay Area Rapid Transit (BART). As the area's population ballooned in the aftermath of World War II, the necessity of regional transportation became apparent, and in 1957 a five-county transit district was set up (unfortunately, San Mateo and Marin counties didn't join). Construction began during the 1960s, and in mid-1972, the first phase of BART began to operate. Today, rail lines

Art Deco architecture mixed with that of ancient cultures at the Golden Gate International Exposition of 1939–40. The main concourse featured the 400-foot Tower of the Sun.

The Great Bridges

The decade of depression became the time when San Francisco's skyline was dramatically changed by the construction of two great bridges.

In the years before the bridges were built, an efficient system of ferryboats conveyed San Franciscans and visitors to and from the city to various points in Marin, Alameda and Contra Costa counties. As the automobile became a popular conveyance in the aftermath of World War I, the ferries adapted to carrying them, as well as their drivers.

But as the use of the automobile expanded, there was increasing pressure to build bridges to connect San Francisco with the areas to the north and to the east. The 1920s saw propaganda and planning for these proposed bridges.

The second of the bridges to begin construction — but the first to be completed — was the San Francisco–Oakland Bay Bridge. Construction began on this bridge, which would connect San Francisco with the East Bay, in May 1933. It was completed and opened to traffic on Nov. 12, 1936. It is 8.6 miles long and constructed in two sections, which are connected mid-bay by a tunnel that passes through Yerba Buena Island. The western half of the bridge passes in a series of arches from San Francisco to Yerba Buena Island. The eastern half is a cantilever-type bridge extending to Oakland in Alameda County.

The tunnel bored through Yerba Buena Island was the largest that had ever been constructed. It was 76 feet high and 58 feet wide. The bridge and its approaches cost $77 million; and from the day the bridge opened to traffic, revenue from the tolls made it a financially successful operation. For a time, per-car tolls were reduced from 65 cents to 50 cents and then to 25 cents. The bonds that had been sold to finance the construction of the bridge were paid off earlier than expected. Today, the eastern span of the bridge is about to undergo massive rebuilding to make the structure more seismically sound.

ABOVE: The towers of the Golden Gate Bridge rise nearly 750 feet, with 4,200 feet between them.

BELOW: The Golden Gate Bridge takes shape: While the inlet is spanned, the roadway has yet to be built. Engineers faced difficult engineering problems during the six years it took to build the bridge.

The second bridge to be completed — the Golden Gate Bridge — has become a veritable icon of San Francisco, truly a symphony in steel. It was one of the beneficent fates that decreed such a magnificent structure to span that exquisite entrance to San Francisco Bay, the Golden Gate.

Although there was little need for a bridge to connect San Francisco with Marin County (and the other counties to the north), for there was very little population in those counties, the idea for the

TOP: The San Francisco–Oakland Bay Bridge, completed in November 1936, was the first to connect the city to its eastern or northern neighbors. It cost $77 million to build.

BOTTOM: Opening day on the Golden Gate Bridge brought out thousands, including these celebrants, who are dwarfed by one of the massive towers.

bridge had been seized upon by engineer Joseph B. Strauss, who became the impresario for organizing support for such a bridge.

Strauss encountered stiff opposition, but he persisted, incessantly promoting the project, and galvanized sufficient support so that in early 1929 the state Legislature created a Golden Gate Bridge and Highway District, and in November 1930, the voters of the six counties comprising the district voted $3.5 million in bonds to construct the bridge.

The building of the Golden Gate Bridge is a story of constant problems. Even after all opposition had been overcome and construction begun in 1931, there continued to be political wrangling and the problem of conflicting personalities among those responsible for building the bridge. In addition, there were formidable engineering problems that needed to be solved: the stiff winds, the swift currents, the depth of the water.

Slowly and persistently, the problems were solved; and, despite such accidents as a ship ramming a fender that was being used for the pouring of concrete for one of the towers and a safety net breaking and 10 men falling to their deaths, six years after construction had begun, the Golden Gate Bridge was opened to traffic on May 25, 1937.

Although Joseph Strauss had been almost exclusively praised for the building of the structure, the Golden Gate Bridge would not have become the exquisite icon it is were it not for the substantial contributions of Charles Alton Ellis, the design engineer, who was responsible for solving many of the technical problems associated with the construction, and also was primarily responsible for the bridge's design, and of Irving Morrow, who was responsible for the lighting, architectural details and color.

The Matson Navigation Lines began freight and passenger service between San Francisco and Hawaii in the late 1800s. This luxurious ship, the Lurline, *the most famous of its fleet, made the crossing until 1963, when the company sold it.*

OPPOSITE: A crab stand on Fisherman's Wharf in the late 1940s. Tourists (and some locals) still buy fresh crab along the wharf or get a walking crab cocktail.

(SAN FRANCISCO HISTORY CENTER,
SAN FRANCISCO PUBLIC LIBRARY)

The Lurline is Hawaii

SAN FRANCISCO HISTORY, CENTER SAN FRANCISCO PUBLIC LIBRARY

Always well-connected, columnist Herb Caen covered his beloved Baghdad-by-the-Bay *for nearly 60 years in the San Francisco* Chronicle *and, for a time, in the rival* Examiner.

SAN FRANCISCO HISTORY CENTER,
SAN FRANCISCO PUBLIC LIBRARY

extend into Contra Costa and Alameda counties, and an addition to the San Francisco Airport is under construction.

Another post-war development was federal legislation in 1945 that provided money to cities that wanted to replace their substandard housing. Thus dawned the age of redevelopment in San Francisco.

With federal funds, San Francisco tackled the Western Addition. From Geary Street to Grove, west of Van Ness Avenue, blocks of wooden Victorian houses and stores were bulldozed and replaced by banal concrete multi-unit buildings. If only the old buildings had been left alone they might have been rehabilitated by private interests, fostering a neighborhood revival of a different sort. For about the same time as most of the Western Addition was being torn down, gentrification was becoming the new buzzword. People began buying up old Victorians and returning them to their 19th century glory.

Redevelopment wasn't confined to the Western Addition. The city's produce district, adjacent to the Financial District, gave way to the Alcoa Building and the Golden Gateway.

Another redevelopment area became one of the most controversial in the city's history: Yerba Buena Center. The idea was to demolish the existing structures in a blighted swath south of Market Street. The plan called for the jumble of small brick buildings that had served as residential hotels, small businesses, bars and grocery stores to be replaced by a complex of housing, cultural institutions, gardens and public buildings. Advocates for the area's residents, who were mostly poor and elderly, fought the project for many years. Finally, in 1994, a scaled-down project was completed, and Yerba Buena Gardens began a renaissance of building that is today transforming South of Market into the city's new center of culture and business.

Beatniks in North Beach

One area of the city that wasn't slated for redevelopment but nonetheless saw a great deal of change in the 1950s was North Beach. As many of the old-time residents of the traditionally Italian neighborhood moved to other parts of the city or out to the suburbs, young writers and artists were drawn to the area by its low rents and distinctly European flavor. Coffee houses abounded, where one could read one's poetry or show one's paintings, and small shops bucked the trend toward large supermarkets and department stores.

By the mid-'50s, North Beach had drawn a cadre of artists and writers. Among them were Jack Kerouac, Kenneth Patchen, Michael McClure and Allen Ginsberg. City Lights Bookshop became the center of beatnik culture. Founded in 1953 by Peter Marten and poet Lawrence Ferlinghetti, it was a place where people met, left each other messages, played chess and browsed the books on the shelves. City Lights also published a magazine and books, including Ginsberg's *Howl*, possibly the greatest poem to come out of San Francisco's beatnik era.

San Francisco's beatnik era didn't last long. As tourists invaded the neighborhood, many of the artists fled, and by the late 1950s, conformity returned — but not for long.

City Lights Bookshop owner Lawrence Ferlinghetti was prosecuted for selling Allen Ginsberg's Howl, *deemed obscene by local authorities.*

Trivia

Herb Caen gave the world the term beatnik — a combination of the jazz/drug scene ergot beat and the last syllable of Sputnik, the first Soviet space vehicle — to describe the artists and writers who populated North Beach in the mid-1950s.

SAN FRANCISCO HISTORY CENTER, SAN FRANCISCO PUBLIC LIBRARY

Trivia

The oldest Chinese bank in the country, the Bank of Canton, opened in San Francisco in 1937.

Enrico Banducci was a fixture in North Beach. He was the force behind the Purple Onion and the hungry i, where such acts as Phyllis Diller and the Kingston Trio appeared, as well as the eponymous Enrico's, a sidewalk café on Broadway.

For two months in 1945, San Francisco hosted delegates from 50 counties as they worked out the details for the founding of the United Nations. The signing of the organization's charter, shown here, took place on June 26.

SAN FRANCISCO HISTORY CENTER, SAN FRANCISCO PUBLIC LIBRARY

A sign of the times: As the city's population expanded westward, business kept up. Stonestown, anchored by the Emporium (or the Big E, as it was sometimes called), was completed in 1953. Another postwar development, Parkmerced Apartment Towers, can be seen in the background.

A Riot in the City

A prelude of the decade to come sounded its note when a subcommittee of the House Un-American Activities Committee held a hearing at City Hall in 1960. A demonstration against the hearing ended in a near riot; fire hoses were used to subdue the protesters, and many were arrested.

Around the same time other, peaceful, demonstrations began to take place: against minority hiring practices at the Sheraton-Palace Hotel and at auto dealerships on Van Ness Avenue, where the pickets were crew-cut young men dressed in slacks or khakis, and young women in Brooks Brothers shirts, madras skirts and penny loafers.

The appearance and demeanor of those picketing would undergo radical alteration during the next few years, but these demonstrations were harbingers of vast changes to come.

SAN FRANCISCO HISTORY CENTER, SAN FRANCISCO PUBLIC LIBRARY

1916–1960

Trivia

More than 5,000 gallons of international orange paint are applied to the Golden Gate Bridge each year to protect it from sun, wind and salt water.

For more than 50 years, Playland at the Beach (below) beckoned San Franciscans with its carnival-like attractions such as the Big Dipper roller coaster. Laughing Sal (left) greeted visitors to Playland's Fun House.

SAN FRANCISCO HISTORY CENTER, SAN FRANCISCO PUBLIC LIBRARY

CHAPTER 6

Transformation
1960–1989

Transformation

The next three decades marked a period of change for San Francisco unlike any other in its history except, perhaps, for the period immediately following the gold strike in 1848. Small manufacturers left the city, seeking cheaper facilities elsewhere. Redevelopment continued to make its mark: Downtown underwent what critics called "Manhattanization," as its new buildings reached higher into the sky. The residential areas of the city were transformed, too, as ethnic migration patterns changed. Always an important presence in San Francisco, the Asian population grew into one of the largest minorities in the city. Hispanics, largely from Central America, populated the Mission district, once mostly Irish. Neighborhoods began to develop character along non-ethnic lines as well: Gays and lesbians began to form a community in the Castro area. And the city's establishment — its Anglo-Saxon corporate leaders, old German-Jewish families and Italian and Irish powerbrokers — saw its power diminish.

San Francisco was rocked by the student unrest that characterized the 1960s in the United States. As students protested against the war in Vietnam and racial injustice at home, they questioned virtually every value of the mainstream society and culture. Even after the demonstrations ended in the 1970s, their effects were still felt far and wide.

Freeway Battles

As San Francisco's suburbs grew, people became increasingly reliant on the automobile. This was a national trend and one that was widely supported as a symbol of the country's affluence. With cars, though, came traffic and the need to find an efficient way to keep it moving.

In San Francisco, the Bayshore Freeway was built from Army to Bryant/Seventh streets in 1953, nearly linking it with the San Francisco–Oakland Bay Bridge, which would be accomplished later. By 1958, the Embarcadero Freeway was about to begin construction, and the Central Freeway was completed in 1959.

The state's highway construction projects were applauded by the city's pro-growth forces: many politicians, downtown interests and, usually, the labor unions. But others began to question the wisdom of destroying homes and businesses and dividing neighborhoods to erect freeways. Grass-roots neighborhood groups began to protest the freeway program. They found a strong ally in Supervisor William Blake, and in 1959, the board voted to cancel seven of the 10 planned freeway routes through the city.

The California Department of Highways was not about to give way so easily. During the next several years, it continued to put forth plans for more freeways in the city, plans San Franciscans would continue to protest.

The biggest revolt began in 1962. The Board of Supervisors had lost four anti-freeway members during the previous two elections, and now the state's highway bureau-

PREVIOUS SPREAD: After the Embarcadero Freeway, under construction here, cut the northern waterfront off from the rest of the city, residents began to balk at the idea of more mammoth concrete roadways. Anti-freeway fervor gained support until the Board of Supervisors finally rejected the last of the roadway proposals in the mid-'60s.

(STATE OF CALIFORNIA DIVISION OF PUBLIC WORKS)

MORTON BEEBE, SF/CORBIS

The Jefferson Airplane (pictured here before Grace Slick joined the band) was but one group that pioneered the San Francisco sound of the 1960s.

Trivia

Tower Records, opened by Russ Solomon in 1968, was one of the first stores in the country devoted exclusively to records. Later on came the Wherehouse and, of course, Virgin Megastore.

cracy, backed by the city's pro-growth element, proposed the Panhandle Freeway. The plan called for an extension of the Central Freeway up the Oak/Fell corridor, taking 60 percent of the panhandle for the roadway and tunneling under the north edge of Golden Gate Park before turning onto Park Presidio Boulevard toward the Golden Gate Bridge.

The proposal was a divisive element in San Francisco for two and a half years. In May 1964, anti-freeway forces brought together thousands of San Franciscans in Golden Gate Park to rally against the project. Then, on Oct. 13, in a dramatic six-to-five vote, the Panhandle Freeway was defeated.

That didn't end freeway planning, though. Local, state and federal politicians joined forces to keep open the option for two more highways in the city. City and state planners recommended that both freeways be built; the freeway opponents kept up their political pressure. Finally, on March 21, 1966, the San Francisco Board of Supervisors voted down the freeway proposals once and for all.

Hippies in the Haight

Like many areas of San Francisco after World War II, the Haight-Ashbury had been undergoing a transformation. Long-time residents of the working-class neighborhood were moving out, leaving behind an area on the brink of decay. By the mid-'60s, young people — college students, dropouts, runaways — drawn by cheap rents and easy access to Muni, the city's public transportation service, were drawn to the neighborhood.

They listened to the British rock 'n' roll sound then popular among the young, and dressed in a fashion considered bizarre by many: Victorian and Edwardian outfits, jeans and T-shirts, long dresses (often without underclothing), long hair. As time went on, drugs — especially marijuana and LSD — became ubiquitous, and the invention of the contraceptive pill ushered in the sexual revolution.

Around this time, the San Francisco sound began to develop. Such groups as the Jefferson Airplane and the Charlatans appeared, nurtured by a promotional enterprise known as the Family Dog. The Family Dog brought these bands together in large rented halls — at first, the Longshoreman's Hall and later, the Avalon Ballroom — where hundreds could dance to the music. A new form of entertainment, the dance-concert, was born.

The success of the Family Dog dances prompted the manager of the San Francisco Mime Troupe, a local theater group that presented social satire for free in the parks, to use the same format for a fund-raising event. That manager was Bill Graham, who would go on to become the quintessential rock 'n' roll promoter. His dances at the Fillmore Auditorium — promoted through psychedelic posters and featuring light shows — turned the venue into one of the best-known symbols of the era.

In the Haight-Ashbury, new businesses popped up to serve the youth who descended on the area: Psychedelic shops, crafts stores, exotic food shops, vintage clothing shops and record stores lined Haight Street. The drug culture took hold, as well; marijuana dealing soon became the commercial base of the neighborhood. And new music groups continued to form: Quicksilver Messenger Service, Big Brother and the Holding Company, the Grateful Dead (who had been known successfully as Mother McCree's Uptown Jug Stompers, the Energy Crew and the Warlocks).

The Haight became a destination on the tourist circuit as out-of-towners, as well as locals, came to see the hippies who stood on the street chanting, "Peace" and "Love," while handing out flowers to passersby. By 1967, the Grayline Bus Co. had added a special route to its line called the "Hippie Hop Tour."

Nearby Golden Gate Park was also a gathering place for the so-called flower children. One area of the park, known informally as Hippie Hill, was a favorite place to congregate for music and drugs. And on Jan. 14, 1967, the Polo Field was the chosen spot for a Gathering of the Tribes, or the first Human Be-In.

ROGER RESSMEYER/CORBIS

Bill Graham (left), conversing with the Grateful Dead's Bob Weir, was the master rock 'n' roll impresario. His early concerts at the Fillmore established the auditorium as an icon of the times.

The San Francisco Mime Troupe, founded in 1959, still performs biting social satire in the city's parks.

Jerry Rubin, one of the Be-In organizers, hoped to bring together San Francisco's hippies and Berkeley's radical left to create a community where "new values and new human relations" could thrive. Allen Ginsberg and Gary Snyder chanted Buddhist and Hindu mantras at the event; Timothy Leary spoke; the Quicksilver Messenger Service, Big Brother and the Holding Company, the Grateful Dead, the Jefferson Airplane and several other bands played to the gathered thousands.

The Summer of Love also took place in 1967. Nearly 100,000 people flocked to the Monterey Fairgrounds for the Monterey Pop Festival, where virtually all the hottest US and British rock bands, and blues and folk groups performed. The crowd was expected to turn up in the Haight, and it did.

National media attention drew unhappy teens and young adults from every corner of the country, kids who thought life in the Haight would be problem-free. Unfortunately, they had no money, no jobs, no safety net. They panhandled on the streets. Some sold copies of the *Berkeley Barb* or the *Oracle*. Others dealt drugs.

The Haight soon became a different place, marked by crime, disease and disillusionment. Long gone were the flower children; their message of love and peace had given way to bitterness over the escalating war in Vietnam. The carnival that had been the Haight had shut down by the end of the decade, leaving behind a neighborhood of derelicts and drug addicts.

Getting Around

The seventh-busiest airport in the world, SFO will handle more than 51 million passengers each year by 2006.

Public transit got its start in San Francisco as early as the 1850s, when a privately run line transported passengers in a horse-drawn wagon along wooden tracks that ran from the Mission to Portsmouth Square. In 1912, the city took over, making the Municipal Railway, or Muni, the first publicly owned streetcar system in a major city in the United States. Muni has since grown to some 80 lines, covered by light-rail vehicles (Metro streetcars), electronic trolley buses, diesel buses and cable cars. Muni recently opened its F-line, from Market and Castro streets to Fisherman's Wharf, a route traversed by historic streetcars. The seventh-largest public-transit system in the country in terms of ridership, Muni carries about 220 million riders each year, down from a peak of about 330 million in the 1920s.

In recent years, Muni has been the target of complaints for poor service. In fact, San Franciscans took their gripes to the polls in November 1999, passing Proposition E with more than 60 percent of the vote. Prop E created a new agency to oversee Muni and the Department of Parking and Traffic, with goals of depoliticizing the operation of Muni, guaranteeing a consistent funding stream and improving overall service.

One of Muni's more popular vehicles and an enduring icon of San Francisco, the famed cable car made its debut in 1873, after Andrew Hallidie watched a team of wagon-bearing horses slide down a hill on slippery cobblestones. Applying technology he had used for bringing ore up out of mines, Hallidie designed a car that would be pulled up the hills by an underground wire rope. The initial run of the Clay Street Cable Car Co. took place at 3 am on Aug. 1, down Clay Street from Jones to Taylor. The public soon put aside its mistrust of the new vehicle, and it was a great success, but because of the cost of installing such a line, the mode of transport took a few years to catch on in other parts of the city. By the 1890s, nine cable-car routes transported passengers throughout the city. Many of these lines have been replaced with buses and trolleys, but the three remaining cable-car lines have been designated a National Historic Landmark, and regularly carry both tourists and locals.

Getting into San Francisco from outlying areas is as important to the vitality of the city as getting around inside. After World War II, when more people took to their cars and settled in the suburbs, it became apparent that the bridges and byways connecting Bay Area cities and towns were not enough to handle the onslaught of people

BART was the first computerized and fully automated rapid transit system built in this country.

who needed to make their way to San Francisco each day. The idea of linking the East Bay with San Francisco via an underwater tube and electric trains came up as early as 1947, when it was suggested by an Army-Navy review board. After much study, the state Legislature created the Bay Area Rapid Transit (BART) District in 1957, including representatives from Alameda, Contra Costa, Marin, San Francisco and San Mateo counties. San Mateo eventually dropped out, citing adequate commuter service provided by Southern Pacific (now run by CalTrain). Marin also withdrew.

The remaining three counties went on to build a system that runs five lines along 95 miles of track, including the 3.6-mile transbay tube, which is buried as deep as 135 feet in some places. Today, BART carries 280,000 riders on an average weekday.

In the meantime, the Golden Gate Bridge District developed a bus-transit plan. Golden Gate Transit carries 32,245 people across the bay from Marin and Sonoma counties. Some commuters prefer water transportation, boarding ferries that are also operated by the bridge district in Larkspur or Sausalito.

While travelers in the 1850s arrived by ship and later by railroad, today's passengers come in by airplane. San Francisco Airport is the seventh-busiest airport in the world and is undergoing a $2.4 billion expansion to accommodate the 51 million passengers it expects to pass through by 2006.

Renaissance on the waterfront: A mix of cars and light rail shares the Embarcadero with cyclists, skaters and strollers.

The Haight-Ashbury drew young people from all over the country during the 1960s. An anything-goes attitude prevailed.

BETTMANN/CORBIS

From Peace and Love to Riots and Invasions

The optimism that characterized the Haight-Ashbury during the mid-'60s evaporated as political dissatisfaction swept the nation. Although San Francisco didn't suffered from urban riots to the same extent as such cities as Detroit, Chicago and Los Angeles, 1968 and early 1969 saw riots at one of its universities that almost destroyed that institution.

San Francisco State University had a history of liberal and progressive sentiment. As its student leaders became more radical through the '60s, the state's political leaders were becoming increasingly conservative. A conflict was inevitable.

A student strike was called to begin on Nov. 6, 1968. The leaders' goals were to abolish the Reserve Officers' Training Corps and to ban recruiters from such companies as Dow Chemical from the campus. A relatively quiet few days ensued (during which some students seized classrooms where classes were still being taught), but a week into the strike, a squad of San Francisco police in complete riot gear marched onto the campus, causing rampant disorder.

In the midst of this campus chaos, the university president resigned; his place was taken by a linguistics professor named S.I. Hayakawa, who later became a US senator.

Despite his lack of administrative experience, Hayakawa immediately set about restoring order, closing the campus early for the Thanksgiving holiday. When the school reopened on Dec. 2, student protest erupted into a full-scale riot. Police, including some on horseback, backed up by helicopters, battled the rioters. Soon faculty members were supporting the students, and Hayakawa once again closed the campus. The strike continued after the holiday recess, but by March 21, 1969, a compromise settlement was hammered out.

Dissatisfaction was by no means confined to college campuses, a fact demonstrated by a group of 90 Native Americans who "invaded" Alcatraz on Nov. 20, 1969. The abandoned federal penitentiary was watched over by a lone caretaker, no match for the Native Americans who occupied the island, claiming their ancestors had occupied it for thousands of years.

The invasion of Alcatraz was led by Richard Oakes, a 27-year-old Mohawk who was a Native American Studies student at San Francisco State; its purpose was both to call attention to the wrongs done to Native Americans and to extract substantial funds for a Native American university.

Federal requests to leave the island were refused, and the US government took no further action until June 1971, when, after numerous factional disputes on the island and a fire that destroyed several buildings, federal marshals peacefully removed the remaining Native Americans and once again took possession of Alcatraz.

Double Tragedies

San Francisco's tribulations in the 1960s carried over into the 1970s. The nation was torn and divided; a deep malaise had descended, brought on by the Vietnam War, the oil embargo, the Iran hostage situation, a weak economy and abiding political divisiveness.

The tempestuous times would result in two tragedies in the late 1970s that would focus the country's — and the world's — attention on San Francisco.

The first of these events centered on a minister named Rev. Jim Jones, who had come to San Francisco and built a rather large following, especially among the city's poor, many of them African-American. The community was called the People's Temple.

S.I. Hayakawa, the take-charge president of San Francisco State University, surveyed damage to a campus office during the student strike.

BETTMANN/CORBIS

The Sporting Life

It made sense that the promoters of the X Games, a showcase of extreme sports, chose San Francisco as their venue for 1999 and 2000. San Franciscans, after all, are accustomed to thrill-a-minute sports.

The city is home to two professional teams that know how to deliver on that score. Ever since 1946, when Tony Morabito founded the first Major League professional football franchise on the West Coast, the 49ers have kept fans on the edge of their seats. In its second season, in fact, the team finished only a half-game out of first place. Some of the finest players have worn the red and gold during the years, including Y.A. Tittle, John Brodie and Joe Montana.

It was with Montana at quarterback and Bill Walsh in command that the Niners won their first Super Bowl, in 1981. The team made the playoffs every year between 1982 and 1991. In 1988, with chants of "Three-peat!" from the stands, the 49ers beat the Cincinnati Bengals in Super Bowl 23's final 34 seconds to win the world championship for a third time. In 1994, with Steve Young calling the signals and George Siefert coaching, the team broke the National Football League record, becoming the first team to win five Super Bowl titles.

Baseball has an even longer tradition in San Francisco than football. From 1903 through 1957, the San Francisco Seals entertained the city's sports fans, winning 11 Pacific Coast League pennants. Charles Graham, who owned the team from 1918 until 1946, gave a start to a skinny 17-year-old who, after three seasons, ending in 1935 with a batting average of .398, went on to the New York Yankees. That legendary player was Joe DiMaggio, whose brothers, Vince and Dom, also played for the Seals.

One of the reasons the Seals were so successful was Lefty O'Doul, one of the greatest hitters in baseball history. Originally a pitcher with the team, he also played for the New York Giants. O'Doul was the only Major League player ever to hit more than 30 runs and strike out fewer than 20 times in one season. He returned to the Seals as a manager, occasionally appearing as a pinch hitter.

When the New York Giants came west in 1958, the Seals moved to Phoenix and became a Giants farm team. The first Major League Baseball game in San Francisco was held at the old Seals Stadium, when the Giants beat the recently transplanted Los Angeles Dodgers 8–0. The Giants–Dodgers rivalry was born when both teams were in New York, and it continues today.

One player who came west with the Giants was the legendary Willie Mays, who went on to become the third-greatest home-run hitter, behind Hank Aaron and Babe Ruth. Joined by the big bats of Willie McCovey and Orlando Cepeda, and pitchers Juan Marichal and Gaylord Perry, Mays and the team went on to thrill fans in the 1960s. In 1962, in a move that has become symbolic of the Giants–Dodgers rivalry, San Francisco came from behind in the standings to tie Los Angeles on the final day of the regular season. After splitting the first two playoff games and going into the ninth inning of game three down 4–2, the Giants came up with four runs, winning the game and the pennant.

The Giants continued to draw the fans to cold and windy Candlestick Park. Between 1986 and 1989, the team posted winning seasons, taking the National League Western Division in 1987 and the National League pennant in 1989. In what was known as the Bay Bridge World Series, the Giants faced the Oakland A's. Down two games, the Giants were preparing to take the field at Candlestick for the third game, when at 5:04 pm on Oct. 17, the ground began to shake. The Loma Prieta Earthquake had hit. When play resumed 10 days later, the A's swept the series. Ten years later, the Giants left Candlestick (now 3Com) Park to the 49ers and, on April 11, 2000, started batting balls into the bay at their new home in China Basin: Pacific Bell Park.

Basketball has also touched San Francisco, which played host to the Warriors for nearly a decade. The Warriors' history predates the NBA, covers both coasts and features a range of players that includes the league's first superstar (Joe Fulks), the only player to score 100 points in a game (Wilt Chamberlain), one of the best free-throw shooters (Rick Barry) and the first standout from the former Soviet Union (Sarunas Marciulionis). The team began in Philadelphia in 1946, moved to San Francisco in 1962 and changed its name to Golden State after relocating to Oakland in 1971.

It's not just team sports that define San Francisco athletics. The century-old tennis complex in Golden Gate Park gained prominence in the early part of the 1900s when "Little" Bill Johnston and serve-and-volley pioneer Maurice McLoughlin headed east to grab four national titles between them. In fact, Johnston beat McLoughlin to take the 1915 crown in an

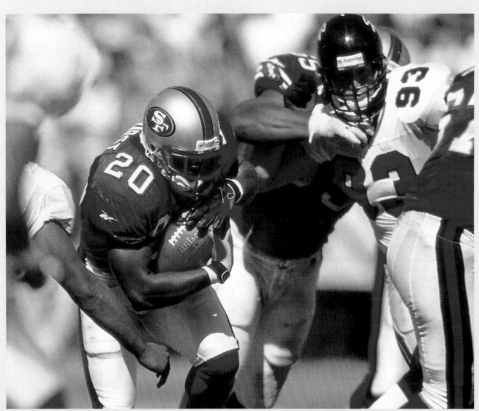

COURTESY OF SAN FRANCISCO 49ERS/TRACY FRANKEL

The San Francisco 49ers was the first professional sports franchise on the West Coast. In 1994, the team made history by winning its fifth Super Bowl championship.

all–Golden Gate Park final. Two legends of women's tennis, Alice Marble and Margaret Osborne duPont, later mastered the game on the same courts. Probably the best of many mid–20th century stars to emerge from the park was Wimbledon and US Open finalist Tom Brown, who also has won more Bay Area net events than anyone else in history.

The city's mild climate has helped to develop great golfers who have played on the city's lush golf courses. The San Francisco city championship once bragged it was the world's largest single golf tournament, with 2,500–3,000 participants on three municipal courses. The Northern California Golf Association, established in 1902, now has more members than any other district association in the United States. The Olympic Club has hosted four US Open championships, starting in 1955; and the Presidio Club celebrated its 100th birthday in 1998. Noted golfers who were born or whose talents advanced here include George Archer, Tony Lema, Lawson Little, Johnny Miller, Bob Rosburg, Ken Venturi, Harvie Ward, Tom Watson and, of course, Tiger Woods.

San Franciscans don't just sit on the sidelines or in the stands. With softball leagues and tennis matches in the parks and ice skating at Yerba Buena Center, there is a wide array of choices. San Francisco is blessed with physical beauty and ample open space, including Golden Gate Park and the Golden Gate National Recreation Area for hiking and cycling. The bay draws kayakers and yachting enthusiasts, from Saturday sailors to America's Cup contenders. And parasailers take to the bluffs above the Great Highway, a jump-off point for soaring above the beach and the Pacific beyond. Now if that isn't extreme…

Special thanks to Lou Spadia, president of the Bay Area Sports Hall of Fame and former president of the San Francisco 49ers.

When it opens in April 2000, the new 42,000-seat Pacific Bell Park will be home to the Giants.

Home to working oil tankers, cargo ships, ferryboats and tugs, San Francisco Bay is also a playground. Sports-minded locals fish, swim, parasail, kayak and, of course, set sail.

FROM THE GOLD RUSH TO CYBERSPACE

Jones was able to galvanize his followers into a powerful political group, which probably contributed to the election of George Moscone as mayor of San Francisco. Many politicians praised Jones' work with the poor, and Moscone appointed him president of the city's Housing Authority.

But it wasn't long before rumors began to circulate of nefarious happenings at the People's Temple. Some were calling the well-respected Jim Jones a demonic cult leader. Two investigative reporters began to research the People's Temple, but their critical story was refused by the *San Francisco Chronicle*. Instead, it was published by a magazine called *New West*.

Fearful of exposure, Jones moved most of the People's Temple adherents and himself to a compound in the jungles of Guyana, in South America. But the publication of the *New West* story fueled the investigations into Jones and his People's Temple. Leo Ryan, a congressmember from San Mateo County, responded to complaints from individuals that their friends and relatives were being kept in the Guyana compound against their will.

In Nov. 1978, Congressmember Ryan flew to Guyana to look into the accusations. When he prepared to leave there with a handful of defectors from the compound, he and four members of his group were ambushed and killed on the airstrip.

Shortly after the story was relayed around the world, even more grisly news followed: After Ryan had left the People's Temple compound, Jones and his followers — nearly 1,000 men, women and children — had committed mass suicide by drinking cyanide-laced punch. There were reports that some bodies had been shot, prompting speculation that at least some of the suicides were forced.

While San Franciscans were still reeling from this news, more tragedy was in store. On Nov. 27, Dan White, a recently resigned member of the Board of Supervisors, entered City Hall through an open basement window and shot and killed San Francisco Mayor George Moscone and Supervisor Harvey Milk.

Native Americans held a demonstration on Alcatraz in 1964, a precursor to the Richard Oakes–led invasion, the aim of which was to repossess the island, as well as to secure funds for a Native American university.

Trivia

Alcatraz was closed as a federal penitentiary in 1962 after serving for nearly 30 years. Before it was home to such famous convicts as Al Capone, the Rock had been used by the military since 1853.

BETTMANN/CORBIS

SAN FRANCISCO HISTORY CENTER, SAN FRANCISCO PUBLIC LIBRARY

1960–1989

Trivia

Tony Bennett first performed "I Left My Heart in San Francisco" at the Fairmont Hotel's Venetian Room in 1962.

Supervisor Harvey Milk was one of the first elected gay officials in the country. When he and Mayor George Moscone were assassinated at City Hall, the city plunged into its darkest days.

OVERLEAF: Begun in San Francisco in 1987 to honor individuals who have died of the disease, the AIDS Memorial Quilt now contains more than 43,000 panels and has been displayed around the world. This was one of its first showings, at City Hall.

(COURTESY OF GERT McMULLIN)

BELOW: The Reverend Cecil Williams, pictured here at a rally in 1978, has long been a fixture among civil-rights activists in San Francisco. Based at Glide Memorial Church, Williams backs causes of the poor and disenfranchised.

White, a former police officer who represented the conservative working-class Visitacion Valley, had been elected to the board during one of the city's reversions to district elections. Milk was the first openly gay official to be elected in San Francisco. They were on opposite sides of the political spectrum in the tense politics of the 1970s.

Shortly before the shooting, White had resigned his seat because of the need for a greater income than his position brought in. He had quickly changed his mind, but Moscone wouldn't re-appoint him. White's revenge for his humiliation was to kill both the mayor and Milk, his former fellow supervisor and political adversary.

The city was shocked when the trial of Dan White for the killings resulted in a verdict of voluntary manslaughter. Following the news, a huge crowd went on a rampage, besieging City Hall, smashing its doors and windows and burning police cars. When Police Chief Charles Gain finally ordered officers to begin to restore order, the maddened police themselves began to rampage among the rioters. By 3 am, San Francisco's streets were empty.

The Jonestown mass suicide, the Dan White killings and the "White Night" riots in the aftermath of his trial, brought San Francisco to a troubling low point.

The president of the Board of Supervisors at the time of George Moscone's death was the twice-unsuccessful candidate for mayor, Dianne Feinstein, who was elected mayor by the board to fulfill the vacancy. She went on to win two subsequent elections (and easily beat a recall attempt), and presided over San Francisco as mayor for nearly a decade.

BOB FARRELL

CHARLIE

STEVE HOLZMAN

JOEY

PAT LESTOCHI

John Walters addio caro

Michael Marshall

WILLIAM ANTON WOODBURN, JR. 12-25-31 3-12-88 WE LOVE YOU 6-18-74

HEAVEN STARRING BABY CLAIRE

BARNABAS WISWELL

AMERICA RESPONDS TO AIDS

CITY

TERRY
COHEN

NEIL PETER
BRENNAN

JOHN
ROMANO

DONALD
J.
TEAHAN

FR

STEVE
MILLER

ALEX

DEDICATED TO
JOHN J. FOX, M.D.
PRACTITIONER AND TEACHER OF
LOVING CARING COMPASSION AND JOY

CARY

CHARLIE

JONATHAN CRAIG HAYWOOD

OCT. 8 & 9 WASHINGTON D.C.

ABOVE: The topping-off ceremony, marking the completion of the steel work at the Wells Fargo building on Montgomery and Sutter streets in 1965 was a cause for celebration. When it was completed, the 43-story building was the tallest west of Dallas.

RIGHT: The Bank of America eclipsed other buildings in the Financial District. Critics of the city's upward growth complained about Manhattanization, eventually leading voters to pass one of the most restrictive growth-control measures in the country.

The middle-of-the-road Feinstein served as balm for troubled San Francisco. She was not as divisive as her predecessor (nor as pugnacious as her successor, Art Agnos). Her predilections were pro-business and pro-growth and, slowly, San Francisco began to recover.

San Francisco's Metamorphosis

The San Francisco of the 1970s and 1980s was a city in flux. Everything, from its physical landscape to its social mores was shifting. The downtown area expanded toward the Embarcadero and south of Market Street, and the skyline changed as smaller buildings erected in the aftermath of the earthquake and fire of 1906 were torn down for high-rises that housed large law firms, investment-banking firms and other businesses attracted by the affluent Bay Area.

Parallel with this explosion of building and business, San Francisco earned the questionable reputation as a center of the sexual revolution, inventing topless dancing, then bottomless dancing and, finally, simulated or real sexual acts on stage. The scene of action was

1960–1989

Broadway, a street once infamous as the Barbary Coast during the Gold Rush days. With a wide array of libido-laden offerings, from the pornographic movies at the Mitchell brothers' O'Farrell Theater to the workshops of the Institute for Human Sexuality, San Francisco appeared to outsiders at least, a highly charged, erotic urban mass.

This period also marked the dawning of the "human potential," or New Age, movement. Werner Erhard's est and its offshoots, the Esalen Institute in Big Sur and countless other body/mind businesses became a minor industry.

As the sexual and New Age movements were achieving international notoriety, the demographics of San Francisco were undergoing a radical transformation. Since World War II, the traditional ethnic groups in San Francisco had been on the move, mostly to the suburbs. North Beach was becoming less and less an Italian enclave. Fewer and fewer Irish lived in the Mission. Gays and Lesbians began to migrate to San Francisco, drawn on the city's reputation for openness and tolerance. The liberalization of federal immigration laws during the 1960s allowed a large number of Asians to immigrate to San Francisco. And a large number of young, single individuals began to call San Francisco home.

As a result, by the 1970s, the tectonic plates of the city's political scene had begun to shift. What had been a relatively conservative city before World War II now increasingly espoused a radical political agenda. Republican voter-registration shriveled. Conservative Democratic voters diminished. In the aftermath of the decade-long mayoralty of Dianne Feinstein, mayors and supervisors were generally ultra-liberal, and city government began rapidly to enact into law this liberal agenda.

SAN FRANCISCO HISTORY CENTER/SAN FRANCISCO PUBLIC LIBRARY

Under Mayor Dianne Feinstein, the city began to heal from fractious politics and the tragedy of the Moscone and Milk assassinations.

Moscone Center, San Francisco's premier convention and exhibition facility, anchors the 87-acre Yerba Buena Center, once the city's skid row and now home to the San Francisco Museum of Modern Art, Yerba Buena Center for the Arts and Sony Metreon, a unique retail-entertainment complex, among other attractions.

OVERLEAF: Pier 39 met with controversy when it was converted to retail use in the late 1970s, but today its mix of restaurants and entertainment is enjoyed by locals, tourists, even sea lions.

(CLIFF CROSS)

SAN FRANCISCO CONVENTION & VISITORS BUREAU

FROM THE GOLD RUSH TO CYBERSPACE

ABOVE: The 1989 Loma Prieta earthquake caused significant damage throughout the city, but none worse than in the Marina, where entire buildings toppled and fires raged.

RIGHT: The Ghirardelli Chocolate Co. moved its manufacturing facility from Jackson Square to this complex of buildings in the late 19th century. When the company was sold and moved again in the 1960s, San Franciscans William Matson Roth and Lurline Roth bought the buildings and converted them to restaurants and shops. Ghirardelli Square remains one of the city's most popular tourist attractions.

1960–1989

GEORGE HALL/CORBIS

The Earth Shakes Again

It was a warm, balmy Tuesday — Oct. 17, 1989. The third game of the first-ever World Series between the San Francisco Giants and the Oakland A's was about to begin in Candlestick Park. Plans to watch the game were soon abandoned when televisions blinked off as the earth rumbled and shook.

The worst earthquake since 1906 hit the San Francisco Bay Area at 5:04 pm, calculated at 7.1 on the Richter scale.

The shocked and confused residents of San Francisco and its environs gathered around battery-powered radios listening to the news. Gradually the story unfurled: significant damage to the area's bridges and highways, and a considerable death-toll from their collapse. In many areas, there was no electricity or telephone service. And in certain areas of San Francisco, there was extensive property damage: both north and south of Market, on the old Yerba Buena Cove, and in the Marina district, on land filled after the Panama Pacific International Exposition of 1915. Fires began in the Marina, and were put out with some difficulty.

San Franciscans, as they had so many times in the past, set aside their differences and rallied to the cause of rescue and recovery. Governmental agencies and private groups galvanized into action. The homeless were sheltered and fed. Utilities were restored. The rubble of destroyed buildings was cleared, and soon new buildings rose on their sites. Within the week, business was being conducted in a normal way. The dead were buried.

San Francisco had survived, though the trauma caused a downturn in the city's fortunes.

The earthquake effectively cut a main artery for Bay Area residents when it caused a section of the Bay Bridge to collapse, killing two people. Commuters resorted to alternate auto routes, BART and ferryboats for the two months it took to repair the bridge.

Trivia

The 1989 Loma Prieta earthquake, at 7.1 on the Richter scale, paled in comparison to the 8.1 quake that rocked the city on April 18, 1906.

CHAPTER 7

San Francisco
at the Dawn of
a new Century
1990–2000

San Francisco at the Dawn of a New Century

The Loma Prieta earthquake of 1989 was a watershed experience for San Francisco. The city mourned its dead, its injured and its dispossessed, and it looked aghast at the destruction the tremor had caused. But the San Francisco spirit, not unlike that which had risen after the earthquake and fire of 1906, was to be its salvation.

The Bay Area's inhabitants faced their deprivations and inconveniences with cheerfulness and a "can-do" attitude. The fractious politics of San Francisco were temporarily suspended. Businesses struggled to bring their operations back to normal.

With a burst of focused energy, both private and governmental groups sought to restore service to San Francisco. The Pacific Gas and Electric Co. strove mightily and heroically — and successfully — to bring gas and electricity to the areas most devastated by the earthquake. The Pacific Coast Stock Exchange traded stocks and options by candlelight. Commuters used ferryboats or drove long distances to get to and from their jobs.

San Francisco's major industry — tourism — was jolted. Tourists canceled their vacation plans to visit San Francisco; conventions canceled their meetings. But quick and decisive action on the part of the city's Convention and Visitors Bureau to reassure travelers successfully reversed the trend.

The earthquake was also the quickening agent for a burst of civic enterprise in San Francisco — what some call San Francisco's renaissance. In 1991, two years after the earthquake, Mayor Art Agnos was defeated by the less confrontational and more centrist Frank Jordan. In an outburst of municipal generosity, voters passed a bond issue for a new main public library. Private donors raised enough funds to construct an award-winning building for the San Francisco Museum of Modern Art and for a proposed new de Young Museum in Golden Gate Park. San Francisco's City Hall, probably the most handsome municipal building in the country, was the beneficiary of hundreds of millions of dollars for seismic retrofitting and burnishing. The earthquake-damaged Embarcadero Freeway was torn down, restoring exquisite vistas of the bay, and the waterfront flanking the Ferry Building was opened up as a promenade.

At the same time, San Francisco was undergoing a shift of a different sort. The early 1990s saw a continued exodus of jobs from the city as large corporate entities merged or moved employees out of town. The Southern Pacific Co., the transportation behemoth, headquartered in San Francisco since the 1870s, merged with its arch rival, the Santa Fe, and its main office moved to Omaha, Neb. Most surprisingly, Bank of America, once the world's largest bank, founded in San Francisco in 1904 as the Bank of Italy by A.P. Giannini, arguably the most creative and innovative banker in history, entered into a merger that moved its headquarters to Charlotte, NC.

These mammoth companies joined the list of large companies that had earlier disappeared from San Francisco's landscape: Ransohoff's, the White House, the City of

PREVIOUS SPREAD: Everybody's favorite city stands majestic under a full moon.

(COURTESY OF MARGE SAMILSON)

GARY STRENG

Paris, Joseph Magnin, MJB Coffee, I. Magnin and Crown-Zellerbach, among many others. And as the century came to an end, a group of small, quintessential San Francisco shops announced their closing: St. Francis Fountain and Candy Store; the Tillman Place Bookshop; Freed, Teller & Freed…and that internationally known spectacle of female impersonators, Finocchio's.

Such corporate departures, especially of very large companies, might have spelled economic disaster for San Francisco, but instead the city has never been more prosperous. It remains a legal and financial center; its tourism makes the hotel, restaurant and retail businesses profitable; and such large employers as the University of California, San Francisco, offer a multiplicity of jobs in health care and biological and life-sciences research.

San Francisco benefits from being the principal city of the San Francisco Bay Area, providing both homes and services to those who work in the businesses of Silicon Valley, the largest wealth-producing area in the world: In 1999 Silicon Valley produced an estimated 64 new millionaires each day.

Further, San Francisco itself has become the principal center of that area of the Technological Revolution in media and telecommunications. Myriad small companies proliferate in the area south of Market Street known as Multimedia Gulch.

This plethora of wealth has brought some problems to San Francisco. The cost for housing — both rental and the purchase of homes — has skyrocketed and, whereas until the last quarter of the 20th century, San Franciscans could rent or own homes no matter how small their incomes may have been, this is no longer true. The rising housing costs have sent those who work in San Francisco farther afield in search of

While the downtown areas of many American cities have lost shoppers to suburban malls, Union Square continues to thrive. Two relative newcomers to the square — Niketown and Levi's — face such longtime tenants as Saks Fifth Avenue, Neiman-Marcus and Macy's.

The annual Bay to Breakers takes place on a Sunday in May. With 75,000 participants — some of them serious runners — the only-in-San Francisco event is billed as the world's largest foot race.

Trivia

More than $2 billion in venture capital went to local start-ups in the second quarter of 1999, almost double the investment for the same period in 1998.

COURTESY OF THE *SAN FRANCISCO EXAMINER*/PETER DASILVA PHOTOGRAPHY

affordable housing, pushing the city's suburbs and creating increasing traffic gridlock on the area's highways and on the city's streets.

One of the results of this prosperity is the possibility that it will increase the chasm between those who are capable of earning the incomes to live comfortably in this area and those who are not, creating an extreme have-and-have-not situation. As the technical, entrepreneurial and educational skills necessary for more-than-subsistence jobs escalate, the problem will become more acute, and San Francisco will need to begin the 21st century with a resolve to overhaul its education system and to seek to offer its young residents opportunities to develop the skills needed for economic sustainability.

The Changing Face of San Francisco

The prosperity of the 1980s and '90s, coupled with cumulative changes in the city's demographics, have altered both the physical landscape and the culture of San Francisco.

The 1960s, '70s and early '80s saw the transformation of the traditional business district of San Francisco. The completion of the Yerba Buena Center sparked a renaissance in the South of Market area: Museums, art galleries, theater and entertainment complexes, hotels, San Francisco's major convention center and numerous residential buildings all rise in what was a badly deteriorated part of the city. The area at the foot of Telegraph Hill, which had consisted largely of warehouses, is now a district of restaurants, small service businesses and condominium complexes, all dominated by the corporate headquarters of Levi Strauss.

And more change is to come. The Mission Bay complex, soon to emerge from decades of planning and controversy, will give life to what had been largely unused land belonging to the Southern Pacific, and a redevelopment project in the former Hunters Point Shipyard will spark renewal in the southeastern portion of the city.

As the cityscape has changed, so has San Francisco's demographics. Today's population hovers somewhere between 750,000 and 800,000. Of this, it is estimated that about one-third is Asian, mostly Chinese, but with a considerable number of Southeast Asians. Aside

This mix of shop signs in the Mission District is evidence of the changing face of San Francisco.

Trivia

San Francisco enjoys five and a half miles of ocean beaches.

Arts & Culture

The countless arts and cultural opportunities in San Francisco reflect the diversity of the city's communities. From murals enlivening the streets of the Mission district, museums centered around Yerba Buena Gardens and children's poetry displayed on street-side kiosks in the Financial District, to the Museum of the City of San Francisco housed at Fisherman's Wharf, the city has become a primary visitor destination for arts and culture in the United States.

From Gold Rush times, San Francisco has had an arts tradition supported by early groups such as the San Francisco Women Artists Collective, an association that has been in existence since 1880 and still operates a gallery in Hayes Valley. In 1894, San Francisco Chronicle publisher MH de Young brought the world's fair to the city and started a permanent museum as a memorial to the exposition. The MH de Young Museum is one of the fine-arts museums operated by the city of San Francisco, as is the Palace of the Legion of Honor, a gift from Alma Spreckels, wife of sugar magnate Adolph B. Spreckels.

For the 1915 Panama-Pacific International Exposition, the Palace of Fine Arts was created to house the works of living artists. Today, the classical building is one of the city's most picturesque spots, as well as home to the Palace Fine Arts Theatre, which hosts events such as the annual Ethnic Dance Festival, and the Exploratorium, a science and arts exploration museum.

The newly renovated War Memorial Opera Center in the Civic Center was built in 1932 and hosts the San Francisco Opera and America's oldest professional ballet company, the San Francisco Ballet. Nearby is Davies Symphony Hall, home of the San Francisco Symphony under the artistic direction of Conductor Michael Tilson Thomas.

Visitors and residents enjoy Broadway shows, improvisational comedy, musical revues and dramatic theater throughout the city. Situated on San Francisco's Union Square is TIX Bay Area, a half-price ticket booth that has day-of tickets to performances at many of the large and smaller houses. Within walking distance are American Conservatory Theater, Cable Car Theatre, Curran Theatre, Mason Street Theater and Theater on the Square.

At the heart of San Francisco's Yerba Buena Gardens, situated south of Market Street near the Financial District, is a bustling

GARY STRENG

San Franciscans raised money through private donations to build the new San Francisco Museum of Modern Art near Yerba Buena Center (above). But not all the paintings are in musuems. Murals, such as this one in the Mission District (bottom left), decorate buildings throughout the city.

center for arts and culture, including the first museum on the West Coast devoted solely to 20th-century art, the San Francisco Museum of Modern Art (SFMOMA). The Jewish Museum and Mexican Museum are two of the many organizations in the process of building their new facilities nearby.

BOB ECKER

From the American Conservatory Theater's offerings at the Geary Theater (top) and the Best of Broadway series to the long-running Beach Blanket Babylon (above) and the offerings of numerous small companies, San Francisco audiences have much to choose from.

Arts organizations of all disciplines and sizes are supported in part by Grants for the Arts, the publicity and advertising portion of the San Francisco Hotel Tax Fund. In 1999, this internationally admired model of municipal funding, established by ordinance more than 38 years ago, granted $10.7 million to the arts. Recipients range from the innovative LINES Contemporary Ballet to the eclectic Cartoon Arts Museum, Hawaiian performers from Na Lei Hulu I Ka Wekiu and the 40-year-old San Francisco Mime Troupe.

Established by city charter in 1932, the San Francisco Arts Commission was established as a city agency that champions the arts. Commissioners are appointed by the mayor and serve four-year terms. The Public Art Division ensures a percentage of new construction is allocated to integrating artworks into the site. Surprises fill downtown parking garages, neighborhood police and fire stations, and bus stops.

The California Palace of the Legion of Honor in Lincoln Park (below) is home to an impressive collection of ancient and European art, as well as traveling exhibitions.

Buddha beckons: Opened in 1894 as part of the Midwinter Fair, the Japanese Tea Garden in Golden Gate Park is still one of the most popular city destinations.

CLIFF CROSS

Trivia

The first out-of-the-park (and into-the-bay) home run hit at Pacific Bell Park was delivered by Barry Bonds on Jan. 21, 2000, during the San Francisco Giants' first batting practice at the new stadium.

from traditional Chinatown, which is inhabited mostly by the elderly and the most recent immigrants, Asians and Asian Americans have expanded into Russian, Nob and Telegraph hills, the Richmond and Sunset districts, the Mission and, more recently, the very southern and the southeastern areas of San Francisco.

The percentage of African-Americans in San Francisco is one of the smallest of any major city in the United States. Only about 10 percent of residents are African-American. One of the reasons for this is that San Francisco was never a major manufacturing center, and traditionally, African-Americans gravitated to factory jobs in their migration from the South. Today, San Francisco's African-American population resides principally in the southeastern portion of the city, in the Western Addition and in the Ingleside District.

The Latino population of San Francisco is 2 to 3 percentage points higher than the African-American population; the city's Latino residents live primarily in the Mission. Unlike Hispanic immigrants to most other major US cities, who hail mostly from Mexico, those in San Francisco are primarily from the countries of Central America.

San Francisco's gays and lesbians are spread throughout the city, but with a heavy concentration in that part of the Inner Mission district known as the Castro.

Because it has had a broadly diverse population since the earliest days of the Gold Rush, San Francisco has escaped the more obvious racial and ethnic tensions that divide many core urban areas. There are tensions, for example, between business and labor and between the ends of the socioeconomic spectrum: those who live marginally or on what are low incomes for San Francisco, opposed to the younger, more affluent individuals moving into working-class or lower-middle-class neighborhoods.

1990–2000

In the booming economic times at the turn of the century, the emphasis is on a San Francisco bustling with prosperity; charged with numerous construction projects, both underway and planned; filled with young men and women delighted with living in the city, buoyant with high-paying jobs, stock options and the expectancy of participating even more in the sparkling economy.

This city on a hill has reinvented itself many times. The Native Americans who populated San Francisco for thousands of years began to change their lives in the latter part of the 18th century with the arrival of Spanish soldiers and missionaries. Spain's rule was replaced by that of Mexico, when the mission and the Presidio were replaced by a trading settlement called Yerba Buena, which, renamed San Francisco in 1847, became an instantaneous metropolis as part of the United States in the aftermath of the Gold Rush.

Destroyed by fire six times between Christmas Eve 1849 and June 1851 — and once again by earthquake and fire in 1906 and 1989 — San Francisco rebuilt each time. And as its demographics constantly shifted, the city accommodated newcomers, not always in exemplary fashion, but in a more harmonious way than any other major US city.

San Francisco will continue to have its problems — whether they be the cost of housing or the effectiveness of municipal transportation — but it is to be hoped that "the city that knows how," as it was dubbed by President William Howard Taft, will respond with the same verve and spirit of innovation that have been hallmark.

Trivia

If a San Franciscan were to eat out every night, it would take 10 years to try each of the city's restaurants.

San Francisco has a history of great hotels, from the St. Francis and the Fairmont to the ultramodern W. But the city also has a number of boutique hotels, such as the Phoenix. The first in a chain of luxury hotels, the Phoenix opened in 1987 and has drawn a Hollywood clientele ever since.

COURTESY OF JOIE DE VIVRE HOSPITALITY

Port of San Francisco

San Francisco Bay is where the economic engines of the greater Bay Area meet the waters of the Pacific. The Port of San Francisco was the *raison d'etre* for San Francisco's rapid growth and economic success.

At one time, San Francisco's port was the third busiest in the United States, but changing modes of transportation and a passing of the port authority from one body to another contributed to a change in usage and prominence.

By 1994, the port had slipped to 26th in the national ranking, and while shipping is again on the upswing, the reasons for the dramatic shifts can be found in the history of port management.

In 1863, the state of California acquired ownership and control of San Francisco's waterfront port as a result of a development scheme put forth by a group of speculators, and for more than a century, the State Board of Harbor Commissioners, exempt from local control, guided the port's operations. Finally, in 1968, the Burton Act transferred ownership and control back to San Francisco. The legislation required that the city assume responsibility for $55 million in general-obligation bonds and agree to invest $100 million (later reduced to $25 million) in harbor improvements.

But the damage had already been done. The state board had been slow to upgrade San Francisco's piers to allow for containerized shipping and other technological changes in the maritime industry. In the meantime, the Port of Oakland had aggressively made the changeover. Oakland also marketed its location and times to continuous rail and truck lines, and took advantage of the rapid increase of Pacific Rim trade. By 1994, Oakland's port ranked fifth in the United States.

The Port of San Francisco's fortunes began to change for the better in the 1990s, when the port authority recognized its decline as a shipping center and adopted a master plan for its 7.5 miles of waterfront. The waterfront plan reserves most port properties for expansion of maritime operations and encourages the creation of new public access, recreation and open space along San Francisco Bay.

Today's port oversees a broad range of commercial, maritime and public activities, and is involved in an incredibly diverse range of businesses: cargo shipping, ship repair, excursion boats, ferry boats, commercial real estate, fishing and fish processing/distribution, tourism, location filming, harbor services and cruise shipping.

Now able to boast of some of the most modern and flexible shipping-terminal facilities on the West Coast, as well as naturally deep water, the port can handle just about any type of cargo, including containers, breakbulk, neo-bulk, automobiles and project cargoes.

Since 1998, the port has doubled its cargo volumes and negotiated contracts with shipping lines that offer services to and from Australia, New Zealand, Asia, South Pacific Islands, Mexico, and South and Central America. Leading import commodities include

Cruise ships put in at San Francisco on their way to Alaska, Mexico and other ports around the world.

Ferries pull in to Pier 1, while cruise ships berth farther north.

coffee, lumber, wine and meat. On the export side, machinery and infrastructure-project cargoes lead the way. The port also houses many of the bay's harbor services, including tugs, pilot boats, barges and a full-service ship-repair facility that can handle the needs of the world's fleet.

In addition, the port's master plan took into account the fact that tourism is San Francisco's No. 1 industry, and many of the city's leading tourist attractions are located at the port, including the Hyde Street Pier, Fisherman's Wharf, Pier 39 and Alcatraz. These attractions draw millions of visitors annually to the port's northern waterfront.

In addition to being a visitor attraction, Fisherman's Wharf is also the center of Northern California's commercial fishing industry. Pier 45 is one of the nation's most modern fish-processing centers. Dungeness crab, Chinook salmon and Pacific herring are some of the leading delicacies landed in San Francisco.

Since it is one of the world's most popular cities, it's not surprising that San Francisco is also a major cruise-ship destination. More than 50 cruise ships call at the port each year, with itineraries including Alaska, Mexico, transcanal and around-the-world cruises. These ship calls and passengers generate an estimated $20 million in economic impact for San Francisco and the Bay Area.

More than one million residents and visitors come to the port each year for special events and concerts. In March 1996, San Francisco voters approved the building of a new baseball park at Pier 46 in China Basin.

The Port of San Francisco has been revitalized in recent years. Today, nearly $1 billion in trade passes through the port.

Afterword

Something new, even by San Francisco standards, hit the streets in late 1999 in the form of Luxor Cab Co.'s purple and yellow Yahoo!-wrapped taxi. The Yahoo! cabs offer San Francisco passengers mobile onboard Web access via wireless laptop computers. The Internet is, indeed, everywhere.

Beginning in the mid-1990s and continuing into the new millenium, San Francisco has once again been transformed, this time by the dot-com entrepreneurs and rapidly expanding technology that propelled the economy into the rarified atmosphere of cyberspace.

A powerful illustration is the changing fate of the venerable Pacific Exchange. Just three years ago, the city's business and political leaders were scrambling to help the exchange find suitable brick-and-mortar space in which to relocate and expand. There were threats and fears the entire operation would pull up roots and move out of the city, taking with it jobs and capital and a certain cachet that enhanced the city's reputation as the financial center of the West.

As this book goes to press, things have changed. The Pacific Stock Exchange, which itself provided the capital that fueled the technology industry, announced it was closing its historic West Coast trading floors — including its 110-year-old operations on Pine Street — and merging with Internet-based electronic marketplace Archipelago. The closure marks the end of an era even as it sets a precedent as the first time a traditional US stock exchange will end the centuries-old practice of completing stock trades face-to-face, auction-style on a trading floor in favor of a fully electronic virtual marketplace. While the news was met with mixed emotions, it certainly signals a change that may have big implications for larger exchanges in New York and internationally.

PHOTO FOR YAHOO! BY COURT MAST

RICHARD LU, MARCH 2000

Powered by technology, e-commerce and the Internet, San Francisco in enjoying unprecedented economic growth. Unemployment is at the lowest ebb ever, and high-paying jobs go begging as the educational system struggles to turn out well-prepared graduates and companies lobby for changes in immigration laws to import more and more tech-trained workers.

The explosive growth in the knowledge-based, global-information economy is changing everything from the city's urban landscape to its demographic mix. The technology business got its foothold in San Francisco in South Park, an old neighborhood of warehouses, small office buildings and old mansions converted to flats and apartments all gathered around a dingy little park that not so long ago was a hang out for the down-and-out. Today, South Park is the city's trendiest address for software developers, e-commerce start-ups, Internet companies and the new breed of publishers that are getting rich off the more traditional paper-and-ink forms of communications. The area bounded by Market Street to the north, the Embarcadero to the east, Townsend Street to the south and Division Street to the west, and including South Park, is known as Multimedia Gulch, the core of San Francisco's 24-hour-a-day, 7-day-a-week economy. The gulch's boundaries have widened to include almost all of SoMa (South of Market), and expanded up the slopes of Potrero Hill, where a spate of Internet music companies have created "Audio Alley," which just may turn San Francisco into the next big music industry mecca.

As the building boom South of Market on once-underutilized industrial land continues, the city's focus is shifting from the traditional northeast quadrant south to new high-rise office complexes, condominiums and apartments. The University of California has broken ground on its Mission Bay campus, the new Pacific Bell Park is a hit with fans and casual visitors alike, and the city's art scene is congregating around Yerba Buena Gardens with its gallery and performance space, the San Francisco Museum of Modern Art, Sony Metreon entertainment-retail complex, theaters and the new Mexican Museum.

Just as the closing of the Pacific Exchange heralds a new day dominated by the dot-com economy and mentality, so does the shift in dining habits of San Franciscans symbolize

This reflection in the glass facade of Sony Metreon's entertainment-retail complex illustrates San Francisco's past in a structure that represents the city's cyber-future.

DANA PAUL, ESPN

More evidence of the growing young influence, the ESPN X Games, held in San Francisco in 1999, attracted a record 268,000 spectators. Shown here are skateboarders Tony Hawk and Andy MacDonald against the backdrop of San Francisco Bay.

changing social mores — driven by high salaries and youth: casually dressed dot-commers in their 20s and early 30s. As reported in the *San Francisco Chronicle* in March 2000: "Prompted by an explosion of Internet riches, these young urban food-lovers are changing every facet of the Bay Area restaurant scene — from the money that backs restaurants to the food that is on the plate.

"Restaurateurs are responding to dot-commers' financial clout and what they want. New restaurants are bigger and louder than ever before. Many feature live entertainment, busy bars and later hours. These restaurants are becoming havens for the young and affluent, promoting a sense of belonging and providing them with a way to escape the pressures of the wired lifestyle."

Won't You be my Neighbor

The booming economy is fueling growth in other sectors that are dependent on affluent demographics. The de Young Museum is planning a new privately funded $135 million facility in Golden Gate Park, the Asian Art Museum has broken ground for its new facility at Civic Center, and filmmaker George Lucas, creator of the *Star Wars* and *Indiana Jones* movies and one of Hollywood's all-time box-office favorites, is developing a $250 million digital movie-making and technology office campus on the grounds of the former Presidio. That Lucas' project was selected over competing projects is another signal of the importance of technology in its many manifestations to San Francisco.

"With its concentration on educational outreach, scientific research and cutting-edge technology, we felt the Lucas plan closely fit goals of the trust," said James Meadows, executive director of the Presidio Trust. Analysts see the move of Lucas to San Francisco as enhancing the city's position as a competitor with Los Angeles to be the West Coast entertainment center.

Lucas is not the only filmmaker to have set his sights on San Francisco. While the city, with its stunning views and cultural amenities, has long been a favorite of filmmakers for on-location shooting, the closing down of three former local military bases — Treasure Island, Alameda Naval Air Station and Mare Island — created opportunities for filmmakers to do everything from pre-planning to post-production work in the Bay Area. Another attraction: stars such as Robin Williams, whom some call "a mini-industry all by himself." Williams and others who live in the area prefer to work close to home, and they are of such significant stature that they can call the shots. The same artists, designers and digital wizards who give life to the Internet are available to create special effects, sound editing and animation for the big screen.

The dot-com mystique is giving lie to the commonly held view that, with the Internet, location becomes irrelevant. Some liken San Francisco, the Bay Area and Silicon Valley to "the water-cooler phenomenon." People in the technology industry like to be close to their peers; proximity allows people to share ideas and keep abreast of the latest innovations, ideas and deals. In fact, some of the nation's biggest and most well-known brick-and-mortar companies are setting up their e-commerce businesses in San Francisco. From Kmart to Macy's, the reason they give is the same: San Francisco has quality workers, proximity to venture capital and a creative atmosphere that breeds innovation and invention.

With the largess of the new economy keeping city coffers flush, San Francisco is seizing the opportunity to reshape its public spaces. The historic Ferry Building is being renovated, and a $46 million transformation of Market Street at the Embarcadero is slated for completion in spring 2000. Municipal railway service has been expanded all along the waterfront, from Fisherman's Wharf on the north to the new Pacific Bell ballpark to the south. The city is renovating Union Square Plaza and transforming the Fillmore into a "Jazz Renaissance District," where the Blue Note Jazz Club will open its first West Coast venue. Also underway is a Gay and Lesbian Community Center on Market Street in a historic, Victorian-era structure.

From Gold Rush to Cyberspace

The new Gold Rush — or Silicon Race — while unprecedented in its magnitude, has distinct similarities to the Gold Rush of the 1850s. In a true "back-to-the-future" scenario, the new economic prosperity is having both positive and potentially harmful effects. Now, as then, new people are surging into the city and earning good wages. As a result, housing is scare and costly. According to the Association of Bay Area Governments, during the next 20 years, San Francisco is expected to add more than 100,000 jobs. That's good for those coming into the job market, but the problem is the city is adding jobs at a ratio of 6.5 to every one unit of housing. As housing becomes more expensive, San Francisco is at risk of losing its wealth of diversity: The population will become more homogeneously affluent, young, single and white. Recent statistics show an increase in the 20–29 age group and a growing proportion of college graduates — up by 23 percent since the 1990 census was taken.

In the 1850s, the bay was crowded with ships; some even abandoned as their crews took off for the gold fields. Today, it's San Francisco's streets that are packed with cars, trucks and Muni buses fighting for space. (So far, the city hasn't had to cope with frustrated drivers abandoning their vehicles in the midst of gridlock!) As big a problem as housing availability and affordability is traffic congestion. San Franciscans, and those who come to the city to work, do business and enjoy its many attractions, find clogged streets, a dearth of parking spaces and a public transit system that, while improving, is still largely unreliable. The regional transportation system is likewise overcrowded with thousands of commuters making their ways each day across packed bridges and freeways and under the bay on BART to their jobs.

In the original Gold Rush days, a willingness to take risks and work hard, matched by a bit of luck, was all that was needed to make a fortune. In the 2000s, access depends on knowledge, skills and training. There is a "digital divide" that separates those who are computer savvy and have regular access to the wired world, and those who do not. While the San Francisco Bay Area far surpasses the rest of the country when it comes to using computers and the Internet — nearly 8 in 10 people use computers regularly and

62 percent have e-mail addresses, compared to only one-third nationwide who have Internet access — the prevalence of Internet use makes the digital divide more acute. With so many people using computers, public services are turning to the Internet, which means people online are getting the full benefit of these services, and the people without computer access are blocked from jobs and the other benefits of a strong economy.

Growing a Strong Economy

What will save San Francisco from the consequences of its own success is its civic-minded, activist population. Many community and business groups are addressing these problems. San Francisco recently re-elected Mayor Willie L. Brown Jr. — the first mayor to be elected to a second term in more than a decade. Brown was able to broaden his appeal beyond his traditional base of registered Democrats and labor, to a new coalition that included downtown businesses, Republicans, and other conservative and middle-of-the-road voters. Brown, a pro-development mayor who has pleased business by holding the line on taxes, is a clear beneficiary of the economic boom that has lowered unemployment and filled city coffers. The coalition that returned him to office should prove helpful as he grapples with traffic, housing and other issues.

On the business front, the San Francisco Chamber of Commerce is providing the leadership to make workforce housing more available and affordable, mitigate traffic woes and attack the issues of better preparing students and others to navigate their way through and into the new digital economy.

The Chamber is a leader in the effort to maintain an economy that addresses the needs of all San Franciscans. Working with city decision-makers, the Chamber is promoting San Francisco's economic vitality and enhancing the livability of our communities. Through initiatives in areas such as workforce housing, congestion and transportation management, and school-to-career education, the Chamber is committed to ensuring that smart and balanced growth continues to elevate our unique quality of life.

With regard to housing, for example, the Chamber has launched a series of housing initiatives to help close the affordability gap and make sure San Francisco continues to support a vibrant middle class. The Chamber is working with city leaders to promote planning changes that protect the character of the city's unique neighborhoods, while allowing for the construction of vitally needed new housing; encouraging the city to streamline the permitting process to reduce the cost and time it takes to develop new housing; and working with finance organizations to deal with the cost of housing through creative financing programs.

The Chamber and a host of other groups representing public-transit riders are also forcing change in the operation of the city's municipal transportation system. The business community's congestion-management agenda also includes fighting for traffic and parking relief, supporting development of a high-speed rail line between San Francisco and Los Angeles, and advocating for an environmentally sound expansion of runways at San Francisco International Airport.

Another change is on the verge of happening as this book goes to press is the changing ownership of San Francisco's two daily newspapers. For the first time in 35 years, San Francisco will have two morning papers fighting it out for the attention of readers and advertisers. The Hearst Corp., publishers for 135 years of the *San Francisco Examiner*, is buying the *San Francisco Chronicle* and, in turn, selling the *Examiner* to Ted Fang, publisher of the thrice-weekly *San Francisco Independent*, a free paper that has an expressed policy of advocacy journalism. The Fang family is, to many in San Francisco, one of the most visible manifestations of Chinese Americans' rise to power in the city. In addition to the *Examiner* and *Independent*, the family owns a chain of eight Peninsula weeklies and the nationally distributed *Asian Week*, and wields considerable clout in San Francisco politics.

Of course, with all the changes and challenges brought on by the technological revolution, the essence of San Francisco — its cultural riches, it physical beauty, its

Mayor Willie Brown, re-elected in 1999, leads San Francisco into the 21st century

RICHARD LU, MARCH 2000

Strollers take in the sites around San Francisco's Museum of Modern Art in SoMa, one of the city's trendiest neighborhoods.

world-class restaurants and venues for recreation and entertainment — remains true. It is a fitting conclusion for this history of a great city, from the Gold Rush to Cyberspace, to end with a passage from a little book published by the San Francisco Chamber of Commerce in 1924:

"Enthroned on hills, San Francisco captivates the stranger who sees it from the bay by the vivacity of its landscape long before revealing any of its intimate lures. Whether you approach in the early morning, when gulls are wheeling above the palette of tones of the bay, or at night, when illuminated ferryboats glide by like the yellow-bannered halls of fable, the buoyancy of San Francisco is manifest.

"It increases as you pass through the Ferry Building, the turnstile behind the Golden Gate... In another moment you are in the surge of Market Street, the long bazaar and highroad of this port of all flags. An invisible presence dances before your footsteps as you sense the animation of the street. It is the spirit of San Francisco, weaving its debonair spell...

"From Richard Henry Dana to Robert Louis Stevenson, from Bret Harte to Henry Mencken, San Francisco has captured the hearts of a train of illustrious admirers. Rudyard Kipling, master of the terse, has tooled a brisk drypoint of the city in a few strokes: 'San Francisco has only one drawback,' he writes, 'tis hard to leave.'" ■

I n purely spatial terms, AMB Property Corporation has been moving steadily down in the world since it opened a small office in 1983 on the 35th floor of Embarcadero Center No. 4. Now occupying the fifth and sixth floors of 505 Montgomery St., AMB will reach sea level in late 2000 when it completes the renovation of Pier 1, just north of the Ferry Building, and moves into its new headquarters.

By every other measure, the company has experienced remarkable success, amassing assets and accolades for its visionary and creative growth strategies. Today, AMB is one of the country's largest industrial real estate investment trusts. It owns a nationwide portfolio of real estate and is one of the Bay Area's largest industrial landlords.

AMB has distinguished itself by maintaining a small corporate team of real estate specialists who focus on strategic decision making, while it outsources day-to-day operations to local property managers and leasing agents.

AMB Property Corporation

Today, AMB is one of the country's largest industrial real estate investment trusts.

It all began when Hamid Moghadam and Doug Abbey partnered 17 years ago to negotiate real estate transactions and investments for San Francisco's largest law firms. The start-up was so successful that Bob Burke, one client's managing director, left his firm to join Moghadam and Abbey, adding the third initial to AMB.

By the end of the 1980s, AMB was managing real estate portfolios for large pension funds, including the City and County of San Francisco Retirement System. In 1997, AMB went public, raising $338 million in what was the Bay Area's largest initial public offering that year.

In 1999, AMB focused its investment strategy "to deliver expedited commerce solutions to companies leading the New Economy," says Moghadam, the chief executive officer. The company committed to sell its $1 billion shopping center portfolio and to redeploy most of the capital into High Throughput Distribution™ properties. These are distribution facilities critical to the supply chain and are located near major

transport corridors, harbors and airports — even on-tarmac at major cargo airports. Currently, AMB leases its High Throughput Distribution™ properties to airlines, air cargo and logistics companies, and major corporations including Dell Computers and Webvan, an Internet grocery retailer.

AMB's strong track record as a developer of distribution properties convinced the Port Authority to select the company to rehabilitate the historic 68-year-old C&H Sugar warehouse at Pier 1. The mission: Transform it into a dramatic open-architecture office building with 30-foot ceilings and uninterrupted views of the city, the Bay Bridge and Treasure Island.

The renovation of Pier 1, the first redevelopment project on the city's waterfront in 30 years, will feature a public promenade around the building and a "history walk" inside. The new headquarters for AMB and the Port of San Francisco will extend 752 feet into the bay — farther over water than any other US office building.

AMB provides other benefits to San Francisco. Company employees make important contributions to cultural and charitable organizations, ranging from the symphony and the opera to the Tenderloin Housing Association. ∎

Academy of Art College

The Academy of Art College "has dispelled the notion of the starving artist. We're not a school that buys into that," says Elisa Stephens, the President of the Academy and the third generation of her family to lead the school. "We believe artists can be productive and make a living at what they love. Thousands of our graduates have proved it."

The Academy was founded in 1929 by Elisa's grandfather, Richard S. Stephens, who was an accomplished painter and a successful commercial artist. He began the Academy of Advertising Art in a single room at 215 Kearney Street, providing professional instruction to 46 would-be art directors. When his son, Richard A. Stephens, took over, he led the first major expansion of his father's dream, building an accredited academic institution and purchasing buildings for the school that provide studio and gallery space for its students, as well as classrooms. Elisa led the Academy into the computer era, foreseeing the important role that artists and designers would play in the technological age.

Today, the Academy of Art College is the largest and fastest-growing private school of art and design in the nation, with more than 6,000 students enrolled. It is one of American's most reputable art colleges, and its programs have won international acclaim. Over the years, the Academy has contributed to a new cultural identity for San Francisco as one of the artistic centers of the would.

The founder's vision has remained at the academy's heart. He was a fine artist who put his skills to commercial use. When the American economy collapsed in 1929, he returned from Paris, where he had been studying painting at the famous Academie Julien, to become a creative director for *Sunset Magazine*. He and his wife, Clara Stephens, opened and operated the Academy while he was at *Sunset Magazine*. Under the leadership of Richard S., the Academy used fine artists to instruct the applied artists in the fundamentals, namely drawing and painting, in an effort to broaden and increase their taste levels. This philosophy reigns today.

To teach them, he hired the best professional artists he could find, many of them personal friends in San Francisco's art community. The founder believed

that, given the opportunity for proper instruction from professionals in the field, artists and designers could learn the skills they needed to become successful professionals themselves. All they had to contribute was hard work and dedication.

But if he created the overall vision, it was his son who provided the executive leadership that built an academic institution. Richard S. was looking to sell the Academy about the time Richard A. was graduating from Stanford University with thoughts about becoming a dentist. Richard A. objected to a potential buyer, whom he believed would not do justice to the school's potential. His father made him an offer: "If you feel that way about it, you run it."

Then 25, Richard A. was ready for the job. He had spent much of his childhood around the Academy, watching his parents teach, and taking some of the Academy's courses. Changing the name to Academy of Art College, he added new department majors: Photography, Interior Design, Magazine Illustration, Filmmaking and Art History. In 1966, the California Department of Education accredited the Academy to offer a bachelor's degree in fine arts. Later, a master's in fine arts degree was approved. Over the years, so many new campus buildings were acquired — all of them around the Financial District and the new art and technology centers south of Market Street — that small vans were purchased to transport students. Enrollment grew to more than 2,000 students.

Richard A. came out of retirement in 1990 to train the third generation to lead the college. An attorney with experience in educational administration, Elisa Stephens took over in 1992, as construction began on the campus' flagship building at 79 New Montgomery

Our ability to marry the traditional with the future is what has made us successful.

Street. A state-of-the-art computer center was in the basement of that building, and the Academy of Art College was among the first to give its students an opportunity to learn how their fine art skills could be applied in the computer environment.

But Stephens saw that the new technology would generate more and more jobs for artists. "I went head-first into computer technology," she says; making rapid advances not just in acquiring new hardware and software, but also in making computers an integral part of the college curriculum. Today, the Computer Arts Department is the largest in the school.

The Academy's eight-story Digital Arts Center at 180 New Montgomery Street, has 700 computer workstations, including 100 Silicon Graphics workstations, 300 Adobe Premier workstations, and 200 auto Cad workstations. A MENSI 3D SOISIC scanner and three Dispos — the latest technology available for digital imaging and output — are also on hand.

Regardless of whether they are seeking computer careers, all students learn how to use the techniques before they leave the Academy. Computer technology

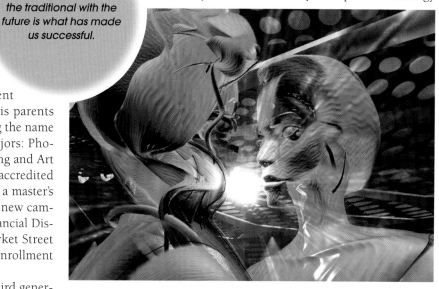

and its applications contribute to all 10 majors now offered: Advertising, Computer Arts, Fashion, Fine Art, Graphic Design, Illustration, Industrial Design Studios, Interior Architecture and Design, Motion Pictures and Video, and Photography.

Other improvements have been made. Predicting an increasing interest in transportation design, Stephens hired Jeff Teague, a former designer at Mitsubishi, Volkswagen and Ford, to set up a program within the industrial design department. International students, an increasing proportion of the student body, are provided with language support.

Though Richard A. or the founder might not recognize the buildings or the work being done in them, he would be right at home with the philosophy, which still insists that all students learn fine arts and the basics of drawing and design. "Our ability to marry the traditional with the future is what has made us successful," Stephens says.

She finds her position at the head of the family business rewarding. "I feel like I'm doing good for students, because I see that education at the Academy changes people's lives." The Academy is justifiably proud of a job-placement record that is as high as 100 percent in some departments and never drops below 80 percent." Teaching students to do what they love for a living. That's what we were all about in 1929, that's what we are about today." ∎

Adolph Gasser Inc.

During World War II, Gasser was the technician on a photographic team that prepared for the bombings at Nagasaki and Hiroshima. When cameras mysteriously refused to work, he advised pilots to turn on the camera heaters well in advance of their use because of the coldness at high altitudes. He developed a camera that could make pictures from radarscopes.

After the war, Gasser opened a store on the 5700 block of Geary Boulevard. As it happened, in the 1950s, Ansel Adams lived just a few blocks away. At the time, he was still earning a living as a commercial photographer while he made the landscape photographs that eventually brought him fame. Gasser did all of Adams' repair and customizing work and, when Adams moved to Carmel, Gasser built the darkroom in his new home. "We got to know each other pretty well," Gasser says with understatement. Adams was the best man at Gasser's wedding.

But Adams wasn't the only professional photographer Adolph helped. Over the years, he became the right hand of local news photographers, developing a range finder that let them "just walk up and snap the picture, and it would come out sharp," he says. "Many of the things we did to make photography easier for professionals later were adopted by camera manufacturers." Nikon asked him to take a look at its first camera, and he made important suggestions to help its marketability in the United States.

A dolph Gasser is a walking museum of photographic history. Founder of the largest, most comprehensive source of photographic equipment in Northern California, he helped develop cameras and their accessories as he worked with professional photographers such as Ansel Adams.

The man who repaired the bellows on early cameras is now chief executive officer of a company that sells, repairs and rents the latest in digital photographic equipment. As he circles the block looking for a parking space near his Geary Boulevard store, he can recall the days when he delivered papers nearby and cars were banned from the streets overnight.

It was 1929 when Gasser graduated from high school and got his first job with a camera-repair shop, building new backs for the European cameras that dominated the market then, so that American-built accessories could be used with them. By 1938, he had developed the reputation — and saved the money — to open his own shop on Post Street, which quickly became the repair mecca for the city's professional photographers.

The man who repaired the bellows on early cameras is now chief executive officer of a company that sells, repairs and rents the latest in digital photographic equipment.

Today, Adolph Gasser Inc. operates two stores. Main store is located at 181 Second St. and satellite store is at 5733 Geary. Though Gasser still reports to work every day, he has turned over company leadership to his son, John.

"I like what I've done in life," the older Gasser says. "I've enjoyed my career, and I've enjoyed my customers — many of them have become personal friends. When they buy from me, I want them to get good value." ∎

Establishing a presence in San Francisco in 1992 was "a great moment" in the development of Alexander Ogilvy Public Relations Worldwide, which was then an Atlanta-based firm specializing in strategic communications for the technology industry.

Back then, "it became apparent to us that to be a player in technology on a national scale, we would need to be in the Bay Area," says General Manager Holland Carney. The agency arrived just as an Internet-driven revolution was brewing in the Bay Area. "Being here in the middle of it has been tremendous for our business," Carney says, "and we feel like we've had a role in making history."

Alexander Ogilvy became a global public-relations presence following an acquisition by Ogilvy Public Relations Worldwide, and now operates in more than 39 markets worldwide. Its Bay Area staff has grown to more than 90 communications professionals, working in San Francisco's Multimedia Gulch and in Menlo Park. Operational headquarters are in Atlanta, and San Francisco serves as a gateway for Alexander Ogilvy to serve technology clients throughout Europe, Asia and other emerging global technology markets.

Alexander Ogilvy
PUBLIC RELATIONS WORLDWIDE

Alexander Ogilvy Public Relations

> The agency's attraction is its extraordinary staff, and the quality of the staff has to do with the city.

Its relationship with Hewlett-Packard was the first important milestone in the agency's history here. Because HP's culture demands personal contact, Alexander Ogilvy knew it needed a Bay Area base to win contracts with the computer giant. Shortly after Carney and the agency's founder, Pam Alexander, arrived, the agency got a last-minute chance to offer a proposal for the launch of HP's Dashboard software. "They awarded us the business on the spot," Carney says, "and that gave us an anchor to build around."

By 1994, Internet-driven businesses became the core of Alexander Ogilvy's work here. Through its work for idealab!, a Los Angeles–based incubator of Internet companies, the agency was chosen for the national and local launch of CitySearch. In short order, eToys, paymybills.com, MindSpring, NextCard, Qwest, Merrill Lynch and Healtheon/WebMD were on Alexander Ogilvy's client list. Today, the agency can't grow fast enough to serve all its would-be clients.

The agency's attraction is its extraordinary staff, and the quality of the staff has to do with the city: "Very smart people come from all over the world to live and work in San Francisco," Carney says. They come to Alexander Ogilvy because "our people have an opportunity to work with — and learn from — the best, smartest, most interesting companies in the industry."

Take one of its newest clients, myCFO.com, a personal financial-services firm targeting technology-made millionaires, founded by Netscape's Jim Clark. "Imagine what it means for a staff person to spend time with Jim Clark," Carney says, "and to be there at the birth of a whole new business concept that's been enabled by the new economy. It's very invigorating."

As Carney sees it, San Francisco and Silicon Valley are at the heart of a new economy that now extends well beyond technology: "Together, they are changing the global economy. The ripples of what happens here are felt everywhere," she says. "Working here really is being part of history." ∎

Asian Week

Florence and John Fang

Florence Fang remembers her days holding up the tail in the dragon her husband John Fang was steering. "John was the head and I was the tail. All I could do was support him and follow along — the tail doesn't know where the head is going. After John died, I was the head and I discovered the burden of the head is very heavy in so many directions. The head has to think about things the tail never imagines."

Florence Fang is the matriarch of the Fang publishing family in San Francisco, whose holdings include the San Francisco Independent Newspaper Group, Asian Week, a Chinese TV Guide and the Grant Printing Co.

In the years since John Ta-Chun Fang died in 1992, Florence Fang has had ample opportunities to feel the burdens of the head as she nurtured the prospering group of innovative publications John had created into what is now considered the paramount Asian-American publishing company in the United States.

The Fang business is a family business. Florence relies on her three sons: James, publisher of The Independent; Ted, publisher of Asian Week and past president of the Bay Area Rapid Transit (BART) board of directors; and Douglas, a computer prodigy who established The Independent's computerized publishing system, which involves the twice-weekly production of numerous editions of eight Independent titles serving San Francisco and peninsula cities.

The Independent is the largest free-distribution newspaper in the United States, delivering more than 379,000 copies twice a week to residences in the city and on the peninsula. The San Francisco Independent's 211,400 twice-weekly home-delivered circulation has established the newspaper as a significant publishing and political presence in San Francisco, rivaling that of the city's two daily newspapers.

John and Florence Fang immigrated to San Francisco from Shanghai in the late 1950s. Their success story is a modern version of the entrepreneurial immigrant spirit that created the fortunes of San Francisco publishing families, the deYoungs, Theriots and Hearsts, among others, in the 19th century. The Fangs' success is representative of San Francisco's new entrepreneurial working class based on achievement, rather than inherited wealth, that has defined and energized the city in the later part of the 20th century.

Florence Fang gives full credit for the family's high rank in publishing to the founder, John Fang. John Fang is an Asian version of Horace Greely; he rose from poverty in China to change the landscape of minority journalism in America. He worked to support himself from adolescence and came to San Francisco in the late 1950s determined to become a publisher after studying journalism at the National Cheng Chi University in Nanking. He continued his studies at UC, Berkeley, and then learned the business from the bottom up, going to Chicago to work in photography, to New York City to work in printing. He returned to San Francisco and launched a series of tourist guides to America's Chinatowns. During this period, Florence, who is today a talented painter and interior designer in addition to her business diplomacy, learned the printing trade by working as a typesetter and page-makeup person in the pre-computer days of hot metal type.

In the 1970s, John boldly eschewed the comforts of the linguistic ghetto and prophetically insisted that English would be the language of the future of Chinese-

Americans. He insisted Chinese-Americans not live on a cultural island but advance their contributions to the economy and politics of the United States in the broader context of Asian-American power. In the late 1970s, he founded Asian Week, which covered the news of the Asian community in the United States entirely in English, when most other publications covered ethnic news only in their native languages.

John Fang was an early and tireless proponent of Chinese-Americans registering to vote and participating in every election — a pioneering political vision that has resulted in the Asian vote becoming one of the most significant voting groups in San Francisco elections.

John Fang published Asian Week and other publications out of the Grant Printing Co.'s two-story building on Sacramento Street in the heart of Chinatown. As it does today, Grant Printing printed a large number of neighborhood and ethnic weekly and monthly periodicals. In 1987, he bought the Lake Merced Independent, a 40,000-circulation

tabloid in the areas adjoining West Portal and Lake Merced, and named as publisher his son, Ted Fang, then a recent graduate of UC, Berkeley, in ethnic studies.

With a formula of emphasizing local community news that affected people's lives, Ted Fang expanded The Independent to citywide distribution and changed its format to a full broadsheet newspaper by 1989. In 1993, the Fangs bought eight peninsula community newspapers and formed the Independent Newspaper Group, with a nearly 400,000 twice-weekly circulation from the Richmond to Redwood City.

In a historical sense, the Fang family's purchase of the *San Francisco Examiner* on March 17, 2000, is a landmark for Asian Americans on the media map. The Fangs will be the only Asian American owners of a major metropolitan daily in California and perhaps nationwide.

James Fang said his family's purchase of the Examiner is beyond what his father would have hoped. "While he never really thought the goal was to buy the Examiner, when the Indy started doing well, I think he was very proud. It showed that Asian Americans could do things successfully that weren't normally associated with Asian Americans."

Florence Fang says, "When I thought of my children, I thought of a relay race. At first, they were too young to run, but I thought that later, if I got tired, I could reach back and put the baton in their hands. But now I find out that my three boys are already running ahead of me." ∎

> All together the Fang family runs and operates one of the largest non-daily newspaper groups in the country.

Ted, Douglas and James Fang

Ascribe Business Services

Just days before the courts were to shut the doors, stop all business operations, sell off its remaining assets and put the employees out on the street, Holly Suzara, then 26 years old, seized an opportunity. She convinced the bankruptcy trustee to sell her the business, and Ascribe Business Services was born. Through an intensive restructuring of operations and marketing, Suzara turned a profit in 18 months.

"Most of my motivation was to save my fellow employees jobs," Suzara says today. It's not surprising that most of those employees are still with the company, whose mission statement reads in part: "Ascribe aims to create an atmosphere for its employees where creativity and innovation can flourish."

"If I can imagine it, I can do it... Courage is the by product of this process."

Uncompromising quality, with competitive prices make Ascribe Business Services the better choice for its clients; repeat business, cost control; and a dedicated work force make Ascribe work for Suzara.

Ascribe had developed a prestigious client base, drawing from some of San Francisco's most successful companies, including Sutro & Co., Orrick, Herrington & Sutcliffe, PG&E, Bank of America, Wells Fargo, Pacific Telesis, Merrill Lynch, Citibank, HBO and Genentech.

Vision and determination on Suzara's part saved the day.

The vision to see that the business could become profitable and the determination to succeed made it happen. "If I can imagine it, I can do it…Courage is the by-product of this process," says the young entrepreneur.

As a further measure of Suzara's vision of what this business could be, and just how successful it could become, three years later, the San Francisco/Bay Area Chapter of the National Association of Women Business Owners honored her as their Woman Entrepreneur of the Year. ■

Ascribe Business Services Inc. provides to its customers the highest standards in printing, graphic design, copying and customer service. Uncompromising quality in products and services, in a highly competitive marketplace, is the hallmark of the company's founder, Holly Suzara.

Suzara was recruited to start a court reporting division for a downtown printing and copying firm looking to diversify. She quickly generated over $300,000 of revenue in her first six months. But as her vision for the court reporting division became more focused and grew, the rest of the company was failing. The former owner declared bankruptcy amid dwindling inventories, equipment repossessions and rapidly declining business.

Bank of America

Bank of America, the first truly nationwide bank in the United States, lives up to its name. Founded in San Francisco's North Beach neighborhood in 1904, the Bank of Italy was to become Bank of America. Now merged with NationsBank of North Carolina, Bank of America has offices coast to coast and in 37 countries. Today, one in three American households banks with Bank of America, and a new home loan is financed by the bank every three minutes. Bank of America is also the nation's top provider of Small Business Administration loans, and it provides financial products and services to more than 80 percent of the global *Fortune* 500.

San Francisco was a fertile environment for a growing bank, and by 1930, Bank of America was playing a key role in the California economy. In the depth of the Great Depression, Bank of America financed the building of the Golden Gate Bridge. Instrumental in developing the state's agricultural and wine industries, Bank of America also played an important role in early Hollywood motion pictures, financing Walt Disney's first full-length animated feature, *Snow White and the Seven Dwarfs*, among other important films.

Today, one in three American households banks with Bank of America.

Over the years, Bank of America has helped Bay Area communities finance schools, housing, libraries and other projects. Nearly $11 billion in the bank's notes and bonds have funded projects such as the Hetch-Hetchy water system, the San Francisco airport renovation and the new Giants baseball stadium.

Bank of America recently helped launch a Microloan Program, with $1 million for small businesses, especially those owned by minorities and women. California nonprofit organizations received more than $18 million in 1999 from the Bank of America Foundation. In January 1999, the bank announced a $5 million contribution toward development of the UCSF Mission Bay campus to be paid over five years.

Today's Bank of America also has roots that were planted in other parts of the country. For example, in 1847, George Knight Budd opened the Boatmen's Bank in St. Louis to help riverboat sailors. In 1858, Chicago business leaders started the Merchants Savings, Loan & Trust Co. to help their frontier town develop. In the 1860s, Dexter Horton bought a safe and began making loans to millhands, trappers and miners in Seattle. All these banks — and their histories of community service — have become part of Bank of America over the years.

Meanwhile, in the Southeast, a North Carolina bank was evolving from a small community bank into a financial powerhouse. In 1960, the merger of two local banks created North Carolina National Bank. In 1988, that company doubled in size with the acquisition of First Republic Bank in Texas. Following a merger with a Mid Atlantic region bank in 1992, the company was renamed Nations-Bank, which merged in 1998 with Bank of America.

The best features of its predecessor organizations are blended into Bank of America's nationwide financial-services franchise. With offices around the world, Bank of America is a hometown bank with a global reach. ∎

bebe

sees a 100+-store chain with boutiques in 24 states, Canada and England. Mashouf says San Francisco was the ideal city for his new stores — it's "a city of firsts," a sophisticated, intellectual city that has spawned many unique offerings.

Although bebe designs more than 70 percent of the clothing in its stores, Mashouf complements those styles by hand-picking other apparel to produce a contemporary collection, "much like selecting flowers from a garden to reflect various occasions and convey specific messages." Mashouf says bebe creates a lifestyle package for women, integrating quality fashion, value, service and environment through bebe's apparel, accessories and the retail experience. bebe's fashions, which he describes as distinctive with an unmistakable hint of sensuality, hipness and sophistication, have attracted such stars as Brooke Shields, Calista Flockhart, Cher, Cindy Crawford and Madonna.

After more than 20 years in business, bebe has kept up with the times. It joined the world of e-commerce by launching the bebe online store at www.bebe.com, which offers a selection of its most popular merchandise. "The website not only enhances our brand

It's hard to imagine that a "for lease" sign would change the direction of Manny Mashouf's life, but that was the case in 1971. The then-successful restaurateur was bored with his business and knew he wanted to explore other options. So when he spotted the rental sign, he hopped out of the car at Polk Street between Bush and Pine, and quickly closed the deal with a handshake. After buying some fabric and a sewing machine, and hiring a master tailor, he found himself in the clothing business nine months later. "I always had a strong sense of fashion," he says.

Mashouf started manufacturing men's clothing, but soon he was filling a missing link in women's clothing — fashions targeting women who did not fall into the junior category but were younger and more stylish than the bridge lines (spanning the gap between junior and missy lines). bebe was born in 1976. The name represents a philosophy of the '70s ("to be or not to be"), as well as the Persian name for the queen in a deck of cards and the Turkish word for *woman*.

Mashouf, president and CEO of bebe, claims he knew nothing about the fashion industry at that time, but after trial and error, he now over-

"bebe creates a lifestyle package for women."

name and gives us a global presence, but also provides our customers with convenience," Mashouf says.

To further provide convenience and access to one-stop shopping, bebe has ventured beyond apparel and added footwear, watch and eyewear collections, all under licensing agreements with manufacturers.

Though bebe has expanded well beyond San Francisco, it has not forgotten its ties to the city. Mashouf and his employees are actively involved in charitable activities, including the annual AIDS Walk, fund-raising for breast cancer and contributing to the Bay Area Foundation for Youth. In addition, Mashouf serves on the board of San Francisco State University's Business School.

Mashouf sees bebe as evolving, something he calls one of the company's constants — changing all the time. "We will continue to do what we are doing now," he says, "growing in leaps and bounds, providing more jobs and contributing to the community as an innovative company in an innovative city." ■

W hether making leaf springs for San Francisco's first cable cars or manufacturing springs for the space shuttle Columbia, Betts Spring Company's chief interest has always been quality.

This family tradition was initially demonstrated when one of founder William M. Betts' ancestors was knighted for inventing a special spring for the queen of England's carriage. After immigrating to the United States and founding the first spring-manufacturing company west of the Mississippi in San Francisco in 1868, Betts was awarded a gold medal at the 1871 Mechanics Exhibition for superior carriage springs. Later, Betts' son Percy diversified the company further to meet the needs of the post–horse-and-buggy era, introducing leaf springs for locomotive, automotive, truck, tractor and industrial applications.

Percy died in 1919. His widow, Emeline, took leadership of the company while raising three young sons. Betts Spring's president, Mike Betts — the fifth generation to join the family business — recalls how his family worshiped his great-grandmother: "She took over after Percy died and then made it through the Depression. What a tremendous accomplishment."

After the Depression, her sons Percy F. and James Shannon Betts took their places in the growing family business. But it was today's chair of the board, William M. Betts III, who pointed it toward new horizons. In 1958, he developed and patented the Betts Spring Mud Flap Holder to serve the trucking industry throughout the United States and Canada. These parts are now manufactured at Betts Spring's ISO 9002-certified plant dedicated to this product.

Under William and his son, Mike's, leadership, the company has become a major supplier to the trucking industry, as well as to diverse transportation, aerospace and other industries. Betts springs stabilize NASCAR and other circle-track race cars,

Betts Spring was awarded a gold medal at the 1871 Mechanics Exhibition for superior carriage springs.

Betts Spring Company

Three generations of Betts.
Left to Right: William Michael Betts IV,
William Michael Betts V and William Michael Betts III

Plant of Betts Spring Company, 1876

and when the new safety barriers are installed on the Golden Gate Bridge, it will be a Betts spring in the mechanism that will enable them to be moved as traffic flow changes.

Betts also manufactures the gate valve springs that regulate water flow from huge dams and municipal water plants. It supplies the fine springs used in watches, silicon-wafer manufacturing machines and medical equipment. And the company pioneered the use of titanium springs in mountain-bike suspensions.

Most recently, the company has come full circle, expanding its truck suspension installations and services to seven locations on the West Coast. True to company tradition, trained craftspeople diagnose and repair truck suspensions and related undercarriage components — a more complex version of the company founder's original buggy-spring business. ■

Blanc & Otus

Blanc & Otus president and CEO
Jonelle Birney

Simone Otus and Maureen Blanc, co-founders

When Maureen Blanc and Simone Otus decided to start their own high-tech public-relations firm, they didn't head for Silicon Valley. Instead, they stayed in San Francisco — a city they love and live in, and one that serves as ideal headquarters for a growing company. Fifteen years later, Blanc & Otus (B&O) is the largest high-tech public-relations agency founded and headquartered in San Francisco, with offices in Mountain View, Boston, Austin and Washington, D.C.

B&O initially chose San Francisco as its home because of its close proximity to the agency's East Bay clients and accessibility to a large pool of potential employees who wanted to work in San Francisco for a high-tech public-relations firm. Started in 1985 at the beginning of the technology boom, B&O is meeting the challenges of the burgeoning e-commerce business world — one dominating the U.S. marketplace and demanding national exposure. Blanc says the firm is one of the top technology PR companies in the world in terms of reputation, revenue and clients.

"San Francisco is a great place for a small company to get started," Blanc says. "The city has always been an asset. It's prestigious to do business with a San Francisco-based company; our clients enjoy spending time in such an exciting, vibrant cosmopolitan city. In return, we do what we can to give back to the city, whether it be

Blanc & Otus is the largest high-tech public-relations agency founded and headquartered in San Francisco.

through contributing to a charity or organization, or participating in a fund-raising event."

Since its founding, B&O has volunteered its services to support community projects such as Project Open Hand and UCSF Breast Cancer Awareness Week. It also helped launch the Entrepreneur's Foundation, an organization dedicated to promoting entrepreneurial involvement in the community. Since its inception, the foundation has attracted 50 companies and 300 volunteers.

One of B&O's primary niches is promoting start-up companies, says B&O President/CEO Jonelle Birney, leading to the successful launch of more than 50 start-ups in the past 14 years. This strong commitment to supporting new companies, as well as B&O's reputation for great service, has positioned the agency to address the needs of companies in South of Market's burgeoning Multimedia Gulch.

Enhancing B&O's cachet was the acquisition of the agency in February 1999 by Hill & Knowlton, one of the world's largest international PR firms. Hill & Knowlton has 59 offices in 34 countries and serves clients in a variety of industries.

Though B&O is caught up in the fast-paced, real-time world of high technology, its mission is pretty direct: Do great work for cool companies, provide a great place for people to work, stay challenged and have fun. These qualities are what Blanc says differentiate the firm from its competitors.

"We stand out because of our strong focus on technology, partner-level involvement with each client, attention to detail and our supportive, team-based culture where the people are fun and smart, and the work is challenging," Blanc says.

As for the future, B&O will continue to participate in the new economy created by the Internet and Silicon Valley. With its roots firmly planted in San Francisco, the agency plans to continue to expand and take advantage of the increasing technological boom in this area and in future emerging markets. ■

The Boudin Bakery philosophy has been, "it does not make sense to reinvent the wheel," or a loaf of bread, for that matter. A San Francisco tradition since 1849, Boudin Sourdough French Bread uses only natural ingredients: flour, water, salt and the original "mother dough," a natural starter that ferments for up to 72 hours. It is the "mother dough" and the time-honored handcrafting process that gives Boudin Sourdough its unique world-renowned flavor.

The sourdough saga originated from modest beginnings when Marie and Louis Boudin, natives of France, opened a French bakery in North Beach. In the early days, their main customers were the miners and adventurers lured to California by the prospect of gold. Isidore Boudin, son of Marie and Louis, is credited with perfecting the sourdough recipe, adopting the idea of saving a portion of the previous day's dough to start the next day's batch. In the 1906 earthquake, which devastated North Beach, lore has it that Isidore's wife and her sons packed the precious "mother dough" in ice and carried it to Golden Gate Park. The bakery was rebuilt at a new location at 10th Avenue and Geary, where, to this day, fresh Boudin bread is baked.

The bakery and Sourdough traditions passed from the hands of the Boudin family to Master-Baker Steve Giraudo in 1935. Giraudo guarded the integrity and quality of the bread by teaching a new generation of bakers the unique process and relationship with the "mother dough." In 1975, the first retail bakery and café was opened on Fisherman's Wharf. Giraudo was ever present, aways checking on his baking staff in the wee hours of the morning, until his death in 1997, at the age of 84.

Boudin Sourdough Bakery

> "The key to Boudin success is the blending of new technologies with a 150-year history of handcrafting bread."

Boudin President Larry Strain explains: "Boudin consistency and well-known quality is driven by the company's longtime bakers, who continue to pass on the Boudin sourdough tradition." Although mechanization has taken over the baking, we are diligent about duplicating the original handmade process. We remain true to our tradition of San Francisco Sourdough French bread, the best loaf possible. We feel strongly that our heritage and the delivery of an exceptional quality product will not be jeopardized by the temptation to increase speed and volume. The key to Boudin success is the blending of new technologies with a 150 year history of handcrafting bread."

Boudin sells its fine array of sourdough and specialty breads through a variety of business outlets. Customers can order the original Sourdough bread through a mail-order catalog, website or cafés. In addition, diners can enjoy a wide range of quality sandwiches, salads and soups served in, on or around our sourdough breads in any one of 29 Bay Area cafés. Boudin also operates cafés in Southern California and Illinois, where the tradition, flavors and impeccable quality have been carefully recreated to be enjoyed by our loyal customers outside the San Francisco Bay Area.

Boudin has recently been selected by The Walt Disney Co. to share in the magic of its new theme park, Disney's California Adventure in Anaheim, Calif. A full demonstration bakery showcasing the history and legend of Boudin Sourdough French Bread and its baking process will open in 2001, sharing the Boudin story and bread with all who visit the Magic Kingdom. ■

Brobeck, Phleger & Harrison LLP

Chairman Tower C. Snow Jr. and San Francisco
Managing Partner Karen Johnson-McKewan
of Brobeck, Phleger & Harrison LLP

Brobeck, Phleger & Harrison is delighted to help San Francisco commemorate its 150th anniversary this year, as the law firm prepares to celebrate its own 75th birthday in 2001.

"One of our main goals is to connect with the businesses of people who are breathing life into the community, namely those at the leading edge of the economy," says Karen Johnson-McKewan, managing partner of the law firm's San Francisco office.

What has been consistent throughout the history of Brobeck has been its close connection to the business of the city, whether it be shipping in the early years, the high-technology whirlwind of the past two decades or a tremendous presence in the financial community, both then and now.

"The Bay Area is the world mecca of high-technology with the greatest concentration of companies in the industry," adds Tower C. Snow, Jr., the firm's chairman. "And we are a leader and driver of change."

To catch the first wave of technology, Brobeck established an office in Silicon Valley as early as 1980, though its seeds were planted much earlier when the firm represented its first high-technology client in 1961. "We wouldn't be doing what we are today if we weren't in the Bay Area, with its prevalence of software and Internet companies," says John Larson, senior partner and former chair of the firm.

As the firm began to target emerging growth companies, it had to radically change its philosophy. "We transformed ourselves from a 19th century business model to a 21st century, cutting-edge firm," Snow says. To keep up with the demands of its high-technology clients, Brobeck has invested $50 million in its own information systems.

Embracing technology to empower people and serve clients is what Snow says differentiates Brobeck from its competitors. "We focus on the success of every member of the firm, and we do what it takes to help everyone do their best," he says. The firm has created three stock-investment funds for its partners, associates and other employees as a testament to their hard work and to the success of the firm.

In addition to doing whatever it takes to encourage its staff, Brobeck also will do whatever it takes to complete a transaction. Larson, who has been with Brobeck for 37 years, recalls how, in the early 1960s, the firm bent over backward for a client in the semiconductor business. "The client's four-member executive team was on its way to New York to meet with investment bankers, but they didn't have suits, the necessary attire for such a meeting. The attorney on the case personally bought them the right clothes," he says.

Brobeck has come a long way since its inception in 1926, when William Brobeck, Maurice Harrison and Herman Phleger formed a partnership after an affiliation

Embracing technology to empower people and serve clients is what differentiates Brobeck from its competitors.

with several other partners. Lore has it that Phleger engineered a dissolution, insisting the firm would be more profitable if the three men practiced alone. In an office coup, the other partners were locked out of their offices on the seventh floor of the old Crocker Building. Not to be deterred, the evicted partners came with fire axes in hand, broke down the doors and confiscated their files.

Today, Brobeck has 650 lawyers, currently serves more than 3,000 high-technology and emerging growth companies, and boasts $314 million in revenue for 1999. It has been ranked by the *San Francisco Business Times* as the most profitable law firm in the Bay Area, with profits up 43 percent for 1999.

Brobeck delivers both transactional and litigation services through nine US offices and one in London. Its transactional business includes IPOs, secondary public offerings, mergers and acquisitions, start-up ventures, financial services, real estate and tax. On the litigation side, Brobeck specializes in products liability, intellectual property, antitrust, securities and labor and employment.

The firm and its staff are not shy about contributing to the community. "San Francisco has given us the platform to be successful and we have given back the fruits of our success," Snow says. The Brobeck, Phleger & Harrison LLP Charitable Foundation not only matches employees' donations to worthy nonprofit organizations, such as the American Red Cross, Habitat for Humanity, the San Francisco AIDS Foundation and Theatre Works, but also makes year-end grants to a variety of other organizations.

In 1999, Brobeck contributed more than $600,000 to educational institutions, legal-services associations, community groups, health and medical research, community youth programs, cultural arts groups and environmental and animal protection agencies. In addition, Brobeck has volunteered thousands of hours of pro bono services to various programs and organizations, while its staff has offered countless hours of community service.

"San Francisco is a special city, and it provides us with access to the best and brightest people," Johnson-McKewan adds. "It is a business-friendly city in a region with excellent transportation systems, so it attracts the kind of people to our firm that help create a vibrant business and legal community."

Brobeck's goal for the future is to become the master of a few rather than the jack of all trades, to represent the most vibrant and exciting high technology and New Economy companies in the world. "Our vision is to become the world leader in representing high-technology companies and venture capital firms," Snow says. So far, the firm is on the right path. In 1999, *The American Lawyer* rated it as the firm mentioned most often as corporate, litigation and securities counsel by New Economy companies, as well as second in the country for company-side and underwriter-side public offerings representation.

"We live in the most exciting age ever with both the greatest risk and the greatest opportunity. We have the brightest imaginable future if (and when) we step boldly into it," Snow says. ■

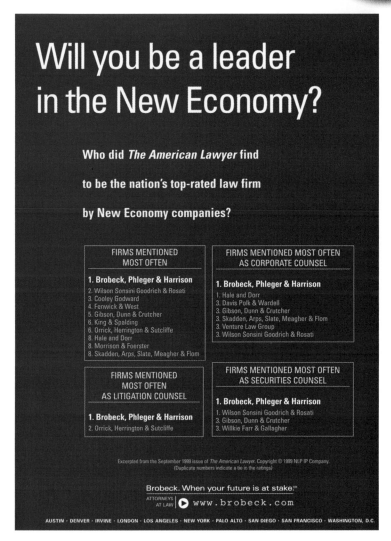

California Host

Service agents, 1,500 employees and 26 Japanese officials who flew in for the unveiling of a satellite they purchased. All details were completed in only two weeks.

California Host also arranges internal corporate events, such as sales meetings, company picnics and employee incentive trips. In today's fast-paced climate, corporations realize the importance of team building to develop camaraderie and build loyalty.

California Host prides itself on "bringing people together to move business forward." "Our goal," says company founder and President Barbara Edwards, "is to motivate, reward and educate attendees." To do that, the company creates innovative environments for their events, helping clients develop themes and searching the globe for the newest venues. "We are a vital resource to our clients," Edwards says. "We have to know about the latest venue openings before our clients do."

Sometimes California Host events seem a little prescient. Several years ago, Edwards produced a product launch for a Silicon Valley corporation, complete with a fake temblor. The event ended at 3 in the afternoon; the Loma Prieta earthquake struck shortly after 5. Undaunted, California Host continues to produce high-impact events.

N
o event is too complex for the event planners at California Host. Launched in Silicon Valley in 1971 by Barbara Edwards, the company was a start-up among start-ups and has grown with many of the valley's top firms, such as Cisco, Apple and Sun Microsystems. Specializing in event planning, California Host has managed everything from product launches to employee incentives to parties to celebrate a corporate client's first billion dollars in sales.

Today, California Host has expanded; about 30 percent of its business comes from outside the United States. It handles IPOs and media events, trade shows and conferences for such clients as Hewlett-Packard, AT&T, Oprah Winfrey's Harpo Productions and American Express. With strong backgrounds in catering, travel, public relations, event marketing and hotel management, the staff of 16 oversee site selection, entertainment, vendor selection, budget management and contract negotiations. California Host is a full-service company in the business of translating a corporate message into an event to be remembered.

Sometimes the details can be daunting. California Host has planned four presidential visits to Silicon Valley companies. For one of those high-profile events, a visit from President George Bush to Ford Aerospace, the company managed everything from the painting and security of nine buildings to coordinating 49 members of the press, 22 Secret

California Host is a full-service company in the business of translating a corporate message into an event to be remembered.

And what better place to do that than San Francisco? Even though California Host produces events all over the world, the city is still Edwards' favorite backdrop. "All the venues are wonderful. There are so many possibilities," she says. "And San Francisco represents what California Host is all about — it's diverse and exciting, the heart of all the energy in California. This is where it's happening, where people are taking the lead." ∎

In the competitive business world of fitness and health centers, Club One has carved out a comfortable niche catering to aging baby boomers where they work and live. Founded in 1991 by Jill and John Kinney, now president/chief operating officer and CEO, respectively, Club One launched its centers with two downtown facilities, targeting Financial District employees.

Today, the business is booming; the company operates 54 fitness centers, including both commercial and corporate sites with clients such as Motorola, 3Com and Intel. Club One is the largest provider of onsite corporate fitness centers on the West Coast. Its current mission is to grow its regional networks in Northern and Southern California with additional convenient, quality fitness centers.

"We look at both the 'health' and 'sports' sides of fitness, and design well-balanced programs which combine mind/body, strength and flexibility exercises," Jill says. The high demand for yoga classes at Club One facilities is indicative of the trend towards integrating the spiritual and physical, she adds.

Befitting today's workaholic with little time, Club One's health and fitness programs include a variety of sports; popular classes such as pilates and yoga; spa treatments; massage therapy; laundry service; certified trainers; child care; physical therapy; and stress management.

Long-time residents of San Francisco, the Kinneys did not spend much time deliberating over a home for their first clubs. "The Financial District is a positive environment for entrepreneurs," Jill says. "The Chamber of Commerce, for instance, has been a source of marketing guidance, networking and educational programs for our staff. San Francisco has also provided us with a wonderfully diverse employee and membership base, a cross section of humanity. We truly serve <u>all</u>

Jill Kinney, president and chief operating officer of Club One Inc.

All Club One locations feature spotlessly clean facilities, spacious lobby and locker-room areas, uncrowded exercise areas, and customer service — driven professional staff.

In the competitive business world of fitness and health centers, Club One has carved out a comfortable niche — catering to aging baby boomers where they work and live.

types of people. The only common denominator seems to be a desire for convenience and professionalism."

Like just about every other industry, fitness has opened its arms to technology which Club One has embraced wholeheartedly. Instituted in January, members at corporate clubs will enjoy individual 12-inch, flat screens offering 60 television stations, 200 digital radio channels, Internet capabilities and access to Club One's video newsletter, providing information on upcoming events and activities.

Club One also recently jumped into the world of e-commerce, selling sporting goods, home fitness equipment and workout clothes via the Internet. In addition, it is designing home pages for each member, who will receive customized information and products and services based on a personal fitness assessment.

In its nine years of existence, Club One has racked up a number of awards. *Inc. Magazine* named it one of the top 500 companies, 1995-1998, while the *San Francisco Business Times* designated Club One as one of the top 100 fastest growing companies in the Bay Area, 1993-1999. In addition, Jill received the 1999 Distinguished Service Award from the International Health Racquet & Sportsclub Association.

As a diversion from baby boomers, Jill, an advocate of helping underprivileged children, is putting her energies into serving on the national advisory board of Operation Fit Kids. The nonprofit organization in Southern California builds fitness centers for children ages 12 to 19 in space donated by communities, refurbishes fitness equipment for the facilities, trains staff, funds programming and underwrites scholarships. Club One is donating equipment, people power and funding to centers underway in San Francisco, Oakland and San Jose. ∎

Congregation Emanu-El

instrumental in establishing the Benjamin H. Swig Camp for Living Judaism in the Santa Cruz Mountains.

Emanu-El has always provided stalwart supporters for the city's opera, symphony, arts museums and other cultural ventures. In the mid-20th century, Cantor Ruben Rinder raised funds to develop new sacred music and foster the careers of several important musicians, including violinists Yehudi Menuhin and Isaac Stern. Today, Emanu-El sponsors its own series of concerts and lectures, with appearances by notable figures, from Eleanor Roosevelt and Martin Luther King Jr., to Maya Angelou and Bruno Bettelheim.

Leadership in social issues is also a feature of Emanu-El's history. In 1921, just a year after women won the vote, Rabbi Martin A. Meyer opened the temple's board of directors to women members. In national forums, Rabbi Alvin I. Fine spoke out against the political witch-hunting of the 1950s and on behalf of black civil rights. Rabbi Joseph Asher was an outspoken advocate of progressive causes through the American Jewish Congress.

Emanu-El also has a long history of leadership in city benevolent activities, among fellow Jews and in the broader community. Under its present rabbi, Stephen S. Pearce, Congregation Emanu-El has expanded its participation in a weekly tutorial program with the Third Bap-

Emanu-El also has a long history of leadership in city benevolent activities.

From the earliest days of San Francisco, members of Congregation Emanu-El, one of the city's founding temples, have been prominent among the city's business tycoons, political leaders and cultural patrons.

Among Emanu-El's early presidents were Abraham C. Labatt, a city alder who helped establish the nation's first Reform congregation, and Henry Seligman, a founder of the Seligman financial empire. Seligman was instrumental in building two temples for the young congregation, first on Broadway in North Beach and, a few years later, on Sutter between Powell and Stockton streets. Built in 1866 — and rebuilt after the great earthquake 40 years later — the Sutter Street temple dominated the San Francisco skyline in those days, with twin towers topped by glittering domes.

In the 1920s, the growing congregation built another city landmark on Lake Street. With its enormous dome and adjacent Temple House, the $1.3 million synagogue was then among the world's costliest. By that time, Emanu-El counted several millionaires among its members. These included Harold Zellerbach, a temple president who led his father's paper-products company, and descendants of clothier Levi Strauss, who donated the huge stained-glass windows added to the temple in 1972.

More recently, California political leaders Benjamin H. Swig and Walter Shorenstein have been members, along with Sen. Dianne Feinstein, whose family home is a neighbor to the Lake Street temple. Swig, a Democrat who was a key figure in mayoral elections of the 1960s, was

tist Church. Elsewhere, volunteers participate in the San Francisco Food Bank, Little Brothers/Self-Help for the Elderly and Christmas/Sukkot in April.

A variety of worship styles are offered to the growing congregation, and unaffiliated Jews in the Bay Area find an open door welcoming them to join this historic community. ∎

T he story of Cresalia Jewelers begins with two Gold Rush pioneers: "Longo" Raffo and Martin Cresalia, who married Raffo's daughter, Clarissa. Although both men soon stopped mining, gold continues to figure prominently in family affairs, along with diamonds, gemstones and pearls.

Traveling by wagon train across the country to California's gold fields, Raffo was undersheriff in Jackson, Calif., in the 1850s. Martin Cresalia arrived by ship from around the Horn. By the 1860s, he had turned from mining to hospitality, opening a hotel and a 24-hour restaurant called Martin's Oysterhouse at Market and Third streets.

One of Martin's six children was Joseph A. Cresalia, a talented musician who wrote music and played in the San Francisco Symphony. In 1912, Joseph A. also became a diamond importer, one of the few in San Francisco at the time. His second-story offices on Post Street eventually sold a wide range of jewelry, silver holloware, flatware, crystal stemware and gift items — as the present store still does. His daughter, Marie Louise, worked at his side and remained with the store for many years after Joseph A. died in 1959.

But it was Marie Louise's brother, Joseph W., who became the head of the business, focusing its stock on the finest jewelry. A veteran of Patton's armored division in World War II, Joseph W. had stayed in Paris to study, then came home to earn his law degree at the University of San Francisco. Joseph W. married Madeline Tracy, another descendant of Gold Rush pioneers. They had three children, Charlie, Lynn and Joseph G. (Jay), who have all worked at the store at various times. Since Joseph W.'s death in June 1999 Mrs. Cresalia has entrusted the management of the store to their oldest son, Jay.

Like his great-grandfathers, Jay spent some time mining gold after graduating from the University of Denver. In 1979, he got a degree at the Gemological Institute of America, thinking he would be a short-term traveling agent for his father. Inflation was high then. Gold, diamonds and gemstones were rapidly increasing in value. Entrepreneurial spirit and hard work were necessary to survive, as they had been in Gold Rush days.

Cresalia Jewelers

Joseph W. and Jay worked side by side for 20 years, as the father passed along his knowledge of jewelry and San Francisco business. Jay is now supported by a staff of long-time employees and his family.

Throughout the years, we have provided quality jewelry at very competitive prices, a gift that is always treasured.

Jay has been married 23 years to his college sweetheart Maryanne Donovan and has nine children. During the busiest times of the year, members of the different generations can be also found helping around the store, as their father and grandfather did. Jay's oldest son, Joseph J. — great-grandson of the founder — designed the store's webpage at www.cresaliajewelers.com. Pictures and prices of some inventory are included, along with information to help customers make sound decisions.

Now located on the ground floor at 111 Sutter St. near Montgomery, the store still has a second-floor style of doing business: That means a reputation for offering quality goods at very reasonable prices with friendly service.

With an extensive inventory, Cresalia Jewelers also creates custom designs for clients and does appraisals and repairs. Most of its business is returning customers and referrals, many from the Bay Area. But to satisfy loyal customers, Cresalia ships jewelry around the country and even overseas. "When someone comes in, we like to think we're making a friend," Jay says. "Throughout the years, we have provided quality jewelry at very competitive prices, a gift that is always treasured." ∎

After 60-plus years, the Golden Gate Bridge is still the most famous icon of San Francisco.

PHOTO COURTESY OF CLIFF CROSS

Del Monte Foods Company™

Orchard Select, Del Monte's new, highly popular line of premium fruits, sold exclusively in the produce section.

Had you been among the exclusive guests savoring a cup of coffee at Monterey's posh Hotel Del Monte in the late 1880s, you might have caught the scent of history brewing. The Oakland Preserving Co., the source of the hotel's specially blended coffee, wisely emblazoned its premium line of fruits and vegetables with the same distinctive red and gold Del Monte Shield used to accentuate those very special products purveyed to the Hotel Del Monte. This tactic launched a brand that became widely recognized and revered for reliable quality and premium value.

The distinctive Del Monte Shield then served as the primary brand for the 18 companies that merged in 1899 to form the California Fruit Canners Association and, subsequently, the California Packing Corp. — "Calpak" — created in 1916. The changes in company ownership succeeded, in part, because the brand values never changed.

Since 1916, San Francisco has been the headquarters city for Calpak — renamed Del Monte Corporation in 1967 to reflect its famous brand. Though Del Monte has been as synonymous with the city as its signature fog ever since, Calpak's first order of business focused far beyond San Francisco. The company quickly set about coordinating the output of 71 previously independent canneries throughout the West, Alaska and Hawaii to step up shipments of food to Allied troops fighting abroad in World War I.

When the war ended in 1918, the new company, then headquartered at 101 California St., began an era of explosive growth, fueled by its reputation for quality among home cooks, as well as the country's now-returned troops. Through acquisitions on the mainland and in the Pacific's lush pineapple belt, Calpak's early prosperity lasted until the Great Depression and carried the "Del Monte" brand even through the world's darkest economic times and a second wrenching war.

Whether times were prosperous or challenging, the company never lost its focus on food safety and quality, its penchant for resourcefulness and productivity, nor its appreciation for loyalty and hard work. Just as the brand has effectively distinguished the company's products, these characteristics define "Del Monte's culture", both then and now.

Innovation has long permeated the business — in operations and marketing, as well as research and development. From the company's inception, its researchers have remained close to the land, working with farmers and suppliers to develop practices yielding the most abundant and flavorful fruits, vegetables and tomatoes.

In the early 1920s, Del Monte realized the critical importance of consistent raw produce quality and began conducting agricultural research studies and supplying proprietary seeds to its growers. The company's new higher-yielding and more flavorful vegetables, such as its famous Blue Lake green beans, won accolades from growers and consumers alike. And its current agricultural research efforts continue to yield coveted results and high praises.

Further, since the healthfulness of the raw crops sprang from the health of the land, studies in low-chemical pest management, cover

On April 21, 1917, the *Saturday Evening Post* carried a full-page ad over the signature of California Packing Corporation. This was the start of an advertising campaign that would eventually change the shopping and eating habits of millions of consumers and make *Del Monte* one of the best-known brand names in the world.

Introduced in 1998, this eye-catching jacket packaging is widely popular with consumers.

cropping, crop rotation and other environmentally sound farming techniques were carried out long before, and well after, "organic" became a rallying cry. Indeed, some of the company's program efforts have become widely used industry models.

In Del Monte's national string of plants, as the machines of war found peacetime applications and technology became an ever-present partner, grueling handwork gave way to mechanical innovations that since have yielded to once unforeseen "high tech" applications. Beyond improving productivity, these technical innovations have unified and optimized finished product attributes such as flavor, appearance and texture.

Though these quality attributes are extremely important to Del Monte consumers, the company is equally aware of and effective in fulfilling another important and growing consumer need: inspiring great meals, at home and on the go.

Today's busy lifestyles mean consumers need healthful and delicious meals whenever and wherever eating occasions arise. Del Monte eagerly

Del Monte has been as synonymous with the city as its signature fog since 1916.

Del Monte employees sort tomatoes to ensure quality.

leads the way in fulfilling those needs. Single-serve packaging, easy-to-open pull-top lids, healthful snacking, dietary foods, uniquely flavored fruits and seasoned vegetables, specialty cuisine tomato products (including Del Monte's recently acquired "Contadina" brand), delicious "CAN DO" meals in less than 20 minutes and the "Freshest Ideas in Italian Cooking" are just some of the ways today's consumers enjoy and are being inspired by Del Monte's products.

With a product line that literally runs from A to Z — apricots to zucchini — Del Monte provides unlimited usage potential throughout each day. With product and recipe help, it's easy for the consumer to "add imagination and serve". And with all those features, it's easy to understand why 80 percent of US households buy Del Monte, and that the average home always has six items at the ready.

To feed these consumer needs, Del Monte employs 2,600 full-time and 12,000 seasonal workers in 14 production facilities and six distribution centers. Supplying those production sites are 2,500 family-owned farms — many second- and third-generation Del Monte growers — growing 129 varieties of fruit, vegetable and tomato crops on 150,000 acres.

This geographic breadth enables the company to expand its headquarters practice of good citizenship throughout the country. A consistent contributor to food banks and feeding programs, it also supports food and agriculture fairs, agricultural research and education, and numerous other efforts aimed at improving the environment and agribusiness.

The first purveyors of those uniquely special and limited "Del Monte"–branded foods had no idea what results ultimately would be derived from their brand strategy. Though, in considering what usually happens when one combines quality, ingenuity and determination, neither this outcome, nor the company's bright future, is surprising. ■

As is still true today, brokers in the early 1900s proudly display their allegiance to Del Monte Foods.

Katie Burke, CEO and Larry Drebes, CTO

What is the next big trend on the Internet? Katie Burke and Larry Drebes, co-founders of Desktop.com, believe they have the answer: a free service, accessible from any PC with an Internet connection, that provides users with an easy-to-use, centralized location for integrating favorite sites, services and files.

"Have you ever tried to use someone else's computer?" asks Burke, Desktop.com's CEO. "If so, you've experienced the frustration of searching for applications and files you know are there somewhere. We make logging onto and using the internet as easy and intimate as logging onto your own personal computer." Desktop.com bring together everything you use and want to store on the web in one portable space.

Desktop.com keeps customers coming back to its site by:

- Offering users the opportunity to cherry pick the best of the Web and bring it all together in a service they can access from any PC
- Using icons and pop-up windows make a user's "Webtop" look and feel like a more interactive PC desktop experience using icons and popout Windows pull down menus and drag and drop customization
- Providing free "portable" storage space for work, personal, audio or other files, eliminating the frustration of being at a home computer without access to files at work, and vice versa
- Giving users the ability to share files such as documents, to-do lists, photos, announcements and invitations with co-workers, family and friends

And there's more. Instead of trying to anticipate all the specialized software needs of its users, Desktop.com provides free infrastructure for developers to write and share innovative new programs they create. Developers can bring their own ideas to life or build on one of the thousands of requests for applications received from Desktop.com users.

"My favorite example is a runner's log," Burke says. "I wanted to be able to record my distance and times of my runs from work or from home. There was no program available, so a developer created one. Now it's available to all Desktop.com users. Other application ideas have included a recipe book, online

polling and surveys, and potluck-dinner invites."

So far, Desktop.com has met with rave reviews. *PC Magazine* nominated the site for its Technical Excellence Award, calling it "a remarkable feat and a trend-setting Web development."

USA Today journalist Tamara Homes writes, "Desktop.com puts forth an idea so logical and so ordinary that I wondered why I hadn't thought of it myself."

And, most importantly, the users themselves have applauded the service. One enthusiastic participant wrote: "Desktop.com is, without a doubt, one of the best ideas for Internet usage I have seen! This is what the Internet needs. I've seen many great free services offered, but Desktop.com, by far and large, offers the most useful Internet application today."

The power behind the concept and business opportunity for Desktop.com inspired its founders to initially shroud the venture in secrecy. When the company was founded in San Francisco in December 1998, it operated under the code name "JumpData" for fear "Desktop.com" would reveal too much to potential competitors. Burke and Drebes were so secretive that job candidates did not learn the nature of the project until the company was ready to extend an offer.

"We were lucky candidates were willing to return for several interviews without knowing our product or vision for the company," Burke

says. "That's where having a strong track record in the industry really helped." (Burke and Drebes were already well-known from their days at Four11, where they launched Web-based e-mail RocketMail, purchased by Yahoo! in 1997.)

The secrecy surrounding Desktop.com was not lifted and the name not changed from JumpData until $29 million in financing from three prominent investment firms, Accel Partners, Kohlberg Kravis Roberts & Co. and Sequoia Capital, was secured in August 1999. A month later,

Desktop.com brings together everything you use and want to store on the web in one portable space.

Desktop.com launched its Webtop for consumers and, by December, the beta version of the platform for developers was up and running. The company lauched its full featured sevice in March of 2000.

Has the pressure let up since these pivotal accomplishments? "We still work hard, but we don't forget to play hard in between the cracks," Burke says. "We recently called all 50 of our employees to a mandatory three-hour company meeting. Everyone showed up very serious, with notebooks in tow. We giggled and said, 'Lock the doors. Everyone's going to the beach!' And boy, did we have a blast." ■

Dodge & Cox

Harry R. Hagey, chair and chief executive officer, and
John A. Gunn, president and chief investment officer

Despite the merger mania of the 1990s, the investment management firm of Dodge & Cox, a San Francisco financial mainstay since 1930, has retained its independence — a well-studied decision. The late Van Duyn Dodge, a San Francisco native, and E. Morris Cox, a Bay Area native who still resides in San Francisco at age 96, were pioneers in the Bay Area investment scene.

A 1915 graduate of the University of California, Berkeley, in accounting, Dodge briefly joined a Boston investment firm and soon after saw a niche in San Francisco for investment management services. He was not deterred despite skepticism that such a company could successfully take root in financially nascent San Francisco.

In the early days, the firm concentrated on managing the financial affairs of individuals. Today, the majority of its business is providing professional investment management services for retirement funds, endowment funds and its own no-load mutual funds, the Dodge & Cox Stock, Balanced and Income funds.

Joining the company in 1946 as a security analyst, Peter Avenali, former president, CEO and chair of the board, retired five years ago and

"We have benefited from the community because of loyal, local institutions and individuals who have looked to us as an investment manager."

was one of the first employees. "You could look out the window of the firm's downtown office and see all our clients," he jokes. Dodge & Cox now has clients all over the United States. Although Avenali (also a San Francisco native) calls himself retired, he says, "I often stick my head in the door to give advice while trying to avoid pontificating too much."

Though the firm has grown from six to 90 employees and now manages assets of $40 billion, its approach to the management of individual, institutional and mutual funds remains the same. "We are an old-fashioned, old-line firm taking advantage of technology but still doing fundamental research in order to provide the best returns to investors," says Harry Hagey, CEO and chair of the board. "We have benefited from the community because of loyal, local institutions and individuals who have looked to us as an investment manager." Both Avenali and Hagey agree that the firm's continued independence has put it in a class of its own, further buoyed by the fact that all shareholders must be active employees of Dodge & Cox.

Working closely with Hagey is John Gunn, president and chief investment officer. Hagey joined the company in 1967, while Gunn came to the firm in 1972. Together they head the Dodge & Cox team of 40 investment professionals.

While *innovative* may not be the operative word for the company, Dodge & Cox was in the forefront of computerizing its business, allowing the company to maintain its administrative efficiency. "If you can't keep good records, you can't give good advice," Avenali recalls Dodge saying.

Dodge & Cox has always had a deep conviction about contributing to the community. Dodge was a founder of the Coro Foundation. Cox, a prodigious fund-raiser, was president of the board of trustees of the California Academy of Sciences and served on many cultural boards. Avenali is past president of the board of St. Francis Hospital and a fund-raiser for UC Berkeley. Many Dodge & Cox employees serve on community boards, such as the Pacific Vision Foundation, Bay Area Discovery Museum, Summer Search, the Asian Art Museum, San Francisco Friends of Chamber Music, the Bay Area Hearing Society and Florence Crittenton Services.

As for the future, Hagey says Dodge & Cox is expanding its research in international companies, which may eventually lead to a fourth mutual fund. "We are proud of our employees, our excellent reputation and the service we have provided our clients over the past 68 years," Hagey says. ■

W ill the Internet change your life? Absolutely, believes Christos M. Cotsakos, Chairman of the Board and CEO of E*TRADE Group Inc., which operates the world's most visited online personal financial services site.

"This business isn't just about transactions, it's about a lifestyle change," he says. "It's about personal financial freedom and growth. It's about putting power and choice back into the hands of individuals."

These are lofty ideals, but E*TRADE is fast making them a reality. Its website, www.etrade.com, enables individuals to quickly and easily access information and financial resources, such as real-time quotes and charts, news and market data, research and financial planning tools, and portfolio tracking; to make a variety of financial transactions, including buying and selling stocks, options and mutual funds and even online IPOs; and to link to a wide range of other financial products, including mortgages, insurance and banking services.

E*TRADE has won a variety of accolades for its site's choice, value, convenience and ease-of-use. In the past year alone, E*TRADE was cited by Lafferty Information and Research Group, *PC Magazine* and Smart Computing as having the most user-friendly website in the industry.

Financial figures for the company are equally impressive. Revenues in 1999 were $621.4 million. More than a million accounts have been added in less than 12 months. And the firm can boast more than $52 million in deposits every business day.

E*TRADE as it is known today was born in 1996, recent by most

Christos M. Cotsakos, chairman of the board and CEO

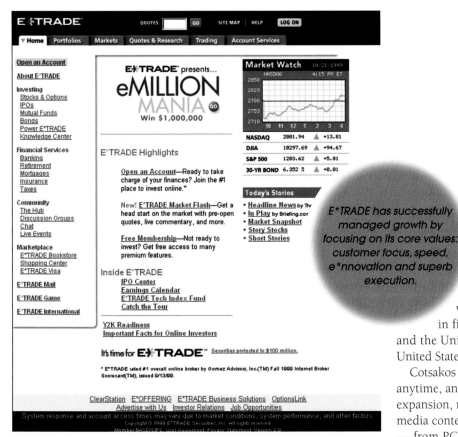

> *E*TRADE has successfully managed growth by focusing on its core values: customer focus, speed, e*nnovation and superb execution.*

values: customer focus, agility, reliability & e*nnovation. Recently, this has meant an aggressive advertising campaign to heighten brand awareness; expansion of customer-service support to 24 hours a day, seven days a week, 366 days per year; and the launch of E*TRADE sites in five additional countries — France, Japan, Korea, Sweden and the United Kingdom — to complement existing locations in the United States, Australia and Canada.

Cotsakos continues to aim high, hoping to soon "serve our customers anytime, anywhere, from any device." In addition to continued global expansion, meeting this goal will involve developing interactive multimedia content and commerce over a variety of channels and platforms — from PCs and cellular phones to digital TV and wireless personal digital assistants.

"The twenty-first century is about the empowerment of the individual," Cotsakos says. "E*TRADE has been both a champion and an innovator for the benefit of tomorrow's consumer today. Bodacious! The revolution continues." ∎

people's standards, but long ago in fast-moving "Internet time." Now with a headcount approaching 2,000, E*TRADE has grown exponentially since its inception to meet the huge increase in demand for its Web-based products and services.

The firm has successfully managed growth by focusing on its core

Esprit

Esprit's corporate headquarters in San Francisco's Potrero Hill

California. The mere mention of the place mails a mental postcard — sun-drenched, wave-splashed, stylish. Forever young. For women who want to dress that part — even if they're far from the state's balmy climes — the quintessential light-hearted California look is easily achieved. It appears nationwide under the label *Esprit*. Just as it has for 30 years.

The company's youthful, strikingly cut casual wear sprang to the fashion forefront in the early '70s, becoming an instant icon of the times. Completely original, Esprit captured the fancy of young women everywhere by offering them a distinctive style that was *so not* their mothers' look.

Credit the design and marketing vision of its forward-thinking founders, Doug and Susie Thompkins, says Esprit's current visionary, Jay Margolis, chair and CEO. "They understood lifestyle marketing before anyone else."

They lived it, in fact, introducing in widely heralded moves such employee benefits as a gourmet cafeteria, greenhouse and gym, company-paid time off for employee participation in community activism, even kayaks for weekend adventuring.

Esprit was "just doing it" before anyone ever thought to articulate what "it" was — which may explain why the company still excels at *it*... still leads the pack, in both lifestyle design and marketing. In 44 countries around the globe.

Having consolidated Esprit's hold on young trendsetters' imaginations with one of the industry's first lifestyle mail-order catalogs (introduced in 1980, three years before Esprit rolled out its first shop-in-shop retail operations), Esprit celebrated its 30th anniversary by relaunching the catalog. This '90s incarnation, revived after a decade's hiatus, bowed hand-in-hand with the essential '90s version of a "store" — an online edition at *www.esprit.com*.

Looking back over three decades, it's hard to fathom that this sure-footed fashion leader — one of the youngest of San Francisco's "historic" headquarters companies — ever faltered. But in true adolescent style, Esprit's turbulent late teens made headlines worldwide and especially at home, where its founders' very public split took the sheen off a Cinderella story that had captured the country's fancy.

Despite fears that the firm would surely lose its way, Esprit not only survived, but started to regain its footing (and its sense of humor, if the 1994 introduction of Dr. Seuss-licensed apparel, footwear and accessories is any indicator). By the mid-90s, the older, wiser Esprit regained its youthful outlook. But it had a sharper focus and a new leader — one hand-picked by Susie Thompkins to pick up where she had chosen to leave off.

A veteran manager of such industry leaders as Liz Claiborne and Tommy Hilfiger, Margolis stepped into a company that surprised him — not for its weaknesses but for its redoubtable strengths, including the high caliber of its "totally committed work force" and the goodwill of its fashionable consumers, for whom the brand still captured a look they liked, whatever its corporate parent's woes. "Everyone," Margolis marvels, "seemed to want Esprit to succeed."

Everyone will be pleased to know that it has, and it will. And that Margolis believes the way to maintain that success is to "remain true to the brand" — a feat more easily aspired to than achieved. "It has been a tough turnaround," Margolis admits.

Lines that had strayed from the Esprit look to one more influenced by the fashion industry itself had to be refocused. Some that made statements more political than fashionable had to be dropped in cost-containment moves. Old members of the Esprit "tribe" often didn't relate to the "new" Esprit — pared down, competitive and totally focused on business. Some members left, and new blood arrived.

Gradually, everything started to click again: Design teams consistently struck gold and a satisfying jump in sales validated the company's re-direction. Still, Margolis says, Esprit had to reconnect in vital ways with its customers. Thus was born the new catalog and, more important, a new marketing "theme."

The "I am Esprit" campaign recognizes that its former junior base is now a lively 20-something, or a youthful spirit who loves that 20-something look, or an Esprit kid with fashion foresight. She is, in short, any woman with a young attitude and a free-spirited fashion focus.

The campaign's images feature close-ups of women and children ranging in age from 12 months to 40-plus and focus on their subjects' unique lifestyles, as well as the individuality of the looks they pull together from Esprit's flexible components. Among those components are accessories with real sparkle and functionality.

Esprit sportwear, swim wear, footwear & accessories spill forth in colorful profusion, swirling into a signature look.

With each passing year, Esprit has regained ground and, since 1997, has even been adding new territory. It bought the Moonstone outdoor "performance brand" and made it a subsidiary in 1997. And, with a flagship store at San Francisco's Stonestown Center, it launched what is now a 41-store chain of free-standing retail shops. Amid the stores' clean, contemporary and fun architecture, Esprit sportswear, swimwear, footwear and accessories spill forth in colorful profusion, swirling into signature looks before your eyes.

"They're happy clothes that people want to wear," Margolis says. "When Esprit does Esprit, product blows out the door."

These days, product is walking out the door, too, and not just on the angular frames of its stylish customers. Its employees proudly sport the Esprit look along with a "come back" attitude that has again made the company an interesting, if intense, place where talented people — 350 in San Francisco and 1,100 nationwide — are happy to work.

Jay Margolis is no longer with the company. ■

The Laurel Court

The Fairmont San Francsico

I f Julia Morgan, the celebrated architect of a century ago, visited San Francisco these days, there's no question where she would stay: The Fairmont Hotel's interior has been restored to look exactly the way she designed it following the 1906 earthquake. She would be right at home.

"We thought the original design was so elegant, that when we decided to renovate, everyone agreed returning our public spaces to the look Morgan had created was the right direction for us to take," says General Manager Mark Huntley, of the extensive $72M project.

With its windows rebuilt and its original white and gray marble floor restored, the lobby is both larger and lighter than it had been in recent years. The walls and moldings are alabaster with gold highlights. Central to the lobby, the Laurel Court has been reconstructed as a beautiful restaurant and bar area, with Ionic columns and chandeliers hanging in three ornate domes.

In part because no documents could be found recording the original plans, the project produced a few surprises. Silverware dating to 1910 was hidden behind some walls and an intricate marble mosaic floor was uncovered and carefully preserved. To satisfy landmark requirements, the lobby's marble floor had to be lifted out slab by slab, with each piece cleaned and restored to its original position.

Every guest room in the original building "was taken back to the brick and rebuilt from there," Huntley says. The flavor of the old design was kept — with marble bathrooms, for example — though in most rooms, fixtures match contemporary tastes. Renovation of the tower, built in 1961 with one of the country's first glass-walled outdoor elevators, is scheduled for completion in November 2000.

The work is being directed by Gensler Architecture, which also restored the ACT Theater and Gump's. Page & Turnbull, the acknowledged expert on historic buildings in downtown San Francisco, has consulted on historical preservation.

The Lobby

Since Theodore Roosevelt stayed there in 1908, The Fairmont has become something of a Western White House. President Clinton is so fond of The Fairmont, he will even use it for a respite on his West Coast schedule. Other world dignitaries and celebrities have made The Fairmont a temporary home. In 1945, the United Nations Charter was drafted at The Fairmont, and in the 1980s, Ronald Reagan and Mikhail Gorbachev met there for meetings that helped end the Cold War.

Wolfe himself is part of The Fairmont's history and a milestone in American hotel hospitality, as well. Arriving at The Fairmont in 1973, he had been fascinated by concierges he observed at work in London and Paris hotels. At the time, American hotels had no concierges. The Fairmont then made hospitality history when it appointed Tom Wolfe as the first concierge in the United States.

It was a challenge at first. Places he would call to make reservations didn't know what a concierge was, and except for those who had traveled abroad, guests also needed to be educated about the service. "In those days, I was looking for customers," Wolfe says. Today, he has a staff to assist him.

The Fairmont's restoration adds new luster to one of the city's grandest grande dames.

It's no surprise The Fairmont was first with this innovation. "We've always been famous for our service," General Manager Huntley says. Today, service is a high priority for the hotel staff, many of them with the hotel 25 years or more. The staff is excited about The Fairmont's return to its original design — as are residents of the neighborhood, who often stop by for a peek.

The Fairmont's restoration adds new luster to one of the city's grandest grande dames, giving it an interior beauty guests are sure to admire as they gather for social, business and political events.

"The Fairmont is truly a work of art," Huntley says. "We're very fortunate to have it." ■

If there were no architectural drawings from the hotel's early years, there are plenty of stories. James Graham Fair, nicknamed "Bonanza Jim" after he discovered one of the world's largest silver strikes in Nevada, bought the property at the crest of Nob Hill in the early 1890s, intending to build a spectacular family estate. In 1902, his daughters, Tessie and Virginia, inherited the property and began construction of the hotel as a monument to their father.

Days before the hotel was scheduled to open, the 1906 earthquake and fire struck the city. After serving as a command post for the mayor and city officials, who sat on crates in the lobby to plot firefighting strategies, the hotel itself fell victim to the blaze. The interior was gutted, but the exterior remained standing. Rebuilt by Morgan, the hotel opened exactly a year later, with a huge celebration at which guests ate 13,000 oysters and drank $5,000 worth of California and French wines.

In 1926, The Penthouse Suite was built as a residence for John S. Drum, president of the American Trust Co., who leased it for $1,000 per month. Later, it was home to mining heir Maude Flood and then to Benjamin Swig, one of The Fairmont's previous owners. With Persian mosaics and lapis lazuli fireplaces, a two-story domed library and its own china and linens, The Penthouse has earned its reputation as the most luxurious suite in America and rents for $8,000 per day. Hundreds of guests have used it since 1981, among them Prince Charles, the late King Hussein of Jordan, Ginger Rogers and Mick Jagger. Today, The Penthouse continues to be the venue of choice for San Francisco's most elegant wedding and holiday gatherings.

Movies and TV shows have been filmed at The Fairmont, and Tony Bennett first sang "I Left My Heart in San Francisco" in the hotel's Venetian Room. Then a nightclub where stars entertained, the Venetian Room is still in use for dinners and private gatherings.

Tom Wolfe, the hotel's concierge, remembers escorting singer/actor Marlene Dietrich to and from the Venetian Room every night. "She never set her foot on anything but red carpet; it was rolled out every step of the way from her room to the stage — even in the service elevator," Wolfe recalls. "She was a marvelous woman. I had a great time working with her."

Family Service Agency of San Francisco

Ms. Kitty Felton, founder of Associated Charities, which later became Family Service Agency of San Francisco

As the oldest and largest multipurpose, non-sectarian social-services agency in the city, Family Service Agency of San Francisco (FSA/SF) is collaborating with hundreds of other agencies and becoming increasingly community-based. What makes FSA/SF unique? The eighth and current director, Lonnie Hicks, answers, "We are one of the few agencies providing services in every part of the city, across ethnic, class and religious groups."

FSA/SF was founded in 1889 as Associated Charities, at that time San Francisco's only nonsectarian relief organization, which was designed to bring collaboration to the city's proliferating charitable agencies. Legendary Kitty Felton, the agency's first director, was among the first to advocate that poor people were at the mercy of social and economic forces rather than morally defective. "Everyone needs a good cup of coffee in the morning, especially if he's out of work," she would say.

Under Felton's innovative and community-based vision, Associated Charities soon created the first foster-home system in California, which ended the appalling Foundling Asylum and reduced San Francisco's infant death rate from 59 percent to 12 percent.

During the 1906 earthquake and fire aftermath, Associated Charities directed the city's entire relief program. During those early years, the agency effectively laid the foundation for San Francisco's social-services

system, and its concepts and programs have been used ever since as prototypes statewide and nationally. In fact, Kitty lobbied into existence the state Board of Charities and Corrections (1903) and organized the San Francisco Community Chest (1922), forerunners of the state Department of Welfare and the United Way.

During the Depression, the agency aided San Francisco by providing food, housing and medical and employment assistance — food boxes for 22,000 people in a year and medical care for 6,000 – 8,000 people monthly.

In the 1960s, FSA/SF became more proactive in neighborhoods and began speaking out more on controversial social issues. Through a model program, staff went door to door in the Western Addition ghetto to bring residents to the agency for counseling, job training, child care and other forms of assistance. The approach was successful: The majority of clients, most of whom had been life-long welfare recipients, became employed and self-sufficient.

"In every neighborhood and community of San Francisco... we'll be where the need is."

Foster grandparent Rosy Caston at FSA/SF's Family Developmental Center in the Mission

Where is FSA/SF going? Hicks says: "We operate from the vision that functional families build functional communities, neighborhoods and ultimately functional nations. And our definition of family encompasses all families, of any orientation and make-up, including affinity groups. In every neighborhood and community of San Francisco…we'll be where the need is."

FSA/SF is the fourth-largest nonprofit working exclusively in San Francisco, operating 41 programs from 40 sites throughout the city and serving approximately 16,000 residents annually. Through a comprehensive array of services, FSA/SF assists low-income children and youth, teen parents, families in crisis, seniors, individuals with HIV, and mentally ill, disabled and abused adults and children. ∎

W hat do you get when you cross the talents of chef Mark Franz and restaurateur/designer Pat Kuleto? Farallon, an upscale seafood restaurant that debuted in June 1997, just off Union Square in the historic Elk's Club headquarters. Friends and co-owners of Farallon, Franz and Kuleto share a love for fishing, sailing, diving, good food and San Francisco.

"Farallon would really only work in San Francisco," Kuleto says, referring to the city's ethnic diversity, its location as a port town and its proximity to the real Farallon Islands. "We believe we have filled a niche by developing a first-class and exotic seafood restaurant."

"San Francisco is doing things on the outer edge, leading the world in the way food is perceived," Franz adds. "We're light years ahead of most of the country, just with the availability of diverse products and fresh produce. It doesn't get any more special than here."

Franz has had the restaurant business in his blood since he was a child. Dating back to his great grandfather, his family has owned restaurants, including one right on Union Square. A Bay Area native and graduate of the California Culinary Academy, Franz spent more

Farallon

Mark Franz and Pat Kuleto

"Farallon is a whimsical undersea fantasy..."

than a decade as executive chef at Stars and also created his culinary specialties at Ernie's in San Francisco, and at Berkeley's Santa Fe Bar & Grill. Kuleto's imprint can be found on many successful Bay Area restaurants: Boulevard, Jardiniere, Postrio and the Fog City Diner.

"We're like brothers; we have the same kinds of ideas but, while Pat takes me further in design, I complement him in the food area," Franz says. Farallon is a whimsical undersea fantasy with its exotic jellyfish sculpted lights, octopus stools, bronze "caviar" staircase, mosaic arches, hand-painted fabrics and stained glass — all of which Kuleto says represent the rebirth of arts and crafts. The food reflects the diversity of the sea, offering sea urchins, mackerel tartar, peeky-toe crab, salmon pillows and prawn mousse. Meals are capped off by the divine creations of executive pastry chef Emily Luchetti, who also hails from Stars.

Franz and Kuleto are quite aware of the many homeless and hungry people in the Bay Area, which is why they continually donate food and make other contributions to a number of worthy causes, including AIDS benefits, Meals on Wheels, and San Francisco Bay-keepers, which advocates keeping the bay clean and preserving it for future generations.

While the partners are quite pleased that both the community and visitors to San Francisco are praising Farallon, they have made some changes. Most notably, they upgraded the banquet facilities by creating what Kuleto describes as a "wild ballroom á la the Titanic, with bubble walls and fish cavorting on the walls."

As the new millennium gets underway, Kuleto sees Farallon doing what it is doing now, only better — through a spectacular wine program, a stellar wait staff, an excellent chef and high-quality food. "People will simply continue to come to the restaurant, and Farallon will become part of the patchwork fabric of San Francisco. Even 20 years from now, we will be considered a 'new classic,'" Kuleto concludes. ∎

Fireman's Fund

One of the top 20 property casualty insurers in the country, Fireman's Fund Insurance Co. bears a name steeped in true San Francisco tradition. Its name originated in 1863, during the days when it donated 10 percent of its profits to a fund that benefited the widows and orphans of San Francisco volunteer firefighters.

When the great 1906 San Francisco earthquake and fire destroyed the company's headquarters and all its records, this resilient young organization survived by providing all claimants with settlements of half cash and half stock. Within five years, that stock was worth considerably more than the cash owed on the original claim.

Today, Fireman's Fund is nationally respected as a dynamic customer-oriented company serving a wide range of personal and business insurance needs. Fireman's Fund also enjoys top marks from independent financial-rating organizations — A.M. Best Co., Standard & Poor's and Moody's — for its financial position, capacity, stability and ability to pay claims. Contributing to that stability are annual gross premiums written that exceed $4 billion and total assets of nearly $13.5 billion.

A significant part of the Fund's business is home owner and auto policies, but it also provides coverage for those with expensive homes requiring very high limits who may need to protect fine art or expensive collectibles. Fireman's Fund has developed special insurance coverage for professionals and entrepreneurs, offering policies that can extend to home offices, as well as to professional liability. The company is also known for its unique Private Event Cancellation Insurance, which can cover loss from canceling or postponing private parties and receptions such as weddings, retirements or bar and bat mitzvahs.

As for business coverage, Fireman's Fund is one of the top underwriters of "package" insurance policies, a concept the fund pioneered in the early 1960s, which allows companies to consolidate a broad range of diverse coverage choices into a single policy. Fireman's Fund packages have protected some of the most recognized institutions in America, such as Sunkist Growers, YMCA, See's Candies and the San Diego Wild Animal Park.

Fireman's Fund also dominates the highly specialized world of motion-picture insurance. Beginning in the era of the Silent Screen, the Fund covered props and sets and, over the years, developed so many film coverages that its entertainment packages have become the most desired policies in Hollywood. Take any week's top five major box-office films and, chances are, Fireman's Fund will have insured at least one of those blockbusters.

Another special Fund niche is ocean marine, a coverage the company has been underwriting ever since it insured schooners which brought goods around the Horn back in the late 1800s — an enterprise that turned the rough-and-tumble post–Gold Rush town of San Francisco into a refined international port city and a commercial center.

Fireman's Fund was founded in 1863 by a retired sea captain. The Fund has consistently been a leader in the marine industry and recently added to its luster in this area by purchasing Wm. H. McGee & Co., one of the top ocean marine cargo insurers in the country.

Another of the founding fathers was a hay-and-grain merchant, so it is no surprise that insurance for farm operations was an early expertise. Pioneering crop-hail insurance in the 1870s, the company recently unveiled a global satellite positioning system to help growers map their fields — without charge if they buy fund policies. That mapping service is especially important to the many vintners in the world-famous Napa and Sonoma valleys. Fireman's Fund agribusiness is also a national leader in coverage for farmers and growers who need to insure business property and standing crops in the field.

The Fund covers small business, as well. In recent years, it has developed ABC (American Business Coverage). In fact, Fireman's Fund

"As communications technologies shrink the world to the size of a desktop terminal, Fireman's Fund will be there with coverage from every avenue of business advancement."

has the flexibility of growing with small companies until they qualify for larger business-portfolio packages and can even help if the customer develops the need and capability — as many do these days — to offer its wares internationally. That's possible because Fireman's Fund is a subsidiary of Allianz AG of Munich, one of the top five insurers in the world.

"Besides serving as a backdrop for our colorful history, San Francisco is a vibrant part of the Fireman's Fund future because so many of the city's businesses are now extending their reach into the global marketplace — a strategy that perfectly tracks with our new international business-coverage policies," says David Kliman, vice president of corporate communications for Fireman's Fund. "As communications technologies shrink the world to the size of a desktop terminal, Fireman's Fund will be there with coverage from every avenue of business advancement."

Now based just 25 miles north of San Francisco, the Fireman's Fund headquarters campus is set in the quiet rolling hills of Marin County, where the 8,700-person company directs national operations across all 50 states. The site is also home to the company's large information-technology unit. In 1998, the Fund launched the first wave of development against an aggressive five-year, $150 million plan to support agents and customers with streamlined processing, reduced long-term operating costs and innovative systems capabilities.

Giving something back to the community that has supported it during the years is an important part of the Fireman's Fund ethic. That's why the Fireman's Fund Foundation, the company's charitable arm, has contributed more than $30 million to fund projects that support education, human needs and community activities. Similarly, Fireman's Fund encourages participation by employees who volunteer personal time and effort to benefit agencies that help make a better community. ■

First Security Van Kasper

First Security Van Kasper prides itself on relationships, not transactions. That philosophy has paid off handsomely, putting the company in the forefront of San Francisco investment banking and private brokerage firms.

"We provide high-level, personalized service and advice to individuals, businesses and institutions," says the company's president, F. Van Kasper, who founded Van Kasper & Co. with Steve Adams, Hugh Gordon, Joaquin Horton and Jim O'Connor in 1978. Van Kasper was acquired by Salt Lake City-based First Security Corporation in 1999.

"We have a high sense of commitment to our clients, many of whom have been with us since the beginning. We see ourselves as a company that builds wealth through integrity, honesty and respect," Kasper adds.

What started as a six-person firm has blossomed into 275 employees throughout California, with nine offices providing investment-banking, investment-management and brokerage services to more than 25,000 individual and institutional clients.

At its inception, Van Kasper & Co. focused on individual portfolio management, offering advice on individual securities, mutual funds, annuities and unit investment trusts, and emphasizing companies with solid fundamentals that were often overlooked by Wall Street. Backed by solid, bottom-up research, the company created an index that has outperformed the market during its 18-year record.

"We provide high-level, personalized service and advice to individuals, businesses and institutions."

By the mid 1980s, Van Kasper was drawn into corporate services by its clients, helping to bring companies public and offering cash-management and other advisory services. Since 1987, the firm has expanded its services to provide specialized research, sales and trading expertise to support institutional and capital markets.

Today, First Security Van Kasper is assisting aging baby boomers who require investment, insurance, credit and trust fiduciary services, along with financial, tax and estate planning. The company also is committed to offering, on a relationship basis, innovative investment-banking services to emerging growth companies.

Kasper, a Bay Area native, says he is as "San Franciscan as you can get. We are lucky to live and do business in the worldwide center of technology. We are literally in the midst of a revolutionary change, as important as the industrialization of the nation. This is the longest extended period of economic prosperity ever, driven by productivity, growth demographics and favorable policies, but at the heart of it all is education."

Kasper is a strong advocate of education, "the foundation of our social and economic future." For that reason, Kasper's firm has sponsored the Stock Market game in schools around he country, putting students' investment skills to the test and awarding them for their successes. His interest in education also has led him to serve on the boards of the UCSF Foundation and the Exploratorium.

First Security Van Kasper is positioned to expand its services into new marketplaces in the West and to a broader group of clients, including more of corporate Middle America (companies with less than $2 billion in market capitalization). Staying with the wave of technology, the company is accessing its high-net-worth clients and delivering more and more of its services via the Internet.

"Access and information for our clients must be available easily and in the way of their choosing," Kasper says. "We are here to interpret, guide and advise them along the way." ∎

S an Francisco is more than a home to Gap Inc.: it's also one of its most important retail markets. Through the heart of the city's downtown, within walking distance for both locals and tourists, are flagship stores for the company's three brands: Gap, Banana Republic and Old Navy.

Hop off a cable car at the foot of Powell Street near Market, for example, and you're at the entrance to Gap. Housed in a building that withstood the devastating 1906 earthquake, Gap's flagship store offers nearly 24,000 square feet of open, clean selling space of Gap, GapKids and babyGap apparel and personal care. The store features larger-than-life video screens which flank the entrance and run continuous Gap TV ads and brand images. Further inside the store, videos from London, Berlin, Tokyo and Paris stores showcase Gap's presence as a global retailing force. Founded on Ocean Avenue in 1969, today the brand operates more than 3,000 stores in six countries.

A short walk from Gap takes you to the corner of Grant and Sutter streets and Banana Republic's flagship housed in the venerable White House building, one of San Francisco's most noted landmarks. Built in 1908 by renowned architect Albert Pissis, the beautifully remodeled store contains 21,000 square feet of selling space offering modern, versatile clothing and home accessories. Founded in the San Francisco

Banana Republic, Grant Street store

Bay Area in 1978 and acquired by Gap Inc. in 1983, when it was a two-store, mail-order business, Banana Republic now operates more than 300 stores in the United States and Canada. The Banana Republic Catalog and the e-commerce site for U.S. customers extend the brand's reach directly into customers' homes.

Head over to the corner of Fourth and Market, and you'll find the company's newest San Francisco flagship — Old Navy. At 102,000 square feet, the four-level store is the largest Old Navy in the nation and features a DJ booth, mechanical mannequins and a 61-seat Torpedo Joe's restaurant. Offering value-priced fashion in a fun shopping environment, the brand was established in 1994 and offers great clothes at great prices for adults, kids and baby at nearly 500 stores in the United States. Old Navy's entertaining ads, energetic store environments and Item of the Week have made the brand one of the fastest growing in retailing history.

> For more than 30 years, Gap Inc. has been an integral part of San Francisco and the local retail industry.

For more than 30 years, Gap Inc. has been an integral part of San Francisco and the local retail industry. But today — with stores in the United States, Canada, France, Germany, Japan and the United Kingdom, as well as online shopping at gap.com, BananaRepublic.com and oldnavy.com — you don't have to travel to San Francisco; you can shop the company's stores from virtually anywhere. ■

Old Navy on Fourth and Market

Ghirardelli

This history caught the eye of food executive John J. Anton in 1992. "The strongest attraction was the existence of a brand that had a strong reputation for quality and a product awareness that was much larger than the size of the business," says Anton, Ghirardelli's new president and chief executive officer.

Under his leadership, the company has expanded its line of baking chocolate and cocoas, now sold in 90 percent of the nation's supermarkets. Specialty chocolates sold in department stores and a broad array of premium chocolate confections have been added to the line. Most recently, the company has opened a select number of "old-fashioned soda fountains and chocolate shops" in other tourist markets, including Chicago's Michigan Avenue, Orlando's Disney World, San Diego's Gaslamp District, Miami's South Beach, Kalakaua Avenue in Honolulu and Robson Street in Vancouver.

These efforts have been rewarded with a 20 percent growth in sales every year since 1992 — growth unprecedented in the company's history — making Ghirardelli the fastest-growing chocolate company in America. "Everyone here has taken a great deal of pride in that," Anton says.

In 1998, Lindt and Sprüngli, a Swiss chocolate maker only a handful of years older than Ghirardelli, acquired the company.

The Ghirardelli Chocolate Company has been a rich part of San Francisco's history since 1852. For more than 110 years, successive generations of the Ghirardelli family built a significant local following for their premium chocolates. Recently, new management has turned the company into an international success its founder never envisioned.

Domingo Ghirardelli began making chocolate here in 1852, using skills he brought from his native Italy. A year after Domingo retired in 1892, his sons moved the factory to the old Pioneer Woolen Mills on North Point, a site that would make the Ghirardelli name world-famous. Over the years, new structures were added to the complex and, by 1923, 15-foot-high illuminated letters spelling *Ghirardelli* welcomed anyone arriving by ship through the Golden Gate.

In the early 1960s, Domingo's descendants sold the chocolate-making business and the factory property overlooking San Francisco Bay. Because the Ghirardelli sign was so closely associated with the site, the buyers who turned the old factory buildings into a specialty shopping center kept the name, as well as the Victorian architecture.

Today, Ghirardelli Square is a national historic site and a must-see attraction for tourists from around the world. For decades now, visitors have stopped by Ghirardelli's Old-Fashioned Soda Fountain and Chocolate Shop to sample the world-famous hot-fudge sundae and — most crucially — take some chocolate home for family and friends, a gift that symbolizes the excitement of San Francisco.

Recently, new management has turned the company into an international success its founder never envisioned.

Blessed by the highly motivated staff and an owner with a deep knowledge and love of the chocolate business, the company's rapid growth will continue, Anton believes. "As caretakers of this national treasure, our job is to leave it in much better shape than we got it," he says. "I think we're doing that." ∎

Grubb & Ellis

W hat started in 1958 as primarily a transaction-focused brokerage firm, with one office in Northern California, has transformed itself into what is today a global, full-service provider of real-estate services. Grubb & Ellis Company is one of the nation's largest publicly traded commercial real-estate companies, with 4,400 professionals and staff, and offices and affiliates in 90 markets.

While serving international clients through offices in London and Brussels, the firm addresses the needs of its San Francisco clients through its California Street office in San Francisco, which Daniel Cressman, managing director, says has the right combination — natural beauty and talented people with good ideas and creative energy — for a city positioned to prosper in the new century. "There is no better place on the globe to live or do business than San Francisco," Cressman says. Some of the company's San Francisco clients include Levi Strauss & Co., Del Monte, Chevron and AirTouch Communications.

Though transaction services — the leasing, acquisition and disposition of commercial real estate — are the firm's historic strength, Grubb & Ellis also provides management, financial and strategic services. "To succeed long term, we believe Grubb & Ellis must continue to encourage its professionals to adopt a consultative rather than a transactional approach to real estate," says Cressman, who is responsible for directing his office in the completion of more than $1 billion in sale and lease transactions in the downtown San Francisco commercial property market.

To achieve this goal, Grubb & Ellis has integrated its transaction and management-services operations to promote teamwork and establish a consistent standard of professionalism in its marketplaces. Through its management services subsidiary, which offers property, facilities, asset and construction/project management, engineering services and lease administration, Grubb & Ellis manages approximately 125 million square feet of commercial real estate nationwide.

Daniel Cressman, managing director

"In a world driven by deals, we're a company driven by values."

Its sophisticated financial services encompass mortgage brokerage, investment analysis and appraisals, while strategic services include site selection, feasibility studies, market forecasts and research.

Grubb & Ellis takes client service seriously. Its innovative national-accounts management system unites senior-level real-estate professionals and their clients to formulate strategies supporting overall business objectives and then direct clients to appropriate local service-team members.

In addition, Grubb & Ellis takes advantage of an international, proprietary intranet that contains professional biographies and confidential access to client information and enables company professionals to exchange and share resources and information on a business-to-business basis.

High-technology and Internet-related companies are now fueling the commercial real-estate market in San Francisco. "As the city experiences a digital renaissance, it is creating a new business prototype for the rest of the world to adopt in the early years of the new century," Cressman says, "and we have an opportunity to be the leaders and participate in that global business revolution." According to Cressman, as the new millennium begins, rapid growth by new media and Internet-related companies have pulled vacancies down to the low single digits throughout the entire San Francisco office market.

The San Francisco office of Grubb & Ellis has attained its tremendous success because "in a world driven by deals, we're a company driven by values," Cressman says. ∎

Guittard Chocolate

More than a century ago, when Guittard Chocolate was located on prestigious Sansome Street in downtown San Francisco, its founder, Etienne Guittard, would walk over to the waterfront to meet ships bringing his goods to the city. Like other merchants of the day, he would set up shop right there, selling his wares to eager customers as they were unloaded.

Today, his great-grandson, Gary Guittard, no longer meets the ships that provide supplies for the family's chocolate factory, but he still believes that personal contact with his customers and personalized service to meet their needs are essential to his business. One of the few chocolate makers left in the United States, Guittard Chocolate is the "last little guy" left in the industry, Guittard says. The company stays in business by virtue of its service and its ever-increasing quality.

The quality of the chocolate — made using very rare cocoa beans from around the world — has been important to the business since Etienne arrived in San Francisco looking for gold and found that the chocolate he'd brought from the family company in France was a more reliable source of wealth. In 1868, he established E. Guittard & Co., selling coffee, tea and spices, as well as chocolate products. When the founder died in 1899, his son, Horace C. Guittard, ran the company for the next 50 years, moving to Main Street after the original building burned in the 1906 earthquake. In 1950, his son, Horace A., took the reins. When the Embarcadero Freeway was erected in 1954, he moved the factory to its present location in Burlingame.

The fourth generation to head the company, Gary has been president since 1989. Acting on his father's advice, he first gained experience in advertising, food brokering and bakery supply. While one member of each generation is selected to lead the company, all the Guittards are involved. "We've always put the money back into the company," Guittard says. "Everybody in the family has made that commitment."

Guittard selects, blends, roasts and grinds its own cocoa beans.

Thus, while Guittard Chocolate has passed from father to son over the years, attention to quality has remained at the core of its business plan. Unlike some other chocolate makers, Guittard selects, blends, roasts and grinds its own cocoa beans. Every lot is tested to ensure it meets the company's standards, and samples from production runs are taste-tested by a six-member panel including top management and family members.

One result is chocolate with an "Old World flavor." Another is international recognition for Guittard Chocolate, a regular recipient of gold medals awarded by the International Institute for Quality Selections in Brussels, Belgium. Guittard products are used by a wide range of clients who prepare food with chocolate, from small but elite San Francisco restaurants to national brands such as See's, Starbuck's and Dreyer's. ■

For more than 100 years, The Hamlin School has been turning San Francisco's girls into young women prepared to face the academic, professional and personal challenges in their future. Three women had particularly important roles in making this happen.

The first is founder Sarah Dix Hamlin, who bought an existing school in 1896 and indelibly branded it with her philosophy about educating young women. Her father once found the young Miss Hamlin at a neighborhood store, sitting with a half-dozen men discussing presidential politics — and impressing them. She was one of the first women to graduate from the University of Michigan at Ann Arbor.

Hamlin set similarly high intellectual goals for her students, turning what had been a finishing school for girls into one of the leading college-preparatory schools in the West.

The second major contributor was Cornelia McKinne Stanwood, a University of California graduate who headed Hamlin for nearly two decades. Seeing that the school needed room to grow, Stanwood bought the historic building at 2120 Broadway that now bears her name. Built in 1900 for James Leary Flood, son of the Nevada silver king, with a design by Julius E. Krafft, the mansion was constructed so solidly that in the 1906 earthquake, the only reported damage it suffered was caused by a vase of flowers falling off a piano.

After a year-long study of women in history, the fourth graders celebrate at the Famous American Women's Tea.

> For more than 100 years, The Hamlin School has been turning San Francisco's girls into young women prepared to face the academic, professional and personal challenges in their future.

And the third key figure was Arlene Hogan, a woman devoted to the cause of single-sex education, who revitalized Hamlin and brought its excellence to the attention of the San Francisco community. "There were wonderful things happening" when she arrived at Hamlin in 1984, Hogan recalled in an interview for the school's history: "Students were receiving a top-notch education, but the community wasn't aware of it." Hogan quickly remedied that problem, promoting the importance of Hamlin's all-girl environment as a place where young women could fully develop both their talents and character.

Hamlin has changed over the years, from a boarding school for 12 grades to a day school for kindergarten through eighth grade. With a flexible mission — "to educate girls and young women to meet the challenges of their times" — its curriculum has also evolved with the times. In the 1940s, a strong athletic program developed. The Jennie May Hooker Science Laboratory was opened in 1970, and a course in environmental science was added. More recently, the entire curriculum has been updated to facilitate computer literacy and Internet access to information.

Intellectual rigor has always been a high value, and the present head of school, Coreen Hester, sees the Hamlin girl as "a tenacious problem-solver." Being in a single-sex environment, she believes, "helps a girl to have a broader definition of who she is, providing a constellation of opportunities, from athletic hero to student leader to class artist."

Whatever their choice, girls are encouraged "to find the best in themselves and to contribute with energy and distinction to the world around them." ∎

Middle School tie drop in Stanwood Hall. Here, eighth graders drop their ties to the incoming eighth graders standing below.

Frank A. Bennack Jr., president and chief executive officer

The Hearst Corp.

The Hearst Corporation traces its origins to March 4, 1887, the day young William Randolph Hearst placed his name on the masthead of the *San Francisco Examiner* as "Proprietor." On that day, he began a career that would forever change the definition of American journalism.

The *Examiner* had been owned by Mr. Hearst's father, George, a wealthy rancher and miner who was more interested in politics than newspaper publishing. After George Hearst was elected a US senator from California in 1886, he reluctantly turned the newspaper over to his 23-year-old son.

The younger Mr. Hearst, functioning as both editor and publisher, quickly transformed the sedate, unprofitable *Examiner* into "The Monarch of the Dailies." He purchased advanced printing equipment, revised the newspaper's appearance, hired the best journalists he could find, and invigorated the paper with energetic, exciting news stories. Within a few years, the new *Examiner* was an unqualified success.

In 1895, Mr. Hearst purchased a second newspaper, the *New York Journal*, and laid the foundation for one of the legendary American newspaper dynasties. By the 1920s, he owned a nationwide chain of newspapers. Hardly a big city in America was untouched by the inventive, dynamic brand of Hearst journalism. His newspapers pioneered many innovations: multiple-color presses, the first halftone photographs on newsprint, the first color comic sections and the wire syndication of news copy.

Today, in addition to its long history publishing the *San Francisco Examiner*, Hearst Newspapers publishes the *San Francisco Chronicle* through a 1999 purchase agreement, as well as 11 other daily newspapers, including the *Albany Times Union*, the *Houston Chronicle*, the *San Antonio Express-News* and the *Seattle Post-Intelligencer*.

The modern Hearst Corporation comprises five additional operating groups that are involved in every type of media existing at the beginning of the 21st century: Hearst Magazines, Hearst-Argyle Television, Hearst Entertainment & Syndication, Hearst Interactive Media and Hearst Business Media.

Inspired by his 1903 honeymoon trip across Europe by automobile, William Randolph Hearst came home to found *Motor* magazine, the modest beginnings of Hearst Magazines. During the next 10 years, he acquired several popular consumer titles of the day. The first, in 1905, was *Cosmopolitan*, then a popular fiction monthly. *Cosmopolitan* is now the pre-eminent young women's magazine worldwide. International editions of the magazine spread the "Fun Fearless Female" ideal, making *Cosmopolitan* the largest magazine franchise of its kind in the world.

In 1911, Mr. Hearst acquired *Good Housekeeping*, which is today America's leading women's service magazine. The world-famous *Good Housekeeping* Institute, which reviews advertising and helps provide editorial content for the magazine, is a publishing-industry legend.

Hearst Magazines is now the world's largest publisher of monthly magazines. Current Hearst titles, in addition to those mentioned above, include *Classic American Homes*, *CosmoGIRL!*, *Country Living*, *Country Living Gardener*, *Esquire*, *Harper's BAZAAR*, *House Beautiful*, *Marie Claire* (with Marie Claire Album), *Popular Mechanics*, *Redbook*, *SmartMoney* (with Dow Jones), *Talk* (with Miramax Films), *Town & Country* and *Victoria*. International editions are distributed in more than 100 countries.

William Randolph Hearst's interest in communications extended beyond the printed word. He began acquiring radio stations in the 1920s, and in 1948 he became the owner of one of the first television stations in the country, WBAL-TV in Baltimore.

By 1997, Hearst had joined the leading ranks of group television broadcasters with the formation of Hearst-Argyle Television, a public corporation. Hearst-

The San Francisco Examiner Building, Third and Market streets circa 1940

William Randolph Hearst, circa 1930

William Randolph Hearst's legacy, The Hearst Corporation, is today one of the largest diversified communications companies in the world, including more than 100 separate businesses.

Argyle Television (NYSE: HTV) is the nation's second-largest non-network-owned television station group. The privately held Hearst Corporation is the majority shareholder of Hearst-Argyle, which owns or manages 26 TV stations in such markets as Boston, Tampa, Pittsburgh, Sacramento and Baltimore. Hearst-Argyle Television Productions produces the nationally syndicated series *Rebecca's Garden*.

In 1989, Hearst Entertainment & Syndication was formed to combine the company's cable, syndication and other entertainment operations. Hearst's cable interests include A&E Networks, Lifetime Television, ESPN and New England Cable News. Hearst Entertainment is a leading producer of TV series, specials and miniseries. King Features Syndicate, created in 1915, is now the world's largest distributor of comics and text features, including *Blondie*, *Beetle Bailey*, *Hagar the Horrible* and *Hints From Heloise*.

In 1993, Hearst Interactive Media was created to manage the company's growing interests in digital media. Its ventures include Women.com Networks, a partnership with Women.com, the leader in reaching women on the Web. In 1994, the company opened the Hearst Interactive Studio at the corporation's New York City headquarters to facilitate the creation of digital products and services. Hearst also holds interests in several Internet-based companies.

In 1980, The Hearst Corporation acquired a group of business publications and manuals covering such varied fields as automobile pricing and floor covering. Today, Hearst Business Media, formed in 1999, produces a wide variety of publications, books, databases and catalogs serving the professional interests of several industries. Units in this group include: *First DataBank*, a premier supplier of pharmaceutical and drug-interaction information; *Diversion*, a leisure publication for physicians; *Electronic Products* magazine; and *Floor Covering Weekly*. *Motor* magazine, now published for auto-service professionals, is part of this group.

William Randolph Hearst died in 1951, at age 88. Richard E. Berlin succeeded him as president and chief executive officer. Berlin was instrumental in consolidating the basic underlying strengths of The Hearst Corporation. Frank Massi, a longtime Hearst financial officer, served as president from 1973 to 1975, playing a leading role in com-

pleting a financial reorganization that helped the company launch an expansion program in the late 1970s. John R. Miller, one of publishing's most respected executives during his 40-year career, was Hearst president and chief executive officer from 1975 to 1979.

Frank A. Bennack, Jr., Hearst president and chief executive officer since 1979, has provided vigorous and imaginative leadership in implementing the growth strategy he developed with Miller while serving as executive vice president. Under Bennack's leadership, The Hearst Corporation has substantially diversified and expanded its operations nearly seven-fold.

"William Randolph Hearst's legacy, The Hearst Corporation, is today one of the largest diversified communications companies in the world, including more than 100 separate businesses," Bennack says. "Each day, more than 16,000 employees help to inform, educate, entertain and inspire millions of readers, viewers and listeners in virtually every area of communications. Although the company has grown dramatically in recent years, the principle on which it was founded remains the same — a commitment to excellence." ■

Host Marriott Services

Boarding a flight at San Francisco International Airport, circa 1954

Host Marriott Services first left its imprint on San Francisco a half-century ago. The more-than-100-year-old company is headquartered in Bethesda, Md., but has a foot squarely planted in San Francisco with an array of food concessions at the city's international airport.

As a leading food, beverage and retail concessionaire at about 200 travel and entertainment venues, Host Marriott Services has one of the world's largest brand portfolios, with more than 100 international brands, regional favorites and proprietary concepts.

Originally called the Van Noy Railway News & Hotel Co., Host Marriott Services began in 1897, opening a store to provide food, beverages and general merchandise to train travelers. It expanded from train concessions to steamships, installing gift shops on famous lines such as American President, and to restaurants, department-store luncheonettes and hotel gift shops, eventually leading the way to acquiring the Beverly Hills Hotel in 1928. Host Marriott Services celebrated its entry into the airport concession business when it contracted with San Francisco International Airport (SFO) in 1954.

SFO started with an International Room and Cocktail Lounge, Coffee Shop, Mayan Cocktail Lounge, The Hut Cocktail Bar, two snack bars,

"We are a service company, anticipating and serving the needs of our customers — people away from home."

an employee cafeteria, a Pancake Palace dining room, an in-flight kitchen, a commissary, a toiletries/sundries store and TWA's Ambassador Club — concessions representing a $1 million contract at the new $14 million airport terminal building 45 years ago.

In addition to national brands, Host Marriott Services develops regional brands to provide local flavor to its travel and entertainment environments. Today, SFO is home to Crab Pot Restaurant, Crab Pot Brew Pub, North Beach Deli, Boudin's, Noah's Bagels, Jamba Juice, Starbucks, Peet's Coffee, Max's Deli, Sanraku and Pizza Hut. The company currently operates 28 food-and-beverage facilities and seven retail shops at SFO, employing 700 people.

"The company has revolutionized dining at SFO, but strives to keep it simple by serving hot food hot and cold food cold in a speedy manner," says Johnny Chiu, vice president of operations for Host Marriott Services, Western Region. "We are a service company, anticipating and serving the needs of our customers — people away from home."

Besides San Francisco, Host Marriott Services has concessions in more than 70 airport locations — 18 of the 20 largest US airports — as well as in travel and entertainment sites in eight countries worldwide, including Australia, New Zealand, Canada, the Netherlands and the People's Republic of China. It also provides its services at travel plazas near more than 90 toll-road and turnpike locations and through food courts at retail malls, from Texas to Florida to New Jersey.

Host Marriott Services, with approximately 26,000 employees, has been ranked by *Fortune* magazine as one of the top five most admired food-service companies in its annual survey.

Host International was acquired by Marriott in 1982, spun off as Host Marriott Corp. in 1993, and re-emerged as a separate, publicly traded travel and entertainment company, Host Marriott Services, in 1995. During the summer of 1999, the company announced its merger with Autogrill Spa Co., Europe's largest provider of restaurant services to travelers. ∎

When Thomas A. Hughes arrived in San Francisco in 1850, it was not as a mining prospector. Unlike most of the thousands of other immigrants, he saw there was gold to be made in providing the goods and services needed by Northern California's burgeoning population. So Hughes became a customs appraiser, starting a firm that eventually became the customhouse brokerage and freight-forwarding firm that is today's Hoyt Shepston.

Hughes' move was shrewd. As California's population surged, most souls headed for the Mother Lode. Few goods were being produced here; almost everything had to be imported by sea. By 1851, San Francisco had become the fourth-largest port in the United States with respect to the value of its foreign trade. By the mid-1850s, 1,250 ships made port in San Francisco every year, carrying more than 550,000 tons of cargo.

In the early days, the firm, which was headquartered in the Merchant's Exchange on Battery Street, opposite the old U.S. Customhouse and Post Office, oversaw shipments of silks and perfumes, furniture and rugs, and coffee, foods and wines, which were brought in by steamship and forwarded to their final destinations by horse and buggy. The tools of the trade were quill pen and ink and rudimentary telegraph. At one point, the firm owned a fleet that carried lumber from Oregon, Washington and the north coast of California as well as cargo from China, Australia and South America. Today the ships are gone and the commodities handled by Hoyt Shepston include everything from chemicals, semiconductors and high-tech medical devices to sailplanes, all tracked by computers and satellite communications.

Over the years, the firm has altered its name too. Early on, Hughes and Hunter decided that employees would be allowed to buy in and succeed the active management. As a result, the company changed

By the mid-1850s, 1,250 ships made port in San Francisco every year carrying more than 550,000 tons of cargo.

names several times as new managing partners took over its operations. In 1919 it became Hoyt, Shepston & Sciaroni, the name under which it was incorporated in 1960. Since then it has operated under the simplified name of Hoyt Shepston (dba). Through it all, the company has missed only a few days of business — immediately after the 1906 earthquake and fire.

Regardless of the changes, Hoyt Shepston's goal has remained the same: to provide efficient customhouse and freight forwarding services. The company offers services in three main areas: ocean freight, air freight and customs brokerage. Hoyt Shepston's specialized professionals handle all import and export regulations, documentation and licensing, seek the most competitive freight rates, and plan and manage every phase of shipment, including containerization, insurance and customs entry and clearance. Today, with California ranked the eighth-largest "nation" in the world as a trading entity, Hoyt Shepston remains a leader in the field. ■

Kent Hudson, chair and CEO

Indus International

San Francisco-based Indus International is the leading global supplier of Enterprise Asset Management (EAM) software and services solutions that meet the asset management demands of complex industries such as energy, telecommunications, process manufacturing and the public sector. Using Indus best-of-breed solutions enables businesses to gain competitive advantage by reducing costs, increasing productive capacity, ensuring regulatory compliance and improving return on investment. Consistent with its 20-year heritage of leadership, Indus will help its clients and partners capitalize on emerging business opportunities in the new millennium through innovations such as my*indus*.com, an innovative Web portal that will reconfigure the way key industry segments do business.

"Indus offers best-of-breed EAM software, services and support that will help companies prosper and become more competitive in the digital economy," says Kent Hudson, chair and CEO. "By capitalizing on the advantages of Internet technologies, Indus offerings such as my*indus*.com increase our clients' ability to make informed business decisions that are more cost-effective, timely and flexible than ever before."

Ultimately, 300,000 Indus clients in more than 40 countries will be able to meet at my*indus*.com, an innovative Web portal that offers a range of services for companies that need expert advice and information about the EAM market. This site gives companies direct, instant access to the software and consulting services that have made Indus the leader in its field.

Indus' my*indus*.com e-business initiative leverages the core competencies, premier client base and valued partner relationships Indus built by delivering offerings such as the Indus Solution Series. The Indus Solution Series is a complete EAM solution that captures and analyzes critical information within complex industries, supporting the expert consultants who provide advice on systems and implementation. Through the strength of the Indus Solution Series, Indus ranks as the largest single player in EAM, controlling about 20 percent global market share.

"Indus is the global leader in the EAM market, with a stronghold in industries such as energy, communications, transportation, manufacturing and the public sector," Hudson says. In the Bay Area, companies as diverse in style and product as Chevron and Genentech rely on Indus to help streamline their maintenance activities, cut costs and avoid shutdowns.

For Indus clients worldwide, my*indus*.com will become a port of entry to the Internet's universe of information related to asset management, focused on best-of-breed EAM solution offerings, business-to-business, e-commerce and EAM-hosted applications. Extending well beyond the role of Web server, my*indus*.com will help customers find the single drop of information, in a sea of data, which provides the answer they need.

In addition to its role as a reference site, my*indus*.com will provide a discussion forum for companies in the same industry that face similar challenges and issues. With its global client base and extensive experience in complex, capital-intensive industries, Indus is in a position to define and disseminate "best practices." The my*indus*.com site will enhance this process by enabling exchange of information and a trading exchange where clients can shop for materials and get help in an emergency. Ultimately, my*indus*.com will evolve into a one-stop information hub for maintenance professionals.

"In a time when choices and decisions must be made in shorter and shorter timeframes, immediate access to information is key," Hudson says. "To stay competitive, people need the kind of advanced support we offer, to sift through information quickly and ensure their decisions are as informed as possible."

By facilitating communication between companies in similar industries, Indus is promoting values it believes are essential to success in the new millennium: partnership and collaboration. In an increasingly complicated world, where global companies face global problems, no single company can provide all the answers.

"To be competitive and provide the best solutions, you need to have partners with expertise in different pieces of the solution," Hudson says. Indus has strong relationships with leaders who are shaping the future of information technology and e-business, ranging from Ariba, Commerce One, Oracle, PeopleSoft, IBM and Hewlett-Packard to Microsoft and PricewaterhouseCoopers.

Collaboration was key to a groundbreaking partnership Indus signed in 1999 with British Energy, Britain's biggest electric-power generator. The $60 million, three-year agreement was the biggest single contract in the history of EAM. It is unique in that Indus' success in landing the contract is tied to the way Indus and British Energy will work together: not as client and vendor, but as full partners. Rather than defining separate roles for each party, Indus and British Energy will take joint responsibility for defining best practices, implementing solutions, improving business processes and educating users. The Indus Solution Series is the foundation for the work, but it is the commitment to collaborate closely with British Energy that cemented this important win, setting Indus apart from its competitors.

Contracts such as the one with British Energy make Indus one of the Bay Area's 150 fastest-growing companies, according to the *San Francis-*

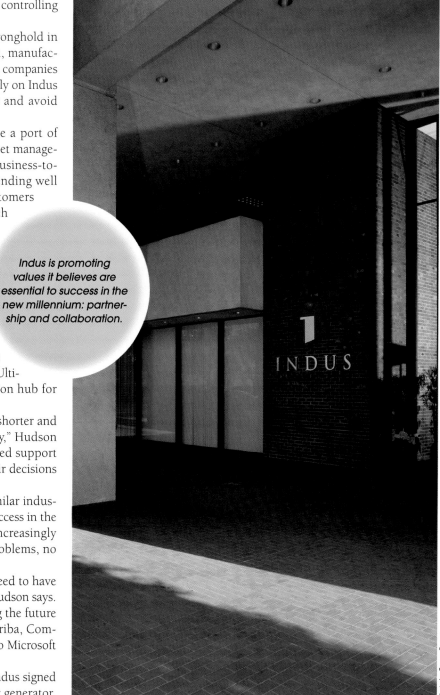

Indus is promoting values it believes are essential to success in the new millennium: partnership and collaboration.

Photo by Susan Spann

co Business Times. With roots in San Francisco dating back to 1988, the company was formed in 1997 through a merger between the Indus Group Inc. and TSW International Inc. Expanding its global reach with offices in Atlanta, Pittsburgh, Dallas, Canada, the United Kingdom, France, Argentina, Abu Dhabi and Australia, Indus will remain headquartered in San Francisco.

"San Francisco's strong international ties make it an excellent global base for our business," Hudson says. "San Francisco is known for its extraordinary local hi-tech talent pool, and its cultural and ethnic diversity, making it an ideal place for a global company that does business in so many different cultural environments." ■

iSyndicate

one point, space was so tight in the company's converted loft by the Embarcadero that Maske moved his office into a bathroom. "It was very convenient," Maske quips. "Anyone who came to see me could just pull up the edge of the tub next to my desk and sit down. And the tub itself offered a great filing system."

Now that the firm is located in more spacious quarters at 455 Ninth St. (at Bryant), Maske works from a more conventional office. iSyndicate employees appreciate having more elbow room, but at first missed being close to their favorite haunt, Red's Java House. This problem was solved when the company purchased a 1978 Volkswagen bus (now painted in iSyndicate's colors) to ferry them back and forth.

Keeping employees happy plays an important role in iSyndicate's plans for the future. "The competition for talent is intense," Maske admits. "But we've built the company on some guiding principals that have helped us attract employees with real intellectual horsepower. First and foremost, we're building a company that is built to last. We value our start-up culture, but we are not going to flame out or be sold, like so many other start-ups.

In 1994, Joel Maske, now president and CEO of iSyndicate, was launching his first Internet startup, a personal finance site. To build an audience, he wanted to post up-to-date stock quotes and news, but to do so was a frustrating and time-consuming task.

"I was faced with the prospect of contacting a variety of sources to get the latest news — over and over and over again," Maske recalls. "I kept thinking, 'Wouldn't it be nice if I could just go to a company that provided this kind of information for me?'"

In 1996, iSyndicate became that company. Founded by Maske and Allison Hartsoe after Intuit (makers of software package Quicken) acquired Maske's first venture, iSyndicate filled the need created by the rapidly expanding Web for timely intelligence.

iSyndicate now boasts syndication of more than 700 sources of information (including Reuters NewMedia, *Time*, *Salon*, CNET, The Associated Press, *Rolling Stone* and CBS SportsLine) and distribution to a network of more than 175,000 websites (including Xoom.com, Citibank, Netscape, PeopleSoft, Nintendo, Nortel and NationsBank). The firm currently employs more than 90 people in its San Francisco headquarters with a sales branch office in New York City.

This rapid expansion has not been without growing pains, though the firm's almost infinitely scalable technology has easily supported the boom in business. A more difficult challenge was accommodating the firm's growing head count in San Francisco's hot real-estate market. At

"In the future, all media will come to rely on information coming off the Net, and iSyndicate will be there to provide it."

"And we have a vision," Maske continues. "That's to become the pre-eminent content and media provider on the Web — and for society. I believe that, in the future, all media — newspapers, magazines, TV — will come to rely on information coming off the Net, and iSyndicate will be there to provide it." ∎

D uring the height of the Gold Rush, August Helbing and a group of fellow Jewish pioneers from Bavaria banded together to meet the needs of their fledgling community. The result was the Eureka Benevolent Society, the first charitable organization west of the Mississippi, founded to care for the poor and the sick. Eureka eventually merged with the Pacific Hebrew Orphan Asylum and its successor, Homewood Terrace, becoming today's Jewish Family and Children's Services (JFCS) of San Francisco, the Peninsula, Marin and Sonoma counties. The tradition of caring has carried on through the generations, as JFCS pioneers new solutions to human problems and continues to alleviate suffering and strengthen individuals and families.

"For 150 years, since the birth of San Francisco, Jewish Family and Children's Services has been serving the needs of the dynamic, growing population of San Francisco and the Bay Area. We have watched the city change and have adapted our services to meet the needs created by those changes," says Dr. Anita Friedman, JFCS executive director. "JFCS is proud to be part of the fabric of this city and part of the history that has made living and working here so exciting and rewarding."

JFCS is a catalyst for change, transforming the community's cherished values into an action plan for saving lives and repairing the world. A national leader in providing innovative and effective social-service solutions to problems facing families and individuals of all ages, the agency offers assistance to more than 40,000 people annually — cradle to rocking chair — through 17 offices around the Bay Area. Integral to this effort are thousands of acts of loving kindness performed by more than 2,100 JFCS volunteers.

JFCS' Parents Place, one of the nation's first family resource centers based on prevention and early intervention, has lent critical support and guidance to countless children, teens and families. Seniors • At • Home enables older adults to sustain their independence through a model con-

Jewish Family and Children's Services

> JFCS is a catalyst for change, transforming the community's cherished values into an action plan for saving lives and repairing the world.

tinuum of community-based care. Dream House, a transitional shelter offering safety, counseling and job training, helps women and children escape homelessness and domestic violence. JFCS' new Rhoda Goldman Plaza and Miriam Schultz Grunfeld Professional Building in San Francisco will provide a state-of-the-art assisted-living and social-service complex for the entire community.

Whether it is providing on-the-job training and health benefits to individuals moving from welfare to work through its Utility Workshop employment-development program; providing small-business loans, scholarships, financial counseling and emergency assistance to help people realize their dreams; delivering meals to those with AIDS and disabilities; or offering leadership opportunities for teens, JFCS proves, time and time again, that it is an effective organization that brings tremendous value to the community.

The agency has given more than 40,000 refugees from many countries, including the former Soviet Union, a new lease on life in the Bay Area by providing the resources to help them resettle and become self-sufficient, fully participating citizens of their new country and communities.

JFCS believes each human life is precious. All the dedicated people, foundations, businesses and organizations make it possible for JFCS to make a difference. Along with its partners, JFCS will continue to pioneer a caring community that turns values into actions — and saves lives — every day. ■

Lennar/BVHP Partners

The urban design and architecture embraces the hillsides and capitalizes on sweeping views of the Bay and downtown San Francisco. The new Hunters Point Shipyard will feature a variety of homes, commercial and industrial uses. The cultural uses will highlight the incredible cultural and ethnic diversity of Hunters Point and San Francisco and capture the rich Naval history of the Hunters Point Shipyard.

As a mixed-use environment, Hunters Point will renovate historic docks and buildings, preserving their original integrity and readying them for the 21st century to be used for waterfront and commercial and industrial enterprises. A unique waterfront marketplace and museum will be focal points for jazz festivals, art exhibits and exciting shopping and dining experiences, as well as provide new economic opportunities for the city's multicultural artists, musicians and local entrepreneurs.

At the essence of development team's philosophy is building communities. To meet that goal, Lennar/BVHP will locate an Economic Renaissance Center at the shipyard, which will provide a place for job training, business education and affordable-housing assistance. The development will create 8,000 jobs over 20-25 years.

It's clear that San Francisco presents the development team with a great opportunity to work with the City in creating an excellent community. "We have created a new partnership with the city of San Francisco which is favorably disposed to bringing new jobs and housing to the community!" Willis says.

"Lennar/BVHP has a grand vision for the renaissance of the Hunters Point Shipyard into an outstanding cultural, industrial, multimedia, entertainment and residential community for the 21st century," says Roy Willis, Lennar/BVHP operations director. "This community promises an exciting and unique opportunity to develop the city's newest and finest jewel on the historic docks of the San Francisco Bay."

Lennar/BVHP, located in San Francisco, falls under the umbrella of Lennar Corp and LNR Partners, the Luster Group and Mariposa Management. Lennar's emphasis is on building communities. LNR's emphasis is on industrial, commercial and multi-family developments. Luster is a local construction management firm. Mariposa is a local development firm with San Francisco expertise.

At the essence of Lennar's philosophy is improving communities.

Lennar/LNR is no stranger to overseeing an enormous redevelopment opportunity in the Bay Area. It is responsible for converting Mare Island Shipyard in the city of Vallejo into a functional mixed-use community and it is applying the same skills to Hunters Point. "It is our goal to redevelop selected urban areas into vibrant mixed-use communities which contribute to an improved quality of life for the citizens," Willis says.

Today, Willis and the growing Lennar/BVHP team are busy transforming Hunters Point into one of the nation's most exciting urban waterfront communities.

"We are bullish on Hunters Point and on San Francisco. As a new stakeholder in the city, we are excited about the opportunity to create new jobs and help solve the housing problems that exist in this constrained market." ∎

The Martin Group

The elegant San Francisco Landmark @ One Market begins the new millennium with a new chapter in its life. Headquarters of Southern Pacific Railway since it was built by world-renowned architects Bliss and Faville in 1916, the unique brick structure at the intersection of Market, California and the bay is now the corporate headquarters of several businesses.

The Martin Group is the developer that facilitated this transition with a renovation that restored the building's historic grandeur while making it ready for the new century. The project provided a number of challenges, which included starting interior demolition while Southern Pacific trains in the western United States were still being operated from a second-floor computer center.

The Martin Group's president, Michael Covarrubias, says: "Historic landmarks have character and beauty you have to preserve and work around. This means finding ways to preserve historic beauty while upgrading to meet seismic standards and the demands of 21st century technology."

Founded in 1984 by David Martin, The Martin Group has experience in doing just that. Thanks to another Martin project, the former Cadillac and Ford car dealership at 1000 Van Ness Ave., a landmark building that stood empty for 10 years, is now a multi-use building with underground parking, 14 movie theaters, a health club, restaurants and residential/work lofts.

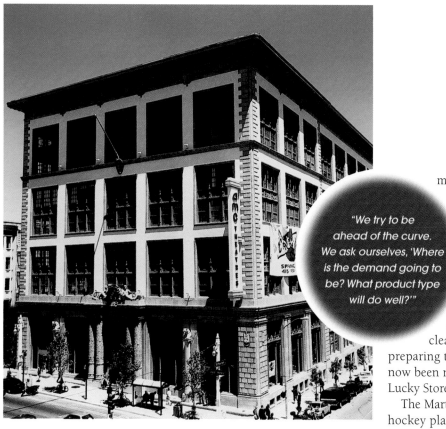

"We try to be ahead of the curve. We ask ourselves, 'Where is the demand going to be? What product type will do well?'"

But the developer doesn't specialize in historic buildings. In fact, it specializes in *not* specializing. "Our product flexibility allows us to develop throughout the Bay Area in whatever location and with whatever product type is appropriate," Covarrubias says.

In Emeryville, that meant the multi-use Marketplace Tower, which combines office, retail and theater space, or more recently, Emeryville Warehouse Lofts. In Redwood City, The Martin Group acquired a half-million square feet of "a frumpy old industrial park" and turned it into a mecca for high-technology and Internet companies, eventually expanding the park to more than 1 million square feet.

In Novato, a new residential community is rising on the land once occupied by Hamilton Air Base. After another proposal was overturned by referendum, The Martin Group went in, listened to community concerns and won approval for a less densely developed project. About $70 million, including $20 million in environmental cleanup, was spent removing the old military structures and preparing the infrastructure for a new community. The property has now been resold to several major home builders, Marriott Hotels and Lucky Stores.

The Martin Group has taken some operating advice from legendary hockey player Wayne Gretsky, who once offered this explanation for his excellence: "I skate to where the puck is going to be." Translated into developer terms, Covarrubias says, "We try to be ahead of the curve. We ask ourselves, 'Where is the demand going to be? What product type will do well?'"

With its history of first-rate execution on multi-use projects in built-up urban areas, Covarrubias says, "We believe there will be a major role for us well into the next millennium." ∎

Robert Bernard, president and CEO

marchFIRST

The Internet is an accelerator of change. It is speeding the globalization of supply and demand, disrupting supply chains, increasing the speed of innovation — all of which translate into a new set of rules, concrete business challenges for traditional businesses, and a new economy. A digital economy.

In the digital economy, companies that want to win have to embrace a new business paradigm that requires an interdependent, dynamic approach to business. The leaders will be those who understand that business models, brands, and systems and processes work together in an ecology that requires a new level of connection.

Today, traditional services companies cannot provide services for the new business paradigm. They lack the scale, execution, imagination or reach to tackle the class of solutions required today by established leaders and dot-com companies alike. They are built on a single discipline — whether they are strategy consultants, technology integrators or creative agencies. Under the traditional business paradigm, businesses treat their business model, their brand, and their systems and processes as independent entities, with little need for interaction.

Enter marchFIRST

marchFIRST (Nasdaq: MRCH) leads the revolution for the new business paradigm by combining the disciplines necessary to win in the digital economy with the global scale and reach needed to take on leading-edge challenges worldwide.

The multidisciplinary focus of marchFIRST helps clients build visionary business models, brands, systems and processes. Blending imagination, know-how, rigor and passion in the work it does, the company seeks to be the strategic weapon of the boardrooms of the digital economy. Its dynamic approach leads to business transformation from the inside to the outside — from business strategy and operations to customers' brand experience. We work with our clients to imagine, build, operate and improve, creating a new way to do business for a new economy.

marchFIRST was created in March 2000 through the merger of two industry powerhouses, Whittman-Hart and USWeb/CKS.

Robert Bernard, President and CEO of marchFIRST, founded Whittman-Hart in 1984 with the goal of providing services and solutions for IBM's midrange computers. By 2000 he had grown the firm into a leading provider of e-business

marchFIRST

profile　　clients　　careers　　investors　　news　　directory

solutions for fast-growing and middle-market companies. Thanks to its origins as an IT consulting firm, Whittman-Hart built deep expertise in business systems integration, ranging from extended supply chain capabilities to ERP systems.

USWeb/CKS was founded in 1995 by three former Novell executives with an ambitious vision: building an Internet-focused services firm that could help companies navigate the transformational effects of the Internet. USWeb/CKS rapidly scaled to become the recognized leader in Internet professional services, with a strong emphasis on the business-to-consumer marketplace and brand building.

The merger of these two companies creates the only Internet professional services firm that combines the disciplines needed to compete and win in the digital economy. Backing up marchFIRST's multidisciplinary expertise is a global organization of more than 8,500 employees in 64 cities and 14 countries worldwide.

marchFIRST's mission is to help its clients make new levels of connections. We create new ways of doing business, new ways of reaching customers and new ways of streamlining operations. We help our clients decide the business they should be in, understand how to win in that business, and then design, build and operate the solutions.

marchFIRST is the only services firm that combines the disciplines needed to win in the digital economy with the global scale needed to take on any size engagement, anywhere in the world. This is our competitive advantage. We can touch the right part of our clients' business at exactly the right time. We are fusing our knowledge of markets and market dynamics with our supply chain and back-office capability to meet the business-to-business challenge head-on. We are also capitalizing on our business-to-consumer expertise to continue advancing those businesses to the next level by integrating their back-end and front-end systems.

San Francisco is the ideal place because it's where Silicon Valley and Madison Avenue intersect. It's where the heart and the brain of the Web come together.

marchFIRST's client base is much more defined by an attitude or desire to win, a sense of urgency and a commitment to invest in the vision. We focus on clients for whom our services can make the most difference. Those clients generally fall into three categories:

Big brands that want to leverage their brand strength to create new markets.

Mid-sized companies that want to transform their market and become the category leader.

Dot-coms — both pure-plays and spin-offs from established businesses — that are changing the face of business.

Our clients represent a wide range of industries including manufacturing, distribution, health care, transportation, financial and business services, retail, and communications. Clients who have turned to us include Williams-Sonoma, Boise Cascade, Apple, Harley-Davidson, Alta Vista, 3Com, Montgomery Ward and many more.

marchFIRST has a large presence in San Francisco. With offices in the Financial district and South-of-Market (SOMA) district, San Francisco is the ideal place because it's where Silicon Valley and Madison Avenue intersect. It's where the heart and the brain of the Web come together. And where marchFIRST will make the winners in the digital economy. ■

m
marchFIRST

McCown De Leeuw & Co. Inc.

DDI, an MDC portfolio company that manufactures fasteners and other small components, is based in Walnut Creek

MDC's West Coast managing directors include (from left to right), Phil Collins, Steve Zuckerman, George McCown and Bob Hellman

In 1996, the founders and managers of private investment firm McCown De Leeuw & Co. (MDC) reviewed the progress they'd made since they began investing to buy and build industry-leading middle-market companies in 1984.

By such standard measures as staff growth, assets managed and return to investors, MDC was a considerable success. For example, San Francisco's Building Materials Holding Corp. had become a billion-dollar public company, the largest supplier of building materials to professional builders in the West.

But MDC had higher goals in mind. For co-founder George McCown, those goals went back to childhood, when he watched his father's career and "how different his life was, depending on whom he worked for." As McCown's own career progressed, he began to see "an incredible opportunity" in being able to influence how people felt about their work.

Co-founder David E. De Leeuw shared this interest. "In an industry that tends to be pretty competitive and cutthroat, we wanted to be known as good people to do business with," De Leeuw recalls. "We also wanted to be a place where people would look forward to coming to work each day. We wanted to give people the opportunity to do what they are most passionate about."

So, in 1996, the MDC management team took a closer look at the 30 companies that had been acquired: What were the characteristics of the businesses of which they were most proud? How had those businesses performed financially?

It turned out the companies sharing MDC's values were also the most successful. "In the process of trying to create a better workplace," McCown reasoned, "you also create great companies."

With this knowledge, the MDC team formulated a new mission: to build companies that make a difference. Then it set about expressing this mission in a clear business strategy applied both internally and to the portfolio companies.

Within MDC, compensation structures have been re-organized so even the best managers are rewarded not only for their personal efforts but also for "their contributions toward building the right kind of environment," Managing Director Steven Zuckerman says, "one that fosters collaboration more than competition."

Open communication is encouraged with extensive reviews and staff meetings. "We talk a lot about making people 'good' as opposed to making them feel good," Zuckerman says. "Sometimes critical feedback is needed, but the idea is not simply to encourage complaints. If employees see something isn't working, we ask them to think about why and offer a solution."

"Modeling this behavior at MDC is one way we extend our philosophy to our portfolio companies," McCown explains. "We also make sure we partner with management teams that share our vision."

Once a company is acquired, the management team is asked to participate in an extensive taking-stock process. "We look at what's working, what's not working and what needs to change in the way the company is functioning," McCown says. "As part of this process, the management team creates a vision, a mission, an articulated set of values and a strategy."

One example of how this effort makes a difference can be found at San Francisco–based Fitness Holdings Worldwide, the holding company for 24 Hour Fitness, Fitness Holdings Asia and Fitness Holdings Europe. Fitness Holdings' mission focuses on helping people in the communities they serve to live healthy and fit lives. "That's a mission that really inspires a lot of people," McCown says. "It is now one of the fastest-growing fitness chains in the world, with 352 clubs on three continents and 2.4 million members worldwide."

At Distribution Dynamics, a Walnut Creek–based manufacturer of fasteners and other small components in the assembly of manufactured products, partnering with MDC meant creating a new management team. Among its members was a senior human-relations professional who developed a program to involve and value employees, giving them an emotional stake in the company. Zuckerman says, "Employees give their best when they find meaning in their jobs — and that's when you get the greatest economic success."

Other Bay Area-based MDC portfolio companies include E-M-Solutions and Aurora Foods. With headquarters in Fremont, E-M-S is a leading provider of electronic contract manufacturing services to high-end data-processing and data-networking OEMs. Aurora (NYSE: AOR), headquartered in San Francisco, is a buildup of leading grocery brands such as Mrs. Butterworth's and Log Cabin syrup and pancake mix, Duncan Hines baking goods, and frozen food products, including Van de Kamp's, Mrs. Paul's, Aunt Jemima and Celeste's.

MDC's investment in building companies extends to the training it provides its employees and portfolio companies. Employees and management teams participate in leadership-development workshops held by San Rafael–based Learning as Leadership. Founded by Claire Nuer, the organization teaches people how to create "eco-system" versus "ego-system" work environments. Historically, the system that runs the world of commerce, the "ego-system" creates destructive competition and me-first thinking. The "eco-system," on the contrary, features authentic communication, shared responsibility, trust and compassion.

Besides Nuer, McCown credits at least two other influences with developing his business philosophy. One is Gen. Georges Doriot, the founder of the venture-capital industry in the United States. McCown

In the process of trying to create a better workplace, you also create great companies.

MDC portfolio company Fitness Holdings Worldwide, headquartered in Pleasanton, is the holding company for 24 Hour Fitness and one of the fastest growing fitness chains in the world.

worked with Doriot at Harvard Business School and at Doriot's American Research and Development Corp., absorbing his "reverence for business." Doriot saw businesses as "living things that involved people, that involved creation," McCown says. The other influence is the World Business Academy, founded in the Bay Area 13 years ago, which McCown has chaired for the past 10 years.

The kind of management system MDC is building not only fosters success, it may be the only strategy for survival in the new millennium. As McCown sees it, the kinds of fundamental changes now taking place are akin to the scientific revolution 300–400 years ago. Technology is just one manifestation of this paradigm shift, he believes. "To be a survivor," he says, "you've got to become a learning organization, one that strives to influence society in a constructive way." ■

A $150,000 grant from the McKessonHBOC Foundation is helping the Tenderloin Community School become a resource for the one of the city's harshest neighborhoods, where children and their families can access dental and medical care service, counseling resources, a community kitchen, a roof-top garden and a family resource center.

Foundation's endowment is now $25 million, and more than $3 million is distributed each year across the country.

Two of his predecessors also established community-oriented programs. Neil Harlan created grants of up to $5,000 that are awarded to programs where employees volunteer. Thomas Drohan established scholarship programs including one for aspiring pharmacists from San Francisco high schools, to assure that the best and brightest people—regardless of family income—continue to enter the field.

Founded in 1833 by John McKesson, the company began as a pharmaceutical distributor and has been the nation's largest for more than a century. It now serves megachains, such as CVS and Rite Aid, as well as thousands of independent pharmacies, small chains, and hospitals. McKesson moved from New York City to San Francisco during a time of extensive corporate diversification. In the 1980s, most of its non-healthcare companies, including Foremost Foods, were divested.

166-year-old McKessonHBOC has been headquartered in San Francisco for almost a third of a century—30 years of that in its current One Post Street building.

When McKesson Corporation moved its headquarters to San Francisco in 1967, it was an important day, not only for the company—which had just merged with Foremost Foods— or for the city's financial district—where in 1970 a new, prominent skyscraper became home to the nation's largest distributor of pharmaceuticals. It also was an important day for thousands of youngsters who weren't even born yet, kids who have benefitted from the company's extensive community outreach programs in San Francisco for more than three decades now.

For example, more than 2,000 homeless kids each year get temporary housing and help at the Haight's Huckleberry House, the country's first shelter for runaway youth. And 500 young residents of the Tenderloin are now attending a public elementary school in their neighborhood—and getting medical services at the on-site McKesson Health Clinic. A first-ever "Child Health and Safety Education Program" pairs UCSF School of Pharmacy students with families in need of medical assistance and guidance.

Through grants from its self-sustaining Foundation and the volunteer efforts of hundreds of headquarters employees, McKessonHBOC provides San Francisco charities with two key resources: time and money. The McKesson Foundation was established in the 1970s, not long after the merger with Foremost. Two decades later, then-CEO Alan Seelenfreund made sure that the Foundation also benefitted when new shareholder values in the company were created. As a result, the

In the late 1970s, McKesson gave customers computer terminals to do their ordering. Like American Airlines SABRE reservations system, this represented a major advance in business uses of information technology. McKesson has continued in the forefront, developing technology that streamlines supply, helps pharmacies make insurance claims, and even assures the hospital nurse that each patient is getting the right medicine.

Its recent merger with HBO and Company, the largest provider of information on health care, is a giant step toward accomplishing McKessonHBOC's goal: to make health care better, faster, and more effective by providing high-quality care and improved clinical outcomes, while managing costs. ∎

The seeds of Weinstein Gallery were planted in 1990, when Rowland Weinstein's parents opened an art gallery in Australia. Weinstein, a CPA at the time, gave them his savings and went over to help set up their books. Weinstein became passionate about some of the master prints in the gallery. He talked to people about them and, to his surprise, started making sales. "I didn't know I was selling; I was simply sharing my passion for the art," he says. His excitement grew with each conversation as he realized he had a talent for connecting with people through art.

A family crisis brought Weinstein back to California, where he took a part-time job at a downtown San Francisco gallery. He thrived. His days as a CPA were over. Weinstein, along with his wife, Julie Michelle, whose passion for art equaled his own, endeavored to open his own gallery. He was 27, and had no money and little history in art. The country was in recession, and the art market was at a low. "Maybe had I known better, I never would have opened," he says. His vision proved persuasive. Artists gave him their paintings, two framers framed them, and he obtained a million-dollar lease — all on spec. With this, and $30,000 in credit-card debt, Weinstein Gallery was born.

Michelle Rowland/Weinstein Gallery

Rowland Weinstein, owner

Weinstein's philosophy is that selling artwork is client service; it is helping someone fulfill a need.

Hard work, vision, a lot of luck and great locations have since turned Weinstein Gallery into one of the most important and successful galleries in the country. "San Francisco was always a world-class city, but who knew that, with the explosion of technology, it would become the center of the world's economy," he says. What makes San Francisco special, Weinstein says, is that it's tiny. The luxury hotels, shopping, restaurants and theaters are all within walking distance of his galleries. He now has three, all in the Union Square area.

The original gallery at 383 Geary St. presents emerging masters, such as Jean-Claude Gaugy, Charles Becker, Andreas Nottebohm and Claude Lazar.

Michelle Rowland Gallery at 353 Geary St. represents living masters who have not been attracted to San Francisco galleries in the past. "We inaugurated the gallery with a show for Robert Kipniss, a master painter/printmaker from New York," Weinstein says. "Kipniss is in most major museums in America but has never before, in his 48-year career, had a show of paintings in San Francisco. This is the caliber of artwork Michelle Rowland Gallery will bring the city."

Weinstein Gallery at 253 Grant Ave. presents the reigning masters of the 20th century: Picasso, Miro and Chagall. "We have chosen to curate only the most important images, in their finest condition, from these masters," Weinstein says.

Weinstein's philosophy is that selling artwork is client service; it is helping someone fulfill a need. "If I take the best care of my clients, my artists and my employees, I may not make as much money on every sale, but the galleries will do much better in the long run," he says.

With this vision for his galleries firmly in place, Rowland Weinstein, at 36, looks with enthusiasm to the future of the art world and the city of San Francisco. ∎

Greg Brown, chairman and CEO

W hat company was recently named *The Times* of London's No. 1 stock of the year? One of *Business Week's* top 10 fastest-growing high-tech companies by revenue? One of the *San Francisco Business Times'* top 10 fastest-growing companies in the Bay Area? And a member of the prestigious Bloomberg Personal Finance 100 and *Forbes* ASAP Dynamic 100 technology lists? Micromuse Inc.

Micromuse offers an application called Netcool, which flags problems in large networks, such as those used by telephone companies, Internet service providers and *Fortune* 500 firms.

"We provide software that consolidates fault data from 150 or more environments onto one screen," says Greg Brown, Micromuse's chair and CEO. "Netcool enables someone in a central operations center — say MCI Worldcom — to see all the potential problems underlying switches, modems and lines throughout the network, around the world. When a red alert appears, the operator can resolve the problem before customers experience an outage in service."

Netcool is one of very few products on the market with a database fast enough to report such faults in real time. Moreover, Netcool can be up and running in a matter of hours. The whole package fits onto a few quickly installed CDs — compared to months of tedious implementation for competitors' products.

Micromuse began in 1989 as a reseller of network-management software. Around 1995, the company developed a solution for British Telecom that inspired the Netcool product. Headquarters were soon established in San Francisco, close to the venture-capital firms funding its expansion, the technical expertise in Silicon Valley and numerous potential clients and partners.

The company went public in 1998 and is traded on the NASDAQ under the ticker-symbol MUSE. Today, Micromuse's client list includes both international household names and local Bay Area firms, such as AirTouch, America Online, AT&T, BART, Cellular One, MindSpring and Pacific Bell.

More than 540 customers worldwide have already licensed Netcool. Investors are looking to Brown, who joined the company in February 1999, to manage the firm's phenomenal growth. To date, the company's

Micromuse offers an application called Netcool, which flags problems in large networks, such as those used by telephone companies, Internet service providers and Fortune 500 firms.

revenues have increased steadily and exceeded analyst expectations every quarter.

Brown, who has a strong telecommunications background, was president of Ameritech's Custom Business Services, a division of the Midwestern telco that provides custom communications to large businesses. He understands the needs of Micromuse's service-oriented clients and the market opportunity provided by the explosion of the Internet-telecommunications sector and the emergence of network-based service industries, such as e-commerce.

According to Brown, one key to managing Micromuse's growth will be to keep hiring the very best people in a timely way. Micromuse currently employs more than 400 sales and technical staff throughout North America, Europe and Asia-Pacific. New offices recently opened in Amsterdam, Paris, Frankfurt and Vienna.

But Micromuse will continue to rely on the Bay Area to provide some of its most important talent — the people who drive the business from the dynamic San Francisco headquarters. ■

N ibbi Brothers General Contractors has been building in Northern California for half a century. The year 2000 marks the company's 50th anniversary. From the beginning, Nibbi Brothers has been known for its work and its word: "A job we accept is a job to be done well by the highest of standards — ours and the client's."

Marino Nibbi, who brought his Old World skills from Italy, started the company in 1950, setting up shop in a building South of Market in San Francisco. The jobs that came to him were small, but friends told friends about the excellence of his work, and the business grew. To meet the increasing demand, Marino was joined by his brother Pete Nibbi and the firm of Nibbi Brothers was born. It expanded rapidly, adding more and more craftsmen. The nature of the work also grew, increasing in scale and diversity.

In time, a second generation of Nibbi brothers took its place alongside their father. Marino's sons Sergio and Larry joined the business in 1957 and 1965, respectively. It is under their leadership that Nibbi Brothers has grown steadily. Today, a third generation of Nibbi's is involved in the management of the firm. Sergio's sons Bob and Michael and Larry's daughter Gina bring their enthusiasm for maintaining Nibbi's tradition and fine reputation.

Nibbi Brothers Inc.

Project Name: Pier One
Owner: AMB Property Corp.
Architect: SMWM

The firm takes a team approach to building projects, which generates innovative ideas about how to get a job done better and more efficiently.

Project Name: Hayes Valley Apartments North Site
Owner: McCormack Baron & Associates, Related Companies of California and
   San Francisco Housing Authority
Architect: Backen, Arrigoni & Ross

The family connection is what separates Nibbi Brothers from its competitors. Sergio says, "You can always call with a problem or question and talk to a Nibbi." It is the younger generation, along with other key management, that has contributed to *Construction Link Magazine's* designation of the company as "a rising star in the industry."

Throughout the past 50 years, San Francisco has called upon Nibbi Brothers to build countless public schools, fire and police stations, federal and city buildings, post offices, churches and hospitals. Nibbi has worked on many San Francisco landmarks, such as Coit Tower,

Candlestick Park, San Francisco International Airport, Moscone Center and Spreckles Temple in Golden Gate Park.

Nibbi Brothers negotiated the contract for the Hayes Valley Apartments, the first replacement of one of the city's dilapidated, low-income public housing projects. Today, Nibbi is leading the way with the renovation of historic Pier One, the first major pier renewal on the waterfront.

The firm takes a team approach to building projects, which generates innovative ideas about how to get a job done better and more efficiently.

Through Nibbi's pre-construction services, costs are controlled through budgeting, value engineering and schedule planning which results in successful projects and satisfied owners.

Nibbi Brothers employs the latest technology throughout its company. The project sites are connected to the home office and clients' offices via the Internet. Nibbi also maintains its website at www.nibbi.com which provides information on current and completed projects.

The company has operated from the same location in Potrero Hill for more than 45 years. In that sprit, the Nibbi family remains very active in the community and philanthropic organizations.

Nibbi Brothers is well known for its work "in the tradition of Old World craftsmanship." Clients know that a job built by Nibbi Brothers is built to last. ∎

Lawrence J. Ellison, chair and CEO

F ew things have remained constant during the past 20 years of computer technology. The presence of software firm Oracle Corp. — and its continuous pursuit of technological excellence and product innovation — are rare exceptions.

"We are a world leader in providing the database, development tools, business applications and professional services necessary for comprehensive, global information management," says Lawrence J. Ellison, chair and chief executive officer of Oracle. "Our market leadership is the direct result of technological leadership — a track record of innovation and firsts."

Today a $9.3-billion, 43,000-person company, Oracle (then known as System Development Laboratories) was founded in the San Francisco Bay Area in 1977 by Ellison, Bob Miner and Ed Oates. The company pioneered the development of the Oracle relational database management system, which allowed the presentation of information in a variety of formats without reorganizing the underlying data. Oracle soon established itself as a leader in the database field, and Oracle can now boast more than twice the market share of its closest competitor in that arena.

In 1987, Oracle also began offering business applications: First for enterprise resource planning (encompassing manufacturing, supply chain, finance and human resources), and later for customer-relationship management (including marketing, sales and service).

As the Internet began to take off, Oracle led the industry in recognizing the enormous impact of the new medium. Today, Oracle offers state-of-the-art e-business solutions. Oracle8i, a powerful new computing platform, can handle huge numbers of users and enormous quantities of information — ideal for developing business applications based on universal Internet standards and for facilitating business operations over the Internet. Oracle also provides business-application hosting services via its Business OnLine division. And the company is expanding its focus on business-to-business trade via the Internet with Oracle Exchange, an online marketplace aimed at facilitating the procurement of goods and services.

"The Internet has created a highly competitive landscape for businesses," says Mark Jarvis, senior vice president of worldwide marketing. "Oracle — with its commitment to customer success, the robustness of its Internet-enabled technology and applications, and its world-class consulting, education and support services — is increasingly seen as more than a vendor. Oracle has become a key business partner, delivering the best e-business solutions and services in the industry."

A wide range of organizations have come to rely on Oracle's products, including:

- Pfizer, the international pharmaceutical giant, which uses Oracle Clinical to streamline the clinical trials process, the most critical and costly stage in pharmaceutical research and development
- Sprint, a leader in advanced data communications, which uses Oracle products in its new Sprint ION Integrated On-Demand Network, a fully integrated broadband network that carries all voice, video, data, fax and Internet communications over a single, high-speed connection
- *The Washington Post*, which uses the Oracle database and *inter*Media as the backbone of its massive Web-based archive, which integrates text, photos and graphics
- The US Department of Justice, which uses Oracle servers, applications and tools in all divisions, including the Federal Bureau of Investigation, the Drug Enforcement Administration, the Immigration and Naturalization Service and the Bureau of Prisons, to automate, simplify and enhance information retrieval and analysis throughout the organization
- Tosco Corp., one of the largest independent US oil refiners and marketers, which uses Oracle Retail for Energy to streamline and automate business processes, as well as manage its diverse retail

"Oracle has become a key business partner, delivering the best e-business solutions and services in the industry."

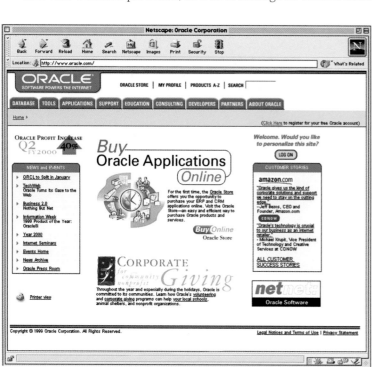

enterprise through improved analysis of merchandising and store performance
- Standard & Poor's, which uses Oracle technology for all economic and financial forecasting, as well as for data delivery
- Princeton University, which uses Oracle WebDB, Oracle Application Server and an Oracle data warehouse to give students, faculty and a core group of administrative staff access to financial and student administration information
- Kaiser Permanente, the largest health-maintenance organization in the United States, which has been using Oracle products to centralize clinical, accounting and care-management information
- The Boeing Co., the world's largest aerospace company, which uses Oracle Internet Procurement to analyze supplier performance and procurement opportunities, as well as develop and maintain key supplier relationships
- Amazon.com, the world's busiest e-commerce site, which relies on Oracle8i to streamline order processing, house information on 4.7 million book titles and supply superior performance and availability in online transaction processing
- Yahoo!, which uses Oracle products to manage Web content, credit-card billing and advertising contracts. Additionally, Oracle data warehouses track and analyze customer demographics and usage, allowing Yahoo! to spot trends and increase advertising revenues

And for the future? The team at Oracle will continue to pursue product innovation and excellence for the benefit of tomorrow's customers. ∎

Orrick, Herrington & Sutcliffe LLP

From left to right: William Orrick, George Herrington,
Eric Sutcliffe and current chairman Ralph H. Baxter Jr.

Leveraging a 137-year history in San Francisco that is infused with the city's spirit of optimism and innovation, Orrick, Herrington & Sutcliffe LLP is using its San Francisco foundation as a springboard to becoming one of the world's premier finance and technology law firms.

Beginning in the 1980s, Orrick planted roots in other cities, first throughout California, then in New York, and most recently in London, Tokyo and Singapore. Thus, the new century will be played on two interconnected stages, Chair and Chief Executive Officer Ralph Baxter says. One is "a continued focus on the San Francisco Bay Area and the wonderful and changing businesses and public entities we have served for more than a century," and the other is capitalizing on "a stunning expansion of our service to global commerce."

As Baxter sees it, that means the firm will "participate as actively in global commerce as we always have in Bay Area commerce." The mission is clear: "Almost everything we do involves finance or technology — or, most of the time, both."

Founded in 1863 by John R. Jarboe, an authority on real-estate titles, Orrick has not only grown with San Francisco, it has helped San Francisco grow. As the leading lawyers in the city — and now in the world — for financing public infrastructure, Orrick's legal advice supported the development of hydroelectric power in the Truckee River/Lake Tahoe region. Among the thousands of major projects the firm has helped to finance, the most famous local example is the Golden Gate Bridge.

Its public finance business led to Orrick's expansion into adjacent financial markets in the 1980s and 1990s. The first office outside San Francisco was in Sacramento; the state of California and its agencies have been major public finance clients. Soon, the firm recognized an office was needed in New York City, "the center of the universe for finance activities," says Peter Lillevand, senior

The PG&E arrangement involved securitization, a procedure for turning various kinds of company loans or receivables into securities. "Bank of America was the first to do it," Lillevand says, "and we helped them do it."

Orrick is also becoming a significant presence in technology law, both in the Silicon Valley and New York's Silicon Alley. "Just as we did the infrastructure for buildings and concrete," partner Gary Siniscalco says, "we're very much involved in the infrastructure for the telecommunications and information age," representing such high-tech leaders as America Online, Microsoft and Lucent Technologies.

Orrick has negotiated a strategic relationship with the Venture Law Group, a Silicon Valley practice dedicated to start-ups. Orrick provides a broad platform of legal services to new tech companies as they become more established. Siniscalco, for example, works in Orrick's Employment Law Department, helping clients adapt to new workplace realities, including the influx of contract employees and the internationalization of the labor force.

We are a firm that has a San Francisco outlook on the world.

Helping Orrick navigate through this period of rapid expansion and change have been core values represented in the careers of the founding partners: William H. Orrick, a precise intellectual analyst; George Herrington, revered for his warmth and generous spirit; and Eric Sutcliffe, who valued client service above all else.

partner and a firm manager during the expansion period. "Although the move to New York was bold and risky, it was nevertheless strategically very logical."

The growth in the New York office from six lawyers to more than 200 is testimony to the wisdom of that decision. Since then, Orrick has handled numerous finance and technology deals in New York, as well as bond issues for renovations of Carnegie Hall and the Rose Bowl, among a host of public projects around the country.

As it expands overseas, Orrick has become involved in "putting together the money and the know-how to deliver electricity, telecommunications, water systems and other public projects to the emerging world" in Asia and Latin America, Baxter says. "No one in the world is more experienced at that than we are."

Orrick is also a pioneer and major player in other kinds of financing. As the 20th century began, partner Charles P. Eells was instrumental in reorganizing the Fireman's Fund Insurance Co. after the 1906 earthquake, and he assembled the corporations that became the Pacific Gas & Electric Co. In 1934, the firm handled PG&E's registration statements, among the first processed by the Securities and Exchange Commission. Adapting to deregulation in the 1990s, PG&E came back to Orrick for help creating a brand-new structure for issuing $2.9 billion in bonds. "We were right there," partner Dora Mao says, "coming up with this new financial product."

The firm's history "is a beacon for those who come to know us today," CEO Baxter says. "We are a firm that has a San Francisco outlook on the world." This outlook has its advantages. In terms of recruitment, New York City lawyers are attracted by "the friendlier, warmer culture" at Orrick, Baxter says. "They join us because we're a better environment in which to build a professional career." The firm's values have also attracted overseas clients who "marvel at the level of cooperation and support Orrick provides to its overseas efforts."

"As we always have in San Francisco, we bring together the highest level of sophistication, expertise and intellect with a culture that befits San Francisco," Baxter says. "That makes us a very potent competitor in other markets in the world."

Orrick's regard for history is expressed in part by its decision to locate its offices in the refurbished Old Federal Reserve Building, a city landmark. But its focus is clearly not on the century behind, but on the millennium ahead. "The pace of change is greater now than it was at the beginning of the 20th century," Siniscalco says. "It's nice to be at the center and forefront of it." ∎

Chinatown is still a bustling neighborhood, as this shot of Grant Avenue attests, even as old ethnic boundaries fall.

PHOTO COURTESY OF PHIL COBLENTZ/
SAN FRANCISCO CONVENTION
& VISITORS BUREAU

"Study the grandest hotels of Europe, and then put them to shame." That was the assignment given to architect JP Gaynor by San Francisco banker William Ralston. When the Palace opened in October 1875, Gaynor had more than fulfilled his contract. Towering seven stories above Market Street, the magnificent hotel was served by four hydraulic elevators, or rising rooms, as they were called. But luxury extended beyond the mere architecture of the Palace. Each room was equipped with an electric call button so the staff could cater to guests' every wish.

Unfortunately, Ralston didn't live to see his finished dream. Committed to building the finest hotel in the world, he had spent $5 million, draining the resources of his Bank of California, leading to its closure. His body was found floating in the bay a few days shy of opening day.

Nonetheless, under the direction of Ralston's partner, Senator William Sharon, the Palace went on to become home away from home for kings, queens and presidents. (In fact, President Warren G. Harding died there — some believe at the hands of his wife and doctor.) It's also been a favorite for actors and entertainers.

Celebrity doesn't protect against natural disaster, though. While the hotel survived the earthquake that struck in 1906, the Palace suffered extensive damage in the fire that followed. Rebuilt at a cost of $10 million, the new Palace was much like its predecessor.

Palace Hotel

Luxury extended beyond the mere architecture of the Palace.

The Garden Court was one dramatic exception. The centerpiece of the hotel, the beautiful dining room was crowned by a stained-glass dome, lighted by chandeliers of Austrian crystal and lined with a double row of Italian marble Ionic columns. Ever since it opened in 1909, this has been the site for important events — from the official banquet honoring the opening session of the United Nations in 1945 to countless marriage proposals.

It was for the reopening of the hotel that Sharon commissioned artist Maxfield Parrish to paint a mural for the Palace Bar. The "Pied Piper," purchased for $6,000, is worth $2.5 million today, and it graces the walls of its namesake, The Pied Piper Bar.

With treasures like this, it's no wonder many in the city were wary when the Palace announced plans for renovation in 1989. Fortunately, the Palace's present owner, Kyo-ya Corp. Ltd., appreciated the jewel. Two years and $170 million later, San Franciscans' fears were put to rest. When the hotel reopened in April 1991, even detractors had to commend the blending of the old and the new. Still opulent with an Old World feel, the Palace also features many modern amenities, including a health spa, video-conferencing capabilities and, in keeping with the tradition of catering to clients' every desire, 24-hour room service. William Ralston would be proud. ■

Peet's Coffee & Tea

Gerald Baldwin, chairman of the board

In an age of instant messages and multi-tasking, Peet's Coffee & Tea still does things the old-fashioned way. The company has changed and grown over the years, but continues to roast its beans by hand to meet the high standard set by founder Alfred Peet.

Peet's was started in April 1966 when Alfred Peet opened a coffee store with a roasting machine at the corner of Walnut and Vine in Berkeley, anchoring what would become that city's legendary gourmet ghetto. Peet had grown up in the family's coffee and tea business in Alkmaar, Holland. After World War II, he lived in Indonesia, where he worked in the tea trade. At the age of 35, he moved to the San Francisco Bay Area and, 10 years later, opened his shop, roasting coffee in the distinctive manner he had been taught by his family. Drawing clientele from the nearby University of California and the adventurous Sixties generation, Peet's was soon successful. No longer satisfied with vacuum-packed canned coffee, Peet's devotees sparked nothing less than a specialty-coffee revolution.

In 1984, Jerry Baldwin, now chairman, bought the company after working with Alfred Peet for several years, learning how to select, blend and roast beans. Joined by coffee buyer and roastmaster Jim Reynolds, Baldwin continues Peet's tradition, which over the years has garnered a loyal following of "Peetniks." Today, Peet's Deep-Roasted™ coffee style still stands apart as a unique brand of coffee sought by people all over the world.

While many coffee companies use computers to roast their beans, Peet's process involves real people, highly trained experts who understand that beans from different regions of the world require different roasting techniques; even beans from the same area vary from harvest to harvest. Peet's expects a minimum commitment of 10 years from its roasters; it takes at least three or four years to master the craft and develop "palate memory." Only by constantly monitoring air temperature and humidity during the roasting process and tasting each batch can the roasters guarantee the quality of Peet's Deep-Roasted™ coffee. Similar care is taken with Peet's unique rare teas and tea blends.

Expansion hasn't changed Peet's commitment to quality. As national coffee-store chains proliferate, Peet's has taken a slow approach, maintaining Alfred Peet's "unfranchised" vision. The original Berkeley store still stands, now joined by nearly 60 others throughout California and in Portland, Boston and the greater Chicago area. These shops bear more than a passing resemblance to the original, not only in their look but in their atmosphere and the esteemed place they hold in their respective neighborhoods.

"We tap the incredible diversity of the people in California and hire people who maintain the unique Peet's culture we have cultivated for more than 33 years," Baldwin says. "Go into any Peet's and you will see employees who represent a wide variety of personal expressions and lifestyles."

Peet's has a tradition of hiring artists, craftspeople, musicians and students. As varied as their backgrounds are, all employees are knowledgeable about coffee and tea, having been trained in Peet's tasting program. Furthermore, most live in the neighborhood where they work and know their customers by name, so each Peet's maintains the friendly nature of a neighborhood market. The stores tend to become widely known landmarks, where people gather to meet and relax.

Today, Peet's Deep-Roasted™ coffee style still stands apart as a unique brand of coffee sought by people all over the world.

And some of those loyalists are far-flung. With that in mind, the company has developed a thriving mail-order operation to serve coffee connoisseurs the world over. By logging on to www.peets.com, consumers can order coffee and tea for delivery and, in keeping with Peet's goal of educating customers, they can get advice on keeping coffee fresh, learn how to brew the perfect cup of coffee and take a virtual tour of Peet's roasting facility.

Even as it continues to grow, Peet's aspires to maintain the quality of its products and stay true to the company's high standards while serving more customers in new communities. Most importantly, Peet's endeavors to provide the best customer service of any coffee company in the world. ■

Christopher Mottern, CEO and president

Peet's has distinguished itself not only for the quality of its coffees and teas, but also for its positioning as a company. In a state known for its high technology, Peet's emphasizes the opposite: artistry and crafts. This attitude applies to everything Peet's does, including its personalized approach to building enduring relationships with customers.

Baldwin believes there is still room for an old-fashioned type of retailer that will continue to thrive as people reject the chain stores that offer mass-produced food and undistinguished beverages.

"The beauty of coffee is that it crosses all demographics and recognizes no cultural boundaries. We see this aspect reflected in the broad range of customers we serve every day," Baldwin says.

Laurel Village, San Francisco

Photo: Najib Joe Hakim

Pillsbury Madison and Sutro

Marking 125 years since its founding in 1874, Pillsbury Madison & Sutro takes the honors for being one of the oldest law firms in California. The 520-attorney firm based in San Francisco is so firmly rooted in the Bay Area that it was responsible for the incorporation of both Pacific Bell and Chevron (formerly Standard Oil Co.) near the turn of the century.

Pillsbury Madison & Sutro also takes credit for being among the top 10 largest law firms in San Francisco and lists many large Bay Area companies as clients, including Bank of America, Wells Fargo, Chevron, Shorenstein Co. LP and Pacific Bell. Though the firm is headquartered in San Francisco, it also has offices in Los Angeles, San Diego, Washington, DC, New York City, Northern Virginia, Orange County, Sacramento, Silicon Valley and Tokyo, with plans to expand to London and other European and Asian cities.

The firm was founded by Evan Pillsbury, whom Mary Cranston, Pillsbury's chair, calls a "man of vision" dedicated to client service. After the 1906 earthquake, he went to the chair of Standard Oil Co. of California and asked for $100,000 to rebuild the city. Cranston says that started a chain of corporate generosity that put San Francisco back on its feet. His son, HD Pillsbury, became a partner in 1905.

Joining the burgeoning firm in the 1890s, Alfred Sutro, another founding partner, became the first of three generations that would be affiliated with Pillsbury Madison & Sutro until 1990. The other Sutros associated with the firm were Alfred's brother, Oscar, his son, John A. Sr., and his grandson, John A. Jr. Frank Delino Madison came on board as early as 1889, but did not become a partner until 1905. His son, Marshall, eventually followed in his footsteps.

Pillsbury prides itself on being a full-service law firm that meets the challenges of the current business environment. Key to the way it conducts business is its

takeover of Gulf, the Pacific Telesis acquisition of Communications Industries Inc. and the joint venture among AirTouch, US West, Bell Atlantic and Nynex.

While Pillsbury has a strong presence in the Bay Area business community, the firm and its staff also are dedicated to the city's civic organizations. Pillsbury not only serves as counsel to the San Francisco Ballet, San Francisco Opera and the board of the Committee on Jobs, a group of Bay Area CEOs who help provide a forum for companies to influence the political system, but its attorneys volunteer time to causes such as the Society for the Prevention of Cruelty to Animals (SPCA), the American Civil Liberties Union (ACLU), various cultural organizations, and state and federal bar associations.

Despite Cranston's full plate, she serves on the Board of the San Francisco Ballet and the St. Ignatius Board of Regents and on the boards of directors of the San Francisco Chamber of Commerce and the Bay Area Council.

Photo: Jan Lundberg

Mayor Willie Brown and chair Mary Cranston celebrate Pillsbury's 125th anniversary on June 23, 1999.

After 125 years in business, Pillsbury is in the process of recreating itself.

emphasis on teamwork, in which each practice's specialty groups routinely tap the know-how and experience of one another. Specializing in litigation and commercial transactions, the firm has added expertise in working with high-technology start-up companies and handling intellectual-property issues.

Pillsbury's other practice areas include employment and labor relations, executive compensation, employee benefits, real estate, political law, tax planning, environmental and land use, bankruptcy, and estate and probate.

"With a renaissance in the United States of innovative digital technology, intellectual-property protection is critical," Cranston says. "As a firm, we want to be able to provide legal support for those companies that need that protection."

To that end, the firm merged with Washington, DC–based Cushman and Darby, a noted intellectual-property firm, giving Pillsbury depth and strength in the discipline. An office in Silicon Valley positions the firm close to the community where high tech is dominant.

Pillsbury has experience in obtaining patents, trademark and copyright registrations; drafting licensing agreements; and advising clients on the protection of trade secrets and confidential business information. *Intellectual Property Today* has named Pillsbury one of the top five patent/trademark firms in terms of successfully obtaining patents and trademarks for its clients.

In addition, Pillsbury has an extraordinary track record in complex commercial litigation. The cases run the gamut from libel and privacy suits for media companies to trade practice and compliance issues to security class-action suits. The company successfully represented AirTouch Communications in a price-fixing suit and Chevron, which was accused of monopoly practices related to retail gas prices. Other cases have involved lender and product liability, consumer fraud and contracts.

The firm also handles sophisticated financial transactions, such as mergers and acquisitions, leveraged buyouts, initial public offerings, tender offers, financing and hostile takeovers. Representing investment companies, venture capitalists, limited partnerships and other business entities, Pillsbury has the ability to take a company from start-up through the development phases. It played an integral part in Chevron's

After 125 years in business, Pillsbury is in the process of recreating itself. "It's easy to fall into static processes," Cranston says, "but you have to tighten up management and look at everything with an open and creative mind."

One of the strategies employed by Pillsbury has been to energize career development. Recognizing that some lawyers want to practice law for a few years and then pursue other ventures, the firm has created lines of business as training grounds to help attorneys move on to new challenges, Cranston says. For instance, they are offered experience in licensing work, an expertise that may later lend itself to joining start-ups.

As the new millennium begins, Pillsbury has set its sights high: doubling its legal staff and becoming one of the largest and most profitable law firms in the United States in the next five years. ∎

Planned Parenthood Golden Gate

Margaret Sanger (second from left) stands outside her first family planning clinic in New York in 1916. Hundreds of women and their families came to the clinic for birth-control information during the 10 days the clinic remained open.

That "something" encompasses extensive educational programs that reach more than 30,000 Bay Area middle- and high-school-age youth and their parents annually. Programs include classes on puberty-related physical changes, responsible sexual decision making, building self-esteem and ending cycles of violence.

But PPGG's services don't end there.

PPGG's health centers' reproductive health care services are offered to both men and women. Primarily women take advantage of PPGG's services, which include family planning, and anonymous and confidential screenings for breast, cervical and testicular cancer, HIV and sexually transmitted diseases. Health services are geared toward meeting women's medical needs at all stages of their lives and ensuring children are born wanted and healthy.

Dian Harrison, president & CEO of Planned Parenthood Golden Gate (middle), sits with teens during "Teen Clinic" at one of PPGG's 11 health centers.

Founded by public health nurse and family planning advocate Margaret Sanger in 1916 in New York City, Planned Parenthood has been woven into San Francisco's social fabric since the late 1920s.

Sanger encountered thousands of women who faced desperate physical and economic burdens due to a lack of family planning services. Sanger and her San Francisco counterparts, Dr. Adelaide Brown and Dr. Florence Holsclaw, formed Planned Parenthood with the backing of the American Association of University Women to advocate women's and children's health rights. This vigorous advocacy has been controversial since the organization's birth.

It still is, more than 80 years later.

Why is a mystery to Dian Harrison, president and CEO of Planned Parenthood Golden Gate (PPGG), which now operates 11 health centers in San Francisco and five other Bay Area counties.

"The United States has achieved a 20-year low in both teen pregnancy and abortion rates," Harrison points outs. "We — and those brave women of the 1920s who first stood up for a woman's right to know how to plan her family — must be doing something right!"

> PPGG's extensive educational programs reach more than 30,000 Bay Area middle- and high-school-age youth and their parents annually.

Health care at Planned Parenthood Golden Gate also includes gynecological exams and pap smears, pregnancy testing and counseling, prenatal care, adoption referrals, sterilization services (for women and men), abortion services, midlife/menopause information and treatment, and primary health care.

For most women, reproductive health is their main health issue from puberty through menopause. So it's not surprising that, for many women, Planned Parenthood serves as their primary health care provider.

"Polling shows that one in four women — regardless of income level — has used Planned Parenthood as a primary provider some time in her life," Harrison says, noting that PPGG is truly a lifeline for many women, but especially for poor women.

"Planned Parenthood Golden Gate has been exemplary in fulfilling the vision of Margaret Sanger. Her vision, that every woman should have the right to decide whether and when to bear children and that every child should be born wanted and loved into a family ready to care for it, is being passionately pursued every day by Planned Parenthood Golden Gate. I salute them for their 80 years of service to the women and men of San Francisco," says Alexander C. Sanger, president of Planned Parenthood of New York City. And coming from the founder's grandson, that's awfully high praise. ■

The fire that followed the San Francisco earthquake of 1906 was one of the largest, most destructive urban fires in history. During three days and three nights, 514 city blocks and 30,000 buildings were turned into smoldering rubble.

Three companies that are part of today's Royal & SunAlliance were among the insurers that faced a total liability of more than $250 million. The task itself was challenging. In the confusion after the fire, not just personal records but many company records had been destroyed. Some insurance companies delayed payment or simply failed to pay.

This was not so with the Royal companies. On June 23, 1906, Rolla Watt, a Royal manager, wrote his agents: "It has seemed to me the situation should be met with fortitude and the obligations satisfied in accordance with the high principles which have governed our great companies to date. We are therefore proceeding with the adjustment and payment of all our claims with such expedition as the circumstances permit."

If the San Francisco fire was a setback for insurance companies, it had a silver lining. As JM Dove, son of Royal's first manager, said in 1908, "A fire like this brings the importance of insurance home to people, and we shall get increased insurances, not only in the new San Francisco, but in the whole of America and throughout the world."

Since then, Royal has grown into a Royal & SunAlliance, one of the world's largest insurers. Its San Francisco office, which opened in 1853, continues to offer Bay Area clients the best of both worlds: a strong, locally based customer orientation matched by the resources of a company that is truly global.

Royal & SunAlliance

Greg Locher, general manager, resident vice president

APRIL 18, 1906

The Bettman Archive, Inc.

ROYAL INSURANCE WAS THERE!

> Our commitment, and the Royal & SunAlliance legacy in the United States, is to provide insightful business insurance solutions, efficiently and effectively.

"We are a company dedicated to our customers. We have experts who know your business, who have the experience to serve your insurance needs and who provide the best underwriting and claims-handling service," says Greg Locher, San Francisco's resident vice president.

As they attend to customers in the Bay Area, Royal & SunAlliance representatives consult with an international network of insurance experts. The company calls it "local touch with global reach." For example, if a large account in San Francisco is wrestling with workers' compensation cost-containment issues, Royal & SunAlliance can seek advice from a global practice team, perhaps in Australia, that has faced similar challenges.

Royal & SunAlliance is among the very few companies that possess the global power and presence to follow a San Francisco business anywhere in the United States and to 132 countries around the world.

"We recognize that each country has its own culture and regulatory bodies," Locher says. "Through our technology and people on the ground around the world, we can put together the best portfolio of products that are tailored to the client's needs."

As the millennium approaches, Royal & SunAlliance draws on a grand tradition. "Our commitment, and the Royal & SunAlliance legacy in the United States," Locher says, "is to provide insightful business insurance solutions, efficiently and effectively." ∎

Salvation Army

Lt. Colonel Richard Love at 133 Shipley Silvercrest Residence for Seniors which provides 257 units of clean, affordable housing with a noon meal and ancillary services.

Every night, several hundred people who would otherwise be homeless sleep in safe warm beds in San Francisco. And every day, hundreds of others are rescued from hunger. After the city's two major earthquakes, thousands were comforted with food and shelter. And every year, hundreds of troubled people, many of them single parents with children, receive counseling that helps them find their way back to useful lives.

All this is true because two Londoners answered the call of Salvation Army founder Gen. William Booth in 1883; just three years after the organization came to America and ventured to San Francisco. Diaries of Major Alfred Wells reveal that he and Captain Henry Stillwell conducted the first Salvation Army meeting at 811 Montgomery Street.

Though Wells and Stillwell couldn't speak the language of many who came, the crowd "remained breathless," he wrote. "Our little hall was nicely filled, and we closed the night with several seekers, all of them for-

In the past, The Salvation Army's most enduring image has often been the soup line, the hand-out. Its outlook for the future builds on helping people live in dignity and in circumstances that strengthen their ability to cope.

eign-born. I did not shed tears of homesickness the second night. If any, they were of joy, for surely heaven honored this Salvation Army meeting in San Francisco."

Since then, key moments in San Francisco have often involved the Army, and key moments in the Army have often involved San Francisco.

Golden State Divisional Headquarters, administrative center for the Salvation Army's work from San Francisco to Bakersfield, including 11 units in the city. The Army uses three floors and rents the rest.

The first Salvation Army Christmas kettle was put out on the streets of San Francisco.

For example, the first Salvation Army Christmas kettle was put out on the streets of San Francisco. Captain Joseph McFee, a sea captain who fed the poor living around the docks, didn't know how he could afford to provide Christmas dinner. So he took an old iron cauldron off the stove and put it outside the Ferry Building, with a sign calling to travelers: "Keep the kettle boiling." An article in the *Morning Call* on December 16, 1891, noted that "wire netting across the top keeps bad boys from emptying the pot of its contents. Quite a snug sum was in the pot last night."

The Salvation Army itself provided another "snug sum" in 1906, when San Francisco was devastated by earthquake and fire. National Commander Evangeline Booth visited the city and "was so moved by the plight of the people here that she pledged the whole Salvation Army budget for the coming year — $4 million — to help the city." Colonel Richard Love, divisional commander, points out. More than 25,000 refugees got help at a Salvation Army camp in Oakland.

When another major quake struck in 1989, nearly a quarter of a million people were assisted by the Salvation Army, with $3.6 million in goods and services distributed in the first two months. Concerned people all over the world sent the Army money to help San Francisco residents. What wasn't used for immediate earthquake relief helped strengthen the system of community centers and residences that still serve the city's needy.

One of the earliest Salvation Army programs in San Francisco, the Harbor Light Center at 1275 Harrison St., helps men and women conquer drug addiction. It is one of two centers in the city that accept patients with AIDS or HIV. Other programs — the Adult Rehabilitation Center on Valencia Street, the Bridgeway Residence and Lifeboat 2000 on Turk Street — help people make the transition from drug dependency and homelessness to independent, enriching lives.

In recent years, Colonel Love says, the Army has enlarged its focus: While it still provides food and shelter for the homeless, it also has programs such as Gateway, that "help them get established" by assisting with childcare and counseling. "They can stay two years, as long as they're making progress," Colonel Love explains. "That gives them a little space in which they don't have to worry about the rent."

An important focus is children: Gateway provides transitional housing for up to 30 homeless single-parent families. At 240 Turk St., in the heart of the Tenderloin, the Salvation Army provides after-school and summer programs for children, along with a day camp and children's recreation program. At Camp Redwood Glen in the Santa Cruz Mountains, more than 2,000 youngsters each year get to spend part of their summer in the country.

In 1998, the Army turned a service center at 517 Stevenson into a seasonal store at Christmas, where the poor can actually shop for presents for their children, rather than accepting a pre-set package. Lt. Colonel Bettie Love, San Francisco administrator, calls it the *Toy and Joy Shop*. A back-to-school program providing clothes and school supplies uses the same space.

Meanwhile, the 300 or so low-income seniors who live at the Silvercreat Residence have seen the enormous changes in their neighborhood since then-Mayor Dianne Feinstein broke ground for the building on Shipley Street in 1974. Residents have had a ringside seat for the transformation of this South of Market community, as its ramshackle buildings and vacant lots were replaced by the Moscone Center, Yerba Buena Gardens, the Museum of Modern Art and, most recently, the Metreon Complex.

Like San Francisco, the Silvercrest Residence has a multi-cultural population and leadership. Since those "foreign-born" souls became seekers at the first Salvation Army meeting here, the diversity of the city's population has been reflected in the Salvation Army's membership. Today, the Army has corps (churches/community centers) that serve the Chinese, Asian, Korean and Latino/Latina communities.

Many of the corps are operated and staffed by people whose lives have been dramatically restored by the Salvation Army. At the Harbor Light Center, Tamesha Sweet found the courage to conquer her addiction to drugs and get a job at Costco. Now a Salvation Army soldier, Sweet counsels residents at Harbor Light every day — and for the Salvation Army," Sweet says. "I never thought I could be so happy." ■

Lt. Colonel Bettie Love at 407 Ninth Street Gateway/Harbor House, transitional housing for drug-dependent single parents and their children.

Photo: Roberto Carra

The San Francisco Foundation

Sandra Hernández, M.D., CEO of The San Francisco Foundation

health, education, cultural arts, neighborhood revitalization, environmental justice and advocacy for under-served populations.

Important and successful efforts catalyzed by the Foundation's support include: KQED, The Trust for Public Land, Bridge Housing, and On Lok Senior Health Services.

"The San Francisco Foundation and the organizations we work with reflect the diversity of the Bay Area's residents and communities," Hernández says.

The San Francisco Foundation is widely considered a primary Bay Area resource for both new and experienced philanthropists. "We bring expertise to donors, helping them reach those most in need, and we also partner with national and regional foundations and contributors. We serve as a vehicle for creating community around charitable giving," Hernández says.

She singles out the improvement of neglected public parks as just one case in point. "We brought together environmentalists, homeless activists, city officials, neighborhood park advocates, and philanthropists — all sorts of people with a common agenda but different ideas. We created an effective plan and strategy to get the job done," she says. "It takes active listening and learning to determine what you need to make a dream a reality."

Photo: Terry Lorant

I n 1948 a small group of forward-looking civic leaders, led by the late Daniel Koshland, started The San Francisco Foundation with the help of a small founding grant from The Columbia Foundation. "Mr. Koshland and his colleagues sought a vehicle to pull the community together to create pride and unity and improve quality of life," says Foundation CEO Sandra Hernández, M.D., noting that this basic mission continues to this day.

From these visionary beginnings, The San Francisco Foundation has become one of the nation's largest community Foundations with $700 million in assets. This growth reflects both strong fiscal stewardship and a vibrant philanthropic spirit in San Francisco and the Bay Area. The Foundation continues to build on Koshland's vision with its $50 million in annual grant making, its Koshland Neighborhood Program, Community Leadership Awards, various neighborhood and affinity-based initiatives, community convenings, and other programs designed to work with community leaders and nonprofits to improve the quality of life in the Bay Area.

The San Francisco Foundation addresses community needs by supporting innovative ideas and strengthening existing nonprofit organizations that lack sufficient resources or infrastructure. As a regional community foundation serving San Francisco, Marin, Alameda, Contra Costa and San Mateo counties, it focuses on community

> The San Francisco Foundation has become one of the nation's largest community foundations with $700 million in assets and $50 million in annual grant making.

Like virtually every other modern organization, the Foundation increasingly focuses on the impact of new technologies. Hernández recognizes the importance of addressing the so-called "digital divide." "The challenge here is helping communities become a part of the digital age, building infrastructure for shared technology, and connecting people and information in new ways," she says.

The "digital divide" project illustrates the wisdom of The San Francisco Foundation's founders. The Foundation is mobilizing funds and expertise to address a need that couldn't have been foreseen 50 years ago. As one of the founders put it, "No one knows today what the best philanthropic use of his or her money will be 25 to 100 years from now."

"Each year we fulfill the vision of the individuals and families who care deeply about the future of our region by giving the community millions of dollars — and valuable leadership — to respond to ever-changing community needs," Hernández says. ∎

The ADCO Group has been a key player in San Francisco real estate for four decades. The San Francisco Development Co., a wholly owned subsidiary of the ADCO Group, acquired six sites in the area of Gough and Geary streets in the early 1960s. At the request of the Roman Catholic Archbishop, ADCO relocated a Lucky store there to make way for St. Mary's Cathedral. Owner Alvin Dworman also lowered the height of one of the residential buildings he was constructing there to leave the cathedral's view to the south unobstructed. The ADCO Group developed three additional buildings in the area, including the Cathedral Hill Tower and Plaza Apartments.

San Francisco Mart

Dworman then sold the remaining sites and plans to the Sequoias for an assisted-living project on Geary. He helped Justin Herman, then head of the Redevelopment Agency, to move the old produce market and develop a new market on Army Street, making way for the Alcoa office building. Recent projects include the Convention Plaza office building at Third and Howard, and the Museum Parc condominiums at Third and Folsom.

The ADCO Group is also the parent company of The San Francisco Mart, an illustrious city institution housed in two buildings on the south side of Market Street between Ninth and 10th streets. The Mart leases approximately 300 showroom/office suites, where nearly 1,000 manufacturers exhibit home furnishings for retailers, buyers and design professionals and where various service professionals and firms have established Bay Area offices.

During two weeks each year — one in January and one in July — more than 8,000 home-furnishings buyers from around the world come to the San Francisco Mart to buy for their retail stores, restaurants, hotels and interior-design clients. About 100 suites are open year-round to interior designers and their clients and to retail-store buyers. In May and November, the "trade only" showrooms are open to the public for sample sales, which attract thousands of people.

Founded in 1915 at Mission and New Montgomery, the Mart moved to its current location in 1929. "Furniture manufacturers found an advantage to showing new products under one roof, enabling retail buyers to compare new styles more easily and select assortments for their stores," says Michael Gennet, president of the Mart. The ADCO Group purchased the Mart I building in the 1960s and developed Mart

During two weeks each year more than 8,000 home-furnishings buyers from around the world come to the San Francisco Mart to buy for their retail stores, restaurants, hotels and interior-design clients.

II in the early 1970s to meet tenant demand. In the 1980s, the first two floors of Mart I were remodeled, and a dramatic two-story rotunda lobby was created.

In recent years, the Mart has been the only home-furnishings market in the West — the only similar markets are in Mississippi and North Carolina. Thus, the Mart is not only a major attraction for West Coast manufacturers and buyers, but also for the many national and international companies that want to do business with them.

In the late 1990s, many offices, including the City of San Francisco's, were moved to the Mart while renovations on City Hall were completed. When City Hall re-opened, some of the original departments moved back to City Hall; others remain in the Mart, and additional departments have moved in, as well. ■

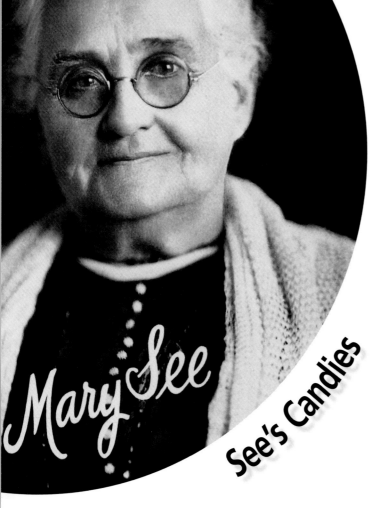

Mary See

See's Candies

See's® Candies may have started in Los Angeles, but its presence in the Bay Area has been enduring since 1935. The first shop, which was also a kitchen and business office, debuted at 160 10th St. in San Francisco, followed by one at 1519 Polk St., which still exists. The confections instantly became a hit at the World's Fair on Treasure Island in 1939.

Founded by Charles See, a visionary and former pharmacist, the company featured his mother, Mary's, favorite candy recipes, handcrafted in the first shop's kitchen in Los Angeles. By the time of Charles See's death in 1949, the single candy shop had exploded into a chain of 78 establishments employing more than 2,000 people. His son, Laurance, then took over the reins, followed by younger son, Harry, for a short stint. It remained a family business until See's sold the company to Berkshire Hathaway in 1972. New owners Warren Buffett and Charles Munger appointed Charles N. Huggins president/CEO, a position he still holds today.

Both the Depression and World War II challenged the company, but See was not deterred; he weathered the Depression by offering customers bulk-rate discounts on candy to encourage gift-giving and fund-raising by charities and clubs. During the war years, when sugar, chocolate from Africa and South America, and pineapple from Hawaii were hard to come by, See limited his store hours rather than compromise the quality of his candy.

Today, See's Quantity Discount Program has translated into significant savings for businesses and others who purchase gifts, employee incentives and promotions. Fund-raisers can make up to 50 percent profit on their sales of candy bars and special holiday items and take advantage of a wide variety of campaign programs, as well as advice from See's seasoned sales consultants.

During the 1950s and '60s, See's jumped on the shopping-mall trend by opening more stores in high-profile locations. Today, the retail candy shops number more than 200 in the Western United States, with six in San Francisco and many others throughout the Bay Area. One of See's two large candy-making facilities is

Charles N. Huggins, President and CEO, stands next to a restored Harley-Davidson motorcycle with old-fashioned sidecar, just like the one used in the '20s and '30s to deliver See's Old Time Candies.

uniforms. Even its packaging has changed very little since the company's inception. It still sports a picture of Mary See, a spectacled, silver-haired woman with a warm smile and an expression of pride. After all, most of her original recipes still fill See's candy boxes.

"See's is truly a California tradition," says Richard Van Doren, vice president of sales and marketing. "We've been in San Francisco so long that people have grown up with our product. It continues to make people happy, and our goal is to maintain this tradition, to always fulfill our promise of 'quality without compromise.'"

See's popular lines of confections made from high-quality, farm-fresh ingredients and the personal See's touch include fudge, assorted chocolates — chocolate butter, molasses chips, caramels, fruit creams — Almond Royal, bridge mix, truffles, nuts and chews, and peanut butter, butterscotch, chocolate and café latte lollypops. One of its latest additions is See's Seegars, rich milk chocolate hand-rolled into a cigar shape, encircled with a Seegar band, individually wrapped and sold in cigar-style boxes.

> *"See's is truly a California tradition. We've been in San Francisco so long that people have grown up with our product."*

See's celebrates each holiday with a special collection of candies, from Irish Potatoes — pure cocoa and cinnamon powder surrounding a whipped walnut-filled divinity center — on St. Patrick's Day, to red-and-white sugar sticks on President's Day.

located in South San Francisco, augmented by a lollypop-manufacturing facility in Burlingame. See's moved off the mainland by opening its first candy shop in Honolulu in 1970 and its first operation outside the United States in Hong Kong in 1976.

In 1989, See's ventured into San Francisco International Airport with a See's kiosk. It proved to be so popular with out-of-towners who wanted a taste of San Francisco once they got home, and with gift-givers, that today the airport houses eight kiosks. To really localize the flavor of See's, the kiosks sport a sign saying, "California's Famous Old Time Candies," rather than "See's Famous Old Time Candies," the familiar slogan gracing retail stores.

There is little doubt why See's has lived up to its philosophy — "Quality Without Compromise" — as it continues to produce hand-made chocolates alongside customized candy-making machines, offer free samples and maintain the homey tradition of salespeople in See's

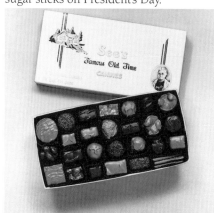

The familiar one-pound box of See's Famous Old Time Candies, a welcome gift on any occasion.

See's has also made it into the hands of some famous people: When George Bush was vice president, he purchased 50 half-pound boxes at the Houston Galleria's See's Candy Shop to bring as gifts to his hosts during a visit to China in 1982. And when former British Prime Minister Margaret Thatcher was addressing the Business Leadership Summit in Stockton, Calif., in 1995, Huggins arranged for the world leader and chocolate-lover to receive a four-pound box of truffles.

Though See's has its beginnings planted in the 1920s and is bound to tradition, that hasn't kept the company from evolving into the 21st century. It has launched a website (www.sees.com), which allows browsers to Go Candy Shopping to order their favorite assorted chocolates and confections, access Shop Locations to find out where See's retail stores are located, obtain information about the company's fund-raising programs at Quantity Discount, and learn more about See's through About Us and Long History.

The Internet may not seem like such an innovative leap, but See's just started accepting credit cards in 1997. It was, however, one of the first companies to advertise on television by sponsoring the musical show, *Beryl by Candlelight*, starring British singer Beryl Davis. For those who are intimidated by buying on the Internet, See's popular Mail Order Catalogue and retail stores offer inviting alternatives. ■

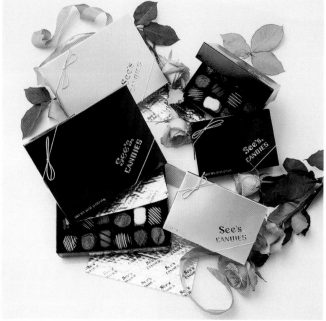

See's Gold and Black Chocolate Truffles...elegant and sublime.

William Lohse, CEO

What do antique dealers, astrologers, printers and gambling ventures have in common? They are some of the small businesses that take advantage of SmartAge.com's Internet products and services.

"Our mission is to help small companies find customers and make money on the Web," says Doug Roseborough, vice president of marketing for SmartAge.com. "SmartAge.com offers tools to level the playing field with big business. We can make the difference between being noticed and being ignored in the electronic marketplace."

Leonard Peake of Leesburg, Va., is one of SmartAge.com's satisfied customers. Peake founded The Coffee Corral, an online gourmet coffeehouse, in 1998 to sell coffee and coffee-related products. CoffeeCorral.com's 40 varieties of gourmet blends were generating positive feedback from customers, but the site did not yet have enough exposure to make the business viable.

"At first, I didn't have enough orders to sell the large amount [of coffee] I was required to buy," Peake says. "And I couldn't keep it for more than a few days before I could no longer conscionably sell it as 'fresh roasted.'"

Peake turned to SmartAge.com. "The goal was to get as many people as possible to our website," he says. "We wanted them to learn who we are and what we are about."

First, Peake enrolled CoffeeCorral.com in SmartClicks, a banner-advertising exchange program. For every two banner ads CoffeeCorral.com displayed, the business earned one credit toward showing its banner ad on another site — and its banners were automatically routed to sites where it was getting the best click-through rate. In addition, Peake took advantage of SmartAge.com's targeted advertising. This enabled Peake to place ads on popular sites with the same delivery options leading advertisers use — search-engine keywords and demographic targeting — without having to place a large order or make a large financial commitment.

Thanks to SmartAge.com, CoffeeCorral.com's user sessions have increased by more than 166 percent — on their way to surpassing Peake's year-end target rates and increasing sales enough to support the large orders required by the wholesaler.

"The potential for Internet sales is enormous," Peake says. "However, tapping it can be difficult. SmartAge and the targeted advertising it uses works for all businesses — big *and* small."

SmartAge.com offers a variety of products and services to small businesses such as The Coffee Corral:

- Create a website: Easy-to-use programs can help individuals build a professional-looking website without writing a line of code.
- Enhance a website: Tools are available to monitor a Web server's response time, shrink graphics to make a site load faster when a customer goes to it, and provide automatically updated content. A free e-mail service can also help build a community of loyal customers on a site.
- Promote a business: In addition to the SmartClicks banner-advertising exchange program and targeted advertising The Coffee Corral used, SmartAge.com can help businesses list a site and track its ranking on top search engines.
- Join a virtual mall: In the SmartAge Store, small-business users have access to store-building tools, merchant accounts, payment processing and secure hosting free of charge for three months.
- Learn e-business strategies: Small-business owners can take advantage of SmartAge.com's expertise by receiving its newsletter

or reading articles posted on the site, such as "What's Your Internet IQ?," "What Type of Website Should Your Small Business Have?" and "Do Your Customers Trust Your Website?" In addition, SmartAge.com is in the process of launching monitored discussion boards and chat rooms. These will enable members to exchange information and ideas among themselves, as well as receive advice from SmartAge.com experts.

Like many of its more than a million members, SmartAge.com is a relatively young business using the Internet to achieve explosive growth. Founded in January 1998 by Chair and CEO Bill Lohse, SmartAge.com is privately backed, most notably by Softbank Capital Partners and Accel Partners. SmartAge.com now employs a total of more than 100 people in its San Francisco headquarters and its North Carolina, Chicago, Boston and New York offices. Overseas branches are scheduled to open shortly in Great Britain, France and Japan.

"SmartAge.com has been highly successful in managing its exponential growth," Roseborough says. "I attribute this to the hiring of seasoned managers at all levels and to having a clearly defined plan — both short- and long-term. We have stayed focused on our overarching goal: to create excellent, easy-to-use products and services for our customers." ■

Like many of its more than a million members, SmartAge.com is a relatively young business using the Internet to achieve explosive growth.

The mayor celebrating Christmas with SmartAge.com

One big happy family

Stacey's

In that year, Stacey's moved to its present location a few doors west. Once again, *Publisher's Weekly* praised the stunning and functional new showcase for books. *San Francisco Examiner* reporter Luther Nichols was particularly taken with elevator doors "the color of raspberry sherbet — the sexiest elevator doors in town."

In 1959, a retail store was opened in Palo Alto, the site of Stacey's wholesale operations. In 1968, the Butler family closed the wholesale business and sold the retail stores to Arthur Brody, founder and proprietor of the Brodart Co. Brody had invented the transparent book jacket while he was a student at Columbia University, and soon the jackets were a staple in libraries everywhere. Brody began moving Stacey's toward general bookselling and, by 1978, after yet another remodel, Stacey's was a full-fledged trade bookseller.

In 1923, botanist John William Stacey, who happened also to be head of The Emporium's book department, raised $20,000 from local medical professionals and opened a small medical bookstore in the historic Flood Building. Since then, the bookstore that still bears his name has added scientific, computer and general-interest books to the medical titles that were his specialty. The company's continuing emphasis on developing the best all-around selection of professional books and bookselling services in the area has given Stacey's a reputation for quality and completeness that extends far beyond the region.

"The book business requires us to be a combination of the traditional and the progressive."

"The book business requires us to be a combination of the traditional and the progressive," says Tom Allen, Stacey's general manager. "The classics always have to be on hand, but tastes change — as do the needs of business. We do our best to provide the mix our customers demand."

Serving customer needs helped build the business, which was well on its way to becoming the largest wholesaler of medical books in the country by the time Stacey died in 1943. The new owner, William Lee Butler, quickly saw that Stacey's had outgrown its birthplace. In 1947, the store moved to 551 Market St., constructing what *Publisher's Weekly* hailed as "the most modern bookstore in the country," and adding technical and scientific books to its stock, which grew by more than 400 titles a year through 1958.

Computer, business and scientific books still represent about half Stacey's business in San Francisco, Palo Alto and the newest store in Cupertino, which opened about 10 years ago. To accommodate its business customers, Stacey's maintains a staff that deals exclusively with corporate accounts and stocks titles that are not found in most bookstores — for example, the building codes of the city and county of San Francisco and the state of California. Both business and mainstream customers benefit from a veteran staff of booksellers, many with the store for a decade or more.

Though it has maintained a website for some time and sells books online, Stacey's intends to remain a local store where customers can test the look and feel of the books they want to buy. "We see ourselves as part of the fabric of San Francisco's Financial District and of Silicon Valley, as well," Allen says. "We've been around a long time and look forward to many more years here." ■

Swinerton & Walberg

Swinerton & Walberg has a rich history of innovation and integrity standing behind the San Francisco–based construction company. Charles Lindgren cultivated the seeds of what would eventually become Swinerton when he started with two partners in Los Angeles in 1888, then helped rebuild Bakersfield after the city was devastated by fire in 1889, and made his way to San Francisco at the turn of the century.

Lindgren and his first Bay Area partner, Lewis Hicks, were pioneers in the development of steel-reinforced concrete construction, a technique that would prove its mettle in the 1906 earthquake, when reinforced concrete buildings were among the surviving structures. Lindgren & Hicks put their expertise to work rebuilding San Francisco and success followed.

That same year, Alfred Bingham Swinerton, a Stanford University student, joined the company and, by 1923, his influence was so strongly felt that the company became Lindgren & Swinerton. The company had downtown's Pacific Telephone & Telegraph Building and Sir Francis Drake Hotel under its belt before the 1929 stock-market crash, a calamity that did not deter the growing company. Soon after, the builders completed the Pacific Coast Stock Exchange and San Francisco's War Memorial Veterans Building and Opera House.

In the late 1920s, Richard Walberg, an engineer, came on board and, by 1942, the company became known as Swinerton & Walberg. The company dominated the San Francisco construction scene with projects such as Ghirardelli Square, Wells Fargo's headquarters and others throughout the West. The building boom continued until 1989, when the commercial real-estate market collapsed. But it wasn't long before the company regained momentum and, in 1996, Swinerton Inc. was formed and became the parent company of Swinerton & Walberg and the firm's other subsidiaries.

The award-winning San Francisco Museum of Modern Art, built by Swinerton & Walberg in 1995, represents a new age in design and construction. Behind SFMOMA stands the Pacific Telephone & Telegraph building, completed by Lindgren & Swinerton in 1925, still one of the most striking structures in the city and an enduring example of time-tested construction.

Ghirardelli Square represents Swinerton & Walberg's work at its finest.

What sets the employee-owned company apart is its people, who are empowered to take responsibility and accountability — a challenge endorsed by the entrepreneurial spirit and diversity of San Francisco.

Since the company's inception in 1888, it has built a reputation for integrity and innovation, from early use of pioneering construction methods to developing Internet-based construction-management tools and "green" building construction and job-site recycling programs.

The company's services are basically the same as its original offerings — construction and construction-management — but today its focus is on office space, public buildings, hotels, and medical, retail, entertainment, and high tech facilities, forgoing the road, pipeline and dam projects of its past. Swinerton has expanded into new geographic markets (Arizona, Colorado, Texas, Oregon, Utah, Hawaii and throughout California) and has added facilities such as assisted-living residences and technology centers to its roster. It heads into the new millennium with two visible projects: Gap World Headquarters on the Embarcadero and Golden Gate Park's new de Young Museum.

What sets the employee-owned company apart is its people, who are empowered to take responsibility and accountability — a challenge endorsed by the entrepreneurial spirit and diversity of San Francisco. CEO Dave Grubb applauds San Francisco as the financial capital of the West — a reason Swinerton set up headquarters downtown to be near many of its clients.

Putting a golden touch on so many construction projects in San Francisco has afforded Swinerton's people the opportunity to become involved in several significant charities, including the renovation of Crissy Field, the Boys and Girls Clubs of San Francisco and Christmas in April. ■

Thomas Weisel Partners LLC

Thom Weisel, chair and CEO of Thomas Weisel Partners

Thomas Weisel Partners LLC, a merchant bank exclusively focused on the next generation of growth companies transforming the US economy, was founded in 1999 by Thom Weisel, Sandy Miller, Frank Dunlevy and Derek Lemke. The transformation of the US economy is driven by agents of change that Thomas Weisel Partners refers to as tailwinds —more commonly known as the Internet, outsourcing or bandwidth. Thomas Weisel Partners is structured around these tailwinds, a strategy that both benefits the firm's clients and gives the firm unique perspective and positioning to build a premier merchant bank for next-generation growth companies.

In its first 12 months, Thomas Weisel Partners grew to more than 450 employees, including 66 partners, and opened offices in San Francisco, New York, Boston and London. The success of its first year of business, completing 106 transactions worth $23 billion, placed the firm at the forefront among local independent investment banks and ranked the firm in the top 20 investment banks nationwide in public stock offerings.

Among its credits are the $117 million IPO for Z-Tel, a provider of advanced integrated telecommunications services, and a $217 million

Front desk of Thomas Weisel Partners San Francisco office

follow-on offering for Proxicom, an information-technology services outsourcing company. Thomas Weisel Partners is responsible for $6.6 billion in mergers and acquisitions alone, following the first advisory transaction for Yahoo!'s acquisition of Geocities.

Thomas Weisel Partners provides investment banking, institutional brokerage, private client services and private equity investing focused on the new frontiers of the growth economy. At the core of the firm is its research capabilities, which allow Thomas Weisel Partners' research analysts to generate timely, insightful views on growth companies, as well as original thought pieces on new areas of growth. The firm currently covers 185 stocks, both listed and over-the-counter, and is focusing its research efforts on Internet, bandwidth, outsourcing, consolidation, education and demographics.

"We have the largest Internet-dedicated research and investment-banking team on Wall Street that fully understands the power of dot-com," says Weisel, CEO and founder of the firm. "In an era when ideas, not capital, will distinguish the winners from the losers, having the smartest, most experienced professionals on the team is a critical asset of the business."

Its Investment Banking Group provides strategic services and equity underwriting to high-quality growth companies, from small to large cap. "We view client relationships as partnerships, not simply transactions," Weisel says. "We engage with our clients along a continuum of their financial and advisory needs, from principal investing to private placements, from merger and acquisition advisory to capital raising in the public markets."

The Sales, Trading and Capital Markets Group has the scale and depth of capabilities in equities trading and global distribution required by large institutional investors. The firm's goal is to be the dominant trader in the growth stocks covered by its research team and to provide liquidity at the best possible price to institutional clients. The firm trades more than 250 stocks, and recorded total trading volume of 1.5 billion shares in 1999.

On the private-equity side, Thomas Weisel Partners raised a growth-oriented private-equity fund to invest in promising opportunities identified through the firm's research and investment-banking efforts. The firm will invest about half the $1.3 billion fund in technology-driven, hyper-growth companies.

The Private Client Department offers clients a full range of strategic wealth-management services, serving the personal needs of clients that do not lend themselves to common solutions. The department is represented by a hand-selected team of seasoned professionals who have experience addressing the unique needs of business-owners and entrepreneurs in the management of their newly created wealth. The services include asset-management consulting, corporate/venture services, fixed-income and corporate cash management, and estate and tax planning.

"We plan to continue building the premier merchant bank dedicated to the frontiers of transformation in the economy."

Tim Heekin, director of trading, on the trading floor at Thomas Weisel Partners

"As a start-up ourselves, we understand the entrepreneurial mindset of growth companies and can identify with the many challenges facing them," Weisel explains. He praises the company's partners, who subscribe to a common vision and culture for the firm and have made a long-term commitment to its future success. "This stability and cohesion provide for unsurpassed teamwork and client-first orientation," he adds.

Weisel has a long, successful career in San Francisco, having started Montgomery Securities 27 years ago, as well as a close affiliation with the cultural world of the city. He serves on the board of trustees of the San Francisco Museum of Modern Art.

To Weisel, there is plenty to appreciate in San Francisco: first and foremost, the rich talent pool in the Bay Area. "Our business is driven by quality people, and we are fortunate to reside in an area with an abundance of highly talented people, the best of whom have been attracted to work at Thomas Weisel Partners," Weisel says.

"Being located in the heart of the venture-capital community has enabled us to build a series of strategic relationships that have benefited the growth of our company. It also helps that we have a high concentration of quality growth companies in the area to target for new business development," he says.

Weisel also sees San Francisco as an ideal place for nurturing entrepreneurship. "There is a culture pervasive in the city that appreciates and values entrepreneurship," he says. "I think people were delighted to see a new independent firm committed to San Francisco emerge after all the acquisitions of the established San Francisco banks. That helped launch the business."

Although Thomas Weisel Partners has grown by leaps and bounds, Weisel says size is not the company's goal: "We plan to continue building the premier merchant bank dedicated to the frontiers of transformation in the economy. Instead of focusing on size, we'd rather be known for quality — as the 'go-to' institution — financing, advising, trading, and distributing and investing in the finest growth companies. We also will expand into some new areas of business that leverage the earnings stream from our existing infrastructure and talent." ∎

A glimpse of the daily activity on the state-of-the-art trading floor at Thomas Weisel Partners.

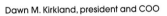
Dawn M. Kirkland, president and COO

Left to right: Betty S. Hui, Jennifer K. Martin, Dawn M. Kirkland

What's the biggest challenge today for many Bay Area businesses? Finding bright, talented technical employees — and that's where Tech-Finders can help.

"We take pride in recruiting hard-to-find applicants for hard-to-fill positions," says Dawn M. Kirkland, president and chief operating officer of Tech-Finders Co. LLC. "For many companies in the Bay Area, recruiting outstanding technical employees, from help-desk support to software developer to chief information officer, is the key to surviving in today's fast-paced economy. We have the tools, services and people to find the right person for a job."

Tech-Finders recruiters draw on their sophisticated database of candidates, extensive network of contacts and resources across the country to fill a position. Throughout the process, those at Tech-Finders put quality first. "We would only submit a candidate to a client that Tech-Finders would also hire," Kirkland says. "We routinely screen 100 candidates before recommending two. Because of our superior level of service, many companies have come to rely exclusively on Tech-Finders to meet their technical staffing needs."

One unique service Tech-Finders offers is the placement of hourly consultants. Consultants are full-time employees of Tech-Finders, but work at the client's site. This gives a company the ability to quickly fill an immediate staffing need. The firm can later hire that consultant for a reduced fee, at which point both the company and the candidate are confident they work well together.

A woman-owned firm, Tech-Finders Co. LLC was founded in 1998. The principals watched companies in the Bay area, the technical heart of the nation, struggle to find experienced technical talent. As a result, Tech-Finder's business has been growing briskly, doubling in revenues during the last year.

Kirkland comes from a technical, as well as a recruiting, background. "I used to be a programmer and still consider myself somewhat of a nerd," she says. "But I think that gives me an edge. I understand the technical side of what companies need and what candidates have to offer."

How has Tech-Finders managed to carve a niche in the competitive field of technical placement? "We work very hard to meet our clients' needs," Kirkland says. "But more importantly, I have a wonderful staff who have the desire, commitment, loyalty and integrity to be very good at what they do. We hear all day why individuals leave their jobs. Issues such as money, growth potential, challenge and recognition come up over and over. We strive to meet those needs and create a comfortable and enjoyable work environment at Tech-Finders.

"We know that having good people is absolutely critical for a business to succeed!" ∎

> "We take pride in recruiting hard-to-find applicants for hard-to-fill positions."

A young Irish immigrant, Richard Tobin was among the men who established The Hibernia Savings and Loan Society in 1859. After just 10 years in San Francisco, Tobin's career was made; elected the society's attorney, he — or his firm, Tobin & Tobin — served the organization for 130 years, as it became The Hibernia Bank and was eventually acquired by the old Security Pacific National Bank.

When Tobin died in 1887, the San Francisco Bar Association noted that "the very extensive business of that vast institution" had prevented him from building a wider practice, but he "had no superior at the Bar" in his chosen field. "His professional conduct was courteous and honorable. He possessed the esteem and respect of his professional brethren," the Bar said. "He rarely and reluctantly spoke ill of any man."

Born in Waterford, Ireland, Richard Tobin came to San Francisco via Valparaiso, Chile, on June 4, 1849, arriving by ship with his father and

Richard Tobin, member of the firm, 1852–1887

From 1892–1977, Tobin & Tobin was "upstairs" in The Hibernia Bank Building.

In 2002, Tobin & Tobin will celebrate its sesquicentennial.

brother. Soon, Tobin was studying law with Judge Barry, and on Oct. 15, 1852, he was admitted to practice before the Supreme Court of California. In 2002, Tobin & Tobin, the firm he founded, will celebrate its sesquicentennial.

Among Tobin's first partners was his oldest son, Robert, who joined him in 1875, and later his other sons: Alfred, Clement and Joseph Sadoc Tobin. The latter was named after the Most Rev. Joseph Sadoc Alemany, the first archbishop of San Francisco, whom his father had served as legal adviser.

In 1901, the younger Tobin was a candidate for mayor of San Francisco. Though he lost, Joseph remained in public service, serving on the

Committee of Fifty after the 1906 earthquake and on the board of the 1915 Panama Pacific Exposition. Joseph also led Tobin & Tobin until his death in 1919, when Cyril R. Tobin, Richard's grandson and Robert's son, took over. Cyril was the firm's dominant force until his death in 1977.

During all those years, The Hibernia Bank remained the firm's principal client. In fact, for a time, the firm's offices were on the second floor of the bank's headquarters at One Jones St. A brass plaque at the front door read, "Tobin & Tobin-Attorneys-Up Stairs."

That plaque has a place of honor in the reception area of Tobin & Tobin today, and a replica is on the building at 500 Sansome St. that is its present home. Since Cyril's death, the firm has expanded in a variety of directions, meeting the litigation and business needs of a diverse range of clients.

Though a Tobin no longer practices there, Tobin & Tobin maintains its old traditions. In 1984, the California Historical Society placed the firm on its register of historic California businesses "in recognition of more than a century of service and contribution to California's economic growth and vitality." ■

United Airlines

Kent attributes United's ranking as the world's largest airline to its also being the largest majority employee-owned company in the world. "Our employees have a real interest in making United a success, which shows up in our high-quality customer service and in the professionalism of our people," he says. The design and implementation of the United Shuttle service in 1994 is the brainstorm of United grass-roots employees. "We are united in values, united in vision," Kent adds.

Though passenger safety is at the forefront of United's philosophy, the airline also is striving to provide simple hassle-free travel, comfort, unsurpassed global access, and warm and genuine attention to customer needs.

Basic yet vitally important customer contact features, including looking the customer in the eye, smiling and thanking them for their business, are just "for openers." Beyond these basics, United is deploying more and more technological advances to customer handling, such as electronic ticketing, portable chariots, boarding-pass gate readers and online bookings, Kent says.

In April 2000, United will launch daily nonstop service from San Francisco to Seoul, South Korea, and new five-day-a-week service to Shanghai; in June, service will begin to Beijing and Frankfurt, Germany — the result of consumer demand, Kent says. United and some of its nine Star Alliance partners will be the primary occupants of an entire concourse (G) in the new SFO international terminal, which will accommodate all the airline's new and existing international flights.

Founded in 1926, United has evolved into a global carrier with 139 destinations in 28 countries and two US territories.

United is proud to invite their First Class International customers to the experience United First Suite created with the lastest design and technology for comfort in the air.

U nited Airlines is the largest airline in the world, and it just might have the San Francisco Bay Area to thank for that. The Bay Area represents the single largest point of revenue production for the company — more than even its home city of Chicago. More than 250 daily flights (54 percent of all departures from San Francisco International Airport [SFO]) connect Bay Area travelers to destinations throughout the United States and around the globe. SFO has been an United hub since 1981, and is the airline's largest international hub.

"The Bay Area as a major business and airline hub makes perfect sense," says Frank Kent, managing director for United in Northern California. "We are an economic lifeline to the community but, in turn, owe our success to demand from Bay Area travelers." That's why SFO is United's largest shuttle and international hub, in addition to having the greatest number of flights to the East Coast, Midwest and other parts of the country.

United is also an airline of "firsts." It introduced the first flight-attendant service in 1930; the first airline flight kitchen in 1936; the first nonstop, coast-to-coast US flight in 1955; the first nationwide, automated reservations system in 1971; and it was the first commercial carrier to use satellite data communication in flight. Founded in 1926, United has evolved into a global carrier with 139 destinations in 28 countries and two US territories.

As the new millennium gets under way, United Airlines will continue to focus on improved on-time performance at SFO. Kent stresses, however, that airline dependability at SFO will not be significantly improved until and unless its existing runway system is reconfigured. "United is 100 percent behind SFO's efforts to ensure that this takes place sooner rather than later," Kent says. ∎

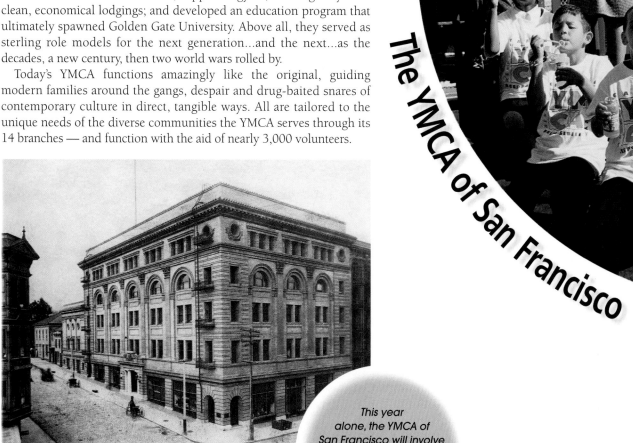

Photo: Michael Mustacchi & Associates

The YMCA of San Francisco

Founded in 1853 to counter the influences of the barflies, floozies and fast-buck artists who swarmed this rowdy city after the Gold Rush, the YMCA of San Francisco — the West's first human-service organization and the nation's 13th YMCA — provided a spiritual and social haven for a generation of young men often far from the homes of their birth.

When these newcomers prayed, "...deliver us from evil," the YMCA responded in direct, tangible ways — all created by volunteers. Christian men conducted Bible studies; supported gyms, bowling alleys and clean, economical lodgings; and developed an education program that ultimately spawned Golden Gate University. Above all, they served as sterling role models for the next generation...and the next...as the decades, a new century, then two world wars rolled by.

Today's YMCA functions amazingly like the original, guiding modern families around the gangs, despair and drug-baited snares of contemporary culture in direct, tangible ways. All are tailored to the unique needs of the diverse communities the YMCA serves through its 14 branches — and function with the aid of nearly 3,000 volunteers.

YMCA of San Francisco's third association building, located on the corner of Mason and Ellis streets, was opened in 1894 and dedicated, debt-free, by President Theodore Roosevelt in 1903. Tradition lives on: Every program and service includes elements of character development — respect, responsibility, honesty and caring.

This year alone, the YMCA of San Francisco will involve 140,000 people — of both genders and all income and educational levels, ages and cultures.

Especially since the YMCA early on broadened its embrace to include not just young Christian men, but women and families of all ages and religions, the YMCA's programs have reflected the times. It now:

- Offers a wide range of programs and services for youth and teens — from licensed child care, learning centers and sports, to job readiness, education, and family and individual counseling programs.
- Creates safe spaces and social supports for seniors, especially in the Tenderloin, Mission, Stonestown and Richmond District neighborhoods.
- Runs resident and environmental education camps, as well as numerous and varied summer day camps throughout the Bay Area.
- Finds new and effective ways to reach troubled or at-risk youth. The YMCA offers an alternative high school, mentoring and tutoring programs, and sports programs with conflict-resolution and prevention elements.

- Maintains a rigorous schedule of recreation, health and fitness programs, with special emphasis on the "ready-to-be-fit." And the YMCA, says its president and CEO, Martie Bolsinger, still teaches thousands of children and adults to swim each year.

And "no one is ever turned away because they can't afford to pay," Bolsinger says.

This year alone, the YMCA of San Francisco will involve 140,000 people — of both genders and all income and educational levels, ages and cultures — through its San Francisco, San Mateo, San Rafael, Suisun City, La Honda and Marin Headlands branches. "We've come a very long way since the first Bible-study group in an office above the post office," acknowledges Bolsinger, "and we've made a world of difference in a great many lives over the years. But just wait until you see what we have in store for the new millennium!" ∎

Photo: Eric Millette

Howard Lester, chair and CEO, and Chuck Williams, founder, of Williams-Sonoma

Williams-Sonoma Inc.

When Chuck Williams moved his "little French kitchenware shop" from Sonoma to San Francisco in 1958, American cuisine and the world of pots and pans were very different from today: The cutting edge of American cooking back then was "convenience" foods such as frozen dinners. And Americans did their cooking with a limited array of utensils made for home use, far inferior to what was then "restaurant quality" and reserved for that use.

On a trip to France in 1953, Williams had marveled at the array of cookware, bakeware and tools being sold to home cooks. He decided to open a small store that would offer American cooks the same choices.

Back then, Williams never imagined his single store would grow into more than 200 Williams-Sonoma stores across the country — and in cyberspace. Nor did he envision a collaboration with Howard Lester, the company's chair and CEO, that would make Williams-Sonoma Inc. a sort of entrepreneurial grandparent for a range of other brands quietly revolutionizing the way people furnish their homes and live their domestic lives.

Pottery Barn storefront

But, perhaps, his store's success was predictable. Williams was a gifted merchant, and in San Francisco, a city that has always savored fine cuisine, he had found the perfect location for his business: "So many people who lived in San Francisco traveled, and they knew French food," he recalls. When they came home, they could visit Williams-Sonoma to get the fine French cookware that was essential for preparing that cuisine.

When Williams opened the store on Sutter Street, a couple of blocks off Union Square, a cluster of elegant shops serving San Francisco residents were his neighbors: a furniture store, a jewelry shop, a dealer in Asian antiques and an Elizabeth Arden salon. The block became one of San Francisco's best shopping destinations.

In those days, Williams was involved in every facet of his business, from annual month-long buying trips to Europe to more mundane tasks,

Williams-Sonoma storefront

such as "wrapping the packages, mopping the floors, sweeping the sidewalks," he says. Like his downtown neighbors, Williams focused on providing his customers not only the best goods, but also the finest service.

Trends in American cuisine favored him: The *James Beard Cookbook* was published in 1959, and its author directed many customers to Williams-Sonoma. In 1961, Julia Child's *Mastering the Art of French Cooking* — and, two years later, her TV show, *The French Chef* — added to the store's client base. In 1971, Alice Waters opened Chez Panisse in Berkeley, giving California cuisine a mecca. Local cooks wanted to be great cooks, and Williams-Sonoma offered the tools.

Then, in 1978, Lester heard about an opportunity to invest in Williams-Sonoma. Retired after 15 years as a pioneer in the computer business, Lester had been looking for "something exciting to do every day." In Williams-Sonoma, he saw a company with a great reputation for quality and good taste, a company that might benefit from better business execution. "I felt I could help there, and I thought it would be a lot of fun," he says.

At the time, Williams had already made a few small steps beyond Sutter Street, opening stores in Palo Alto, Beverly Hills and Orange County. But a more significant step involved the introduction of Williams-Sonoma catalogs in 1971. Jackie Mallorca, a customer who worked in advertising, suggested the idea, and Williams, who had been impressed by the Neiman-Marcus catalog, thought it was a good one. "Between the two of us, we did it all," Williams says.

About 5,000 customers received catalogs that first year. It turned out Williams had a knack "for seeing something on a shelf and visualizing how to sell it in a catalog format," Lester says. Today, Williams-Sonoma Inc. distributes more than 200 million catalogs annually — 30 percent more mailings than all US food and travel magazines put together.

Catalogs have become the company's way of moving into new businesses. In 1983, the first Hold Everything catalog, offering organizational solutions for the home, was issued. When Williams-Sonoma purchased the Pottery Barn stores from Gap in 1986, success came first through catalogs. In 1989, the Chambers catalog, with high-quality furnishings for bed and bath, was issued. Most recently, some young employees, finding it difficult to locate furnishings for their new babies, launched the Pottery Barn Kids catalog.

And the catalog sales permitted an enormous retail expansion. In addition to its 200 Williams-Sonoma stores, the company today also operates more than 100 Pottery Barn stores — all of them enlarged and redesigned — 33 Hold Everything shops and a half dozen outlet stores. And the leap into virtual reality followed as the old century ended, first with a wedding and gift registry website and then with a full-scale e-commerce operation, www.williams-sonoma.com.

Over the years, Williams and the company he founded have made a large contribution to American cuisine and the world of pots and pans. Williams-Sonoma has sold 11 million cookbooks edited by Williams, reflecting the increasing sophistication of American cuisine. Through his stores, American cooks have been able to find all the tools they need to keep up with the latest trends, from balsamic vinegar to food processors. Recently, the company collaborated with All-Clad Metalcrafters to produce Copper-Core, an exclusive line of cookware.

Though Williams no longer wraps the packages or sweeps the sidewalks, he still comes to work every day, helping to shape the company's merchandising strategy.

No one at Williams-Sonoma is looking around for any laurels to rest on. While Williams-Sonoma continues to be "the best kitchen shop in the world," Lester says, the corporation sees itself as the provider of a full range of home furnishings for high-end customers through all its brands.

"As we make our stores bigger and more interesting to the customer," Lester says, "we've discovered that we really don't know how high is up." Though Williams-Sonoma has already grown from one creative fellow in Sonoma to 20,000 employees around the world, Lester says, "We're really just getting started." ∎

> Over the years, Chuck Williams and the company he founded have made a large contribution to American cuisine and the world of pots and pans.

Original Williams-Sonoma store at 576 Sutter street

Xpedior

Gene Rooney, executive vice president

E-commerce is booming. And so are some of the companies that help e-commerce firms succeed — such as Xpedior, which creates, maintains and updates websites for Internet businesses.
"Our clients range from large, well-established companies, such as Hewlett-Packard, Cisco and Sun, to Internet start-ups," says Gene Rooney, Xpedior's Executive Vice President of corporate development and head of international operations. "We help our clients figure out their Internet strategy and website design, as well as provide strong technical underpinnings for a site. What distinguishes us from other firms in the field is our focus on e-business, in which rapid development of a site and the creation of complex, high-transaction systems are often imperative."

The site www.onlineofficesupplies.com, an award-winner Xpedior created in just 14 weeks, is one example of Xpedior's work. When Paula Jagemann, CEO of then-start-up Onlineofficesupplies.com, came to Xpedior in 1998, she had a vision: to create the ultimate online office-supply superstore. However, building such a site was a challenge, requiring a fully searchable database, the capacity to offer tens of thousands of products and the scalability to handle hundreds of thousands of orders per day.

The team from Xpedior worked closely with leadership at Onlineofficesupplies.com to manage the project from two perspectives: technology and business. To launch the site was paramount because the site *was* the business. However, since the site was one-of-a-kind, formulating a unique strategy for the entire value-chain — from purchaser to supplier to manufacturer — was necessary.

On the front end, purchasers could range from small-office and home-office customers to buyers within a large corporation. So Xpedior's team worked to create a design that provided the flexibility to process small and large orders,

"We help our clients figure out their Internet strategy and website design, as well as provide strong technical underpinnings for a site."

Tony Morosini, managing director, Xpedior in London

Rod Volz and Gene Rooney

as well as the ability for a large user to customize a catalog in just two weeks.

On the back end, Onlineofficesupplies.com's distribution partner, United Stationers, lacked the internal infrastructure to use new Internet technology. So Xpedior's team adapted United Stationers' electronic data-interchange process so it could transfer orders to the fulfillment center and obtain customer order information. Xpedior's team leveraged existing tools wherever possible, building new ones only where applications did not exist.

Throughout the development process, the team from Xpedior documented the system architecture, database design, data dictionary, coding standards and user instructions. Xpedior's personnel trained Onlineofficesupplies.com staff on the features that allowed for easy maintenance of the site by non-technical personnel. The Xpedior team also held formal training classes and provided Onlineofficesupplies.com with a wide range of training documents and reference aids.

The results have been impressive. Since Onlineofficesupplies.com's first full month of operation in August 1998, hits to the site have reached 750,000, and sales volume has risen more than 50 percent every month.

Xpedior has successfully assisted many clients across the United States — and now internationally — from 18 locations that include San Francisco, New York, Chicago, Dallas, Denver, Washington, London, Toronto and Perth, Australia.

The San Francisco office, now comprising about 170 people, was started by Rooney, Dave Stanton (now Xpedior's Senior Vice President and Chief Technology Officer) and another colleague in 1994, under the name Sage IT Partners. Initially, the founders aimed to produce customer-relationship management software. However, as the company started building Internet systems, the partners soon realized the company had found another, more lucrative niche: e-business site development. The firm's business soon took off.

In 1998, Sage IT Partners was bought by a Texas firm, Metamor Worldwide Inc. (NASDAQ: MMWW). Metamor merged the San Fran-

cisco firm with three other companies — based in Chicago, Dallas and Washington — with similar business plans. The new, larger company was named Xpedior. Metamor spun out approximately 20 percent of its ownership of Xpedior in a successful initial public offering in December 1999 (NASDAQ: XPDR), with plans to distribute the remaining shares of Xpedior in 2000. This will allow Xpedior to realize its full value as an independent company.

"These frequent changes in ownership can be distracting, but on the whole, we've stayed focused on what is important: serving our clients," Rooney says. "Our rapid growth has presented its challenges, but I believe it would have been more difficult *not* to grow. Growth has enabled us to meet the demands of our customers, as well as to attract and retain top-notch employees in the Bay Area, a competitive environment for talent. It's because of our growth — not in spite of it — that our office has been and will continue to be a great place to work." ■

Index of Profiles

*Members of the San Francisco Chamber of Commerce

Hoyt Shepston, 215
700A Dubuque Avenue
So. San Francisco, CA 94080
650-952-6930
www.shepston@ix.netcom.com

*Indus International, 216
60 Spear Street
San Francisco, CA 94111
415-904-5000
www.indusinternational.com

*iSyndicate, 218
455 9th Street
San Francisco, CA 94103 - 4410
415-896-1900
www.isyndicate.com

*Jewish Family and Children's
Services, 219
1710 Scott Street
San Francisco, CA 94115
415-567-8860
www.jfcs.org

Lennar/BVHP Partners, 220
5960 Inglewood Drive, Suite 220
Pleasenton, CA 94588
415-434-9100
www.lennarcommunities.com

The Martin Group, 221
100 Bush Street 26th floor
San Francisco, CA 94104
415-772-5900
www.themartingroup.com

*marchFIRST, 222
410 Townsend Street
San Francisco, CA 94107
415-369-6717
www.marchfirst.com

*McCown De Leeuw &
Co. Inc., 224
3000 Sand Hill Building 3 #290
Menlo Park , CA 94025
650-854-6000
www.mdcpartners.com

*McKessonHBOC, 226
1 Post Street

San Francisco, CA 94104
415-983-8300
www.mckhboc.com

Michelle Rowland/Weinstein
Gallery, 227
383 Geary Blvd
San Francisco, CA 94102
415-362-8151
www.weinstain.com

Micromuse, 228
139 Townsend Street
San Francisco, CA 94107
415-538-9090
www.micromuse.com

*Nibbi Brothers Inc., 229
1433 17th Street
San Francisco, CA 94107
415-863-1820
www.nibbi.com

*Oracle Corp., 230
500 Oracle Parkway
Redwood Shores CA 94065
650-506-7000
www.oracle.com

*Orrick, Herrington &
Sutcliffe LLP, 232
400 Sansome Street
San Francisco, CA 94111
415-392-1122
www.orrick.com

*Palace Hotel, 235
2 New Montgomery Street
San Francisco, CA 94105
415-546-5098
www.palacehotel.com

*Peet's Coffee & Tea, 236
1400 Park Avenue
Emeryville, CA 94608
510-594-2100
www.peets.com

*Pillsbury Madison and Sutro, 238
50 Fremont Street
San Francisco, CA 94105
415-983-1000
www.pillsburylaw.com

*Planned Parenthood
Golden Gate, 240
815 Eddy Street
San Francisco, CA 94109
415-441-7858
www.pppp.org

*Royal & SunAlliance, 241
595 Market Street, Ste 400
San Francisco, CA 94105
415-495-0700
wwww.roralsunalliance.com

*Salvation Army, 242
832 Folsom Street
San Francisco, CA 94119
415-553-3500
www.salvationarmy.org

*The San Francisco
Foundation, 244
225 Bush Street, Ste 500
San Francisco, CA 94104
415-773-8500
www.sff.org

*San Francisco Mart, 245
1355 Market Street
San Francisco, CA 94103
415-552-2311
www.sfmart.com

*See's Candies, 246
210 El Camino Real
South San Francisco, CA 94080-5998
650-761-2490
www.sees.com

*SmartAge.com, 248
3450 California Street
San Francisco, CA 94118
415-674-3787
www.smartage.com

*Stacey's, 250
581 Market Street
San Francisco, CA 94105
415-421-4687
www.stacys.com

*Swinerton & Walberg, 251
580 California Street, 12th floor

San Francisco, CA 94104-1033
415-421-2980
www.swbuilders.com

*Thomas Weisel Partners LLC, 252
One Montgomery Street
San Francisco, CA 94104
415-364-2500
www.tweisel.com

*Tech-Finders, 254
465 California Street Ste 475
San Francisco, CA 94104
415-732-1270
www.techfinders.com

* Tobin & Tobin, 255
500 Sansome Street
San Francisco, CA 94104
415-433-1400
www.tobinlaw.com

*United Airlines, 256
Bldg 575, 3rd Floor-sfos,z
San Francisco, CA 94128
650-635-2004
www.unitedairlines.com

*The YMCA of San Francisco, 257
44 Montgomery Street Suite 770
San Francisco, CA 94104
415-439-6510
www.ymca.org

*Williams-Sonoma Inc., 258
3250 Van Ness Avenue
San Francisco, CA 94109
415-733-3168
www.williamssonoma.com

*Xpedior, 260
44 Montgomery Street Suite 3200
San Francisco, CA 94104
415-399-7000
www.xpedior.com

*Members of the San Francisco Chamber of Commerce